Wilfred L. Morin
Collection in Archaeology

THE WORLD
OF THE ANCIENT
SLAVS

ZDENĚK VÁŇA

THE WORLD OF THE ANCIENT SLAVS

PHOTOGRAPHS BY
PAVEL VÁCHA

ILLUSTRATIONS BY
PAVEL MAJOR

Wayne State University Press
Detroit 1983

Text by Zdeněk Váňa
Translated by Till Gottheiner
Illustrations and maps by Pavel Major
Photographs by Pavel Vácha (75),
Zdeněk Váňa (35), Zdeněk Bureš (1),
Olga Hilmerová (1), Alois Kleibl (1),
Miroslav Navara (1), Prokop Paul (1), Ann Münchow (1)
Graphic design by Bohuslav Blažej

Designed and produced by Artia for Orbis Publishing
Limited, 20-22 Bedfordbury, London WC2N4BT

CONTENTS

Very few Western publications have appeared that give clear information on the earliest history of the Slavs and their culture. The English reader has at his disposal only Francis Dvornik's book *The Slavs: Their Early History and Civilisation* (Boston 1956), which analyses written records with special regard to the beginnings of Christianity and church history. Then there is the book by Marija Gimbutas *The Slavs* (London 1971), which is limited to a survey of archeological cultures on the territory of the early Slavs from the Iron Age to the period of migration in the sixth and seventh centuries.

In French there exists only the *Manuel de l'antiquité slave* I, II (Paris 1923, 1926) by Lubor Niederle, a work that was pioneering in its time but is today rather out of date.

German literature is in a slightly better position, mainly thanks to the work of Witold Hensel *Die Slawen im frühen Mittelalter* (Berlin 1965), which is, in fact, a translation of a Polish publication and gives a systematic survey of material culture without regard to historical development. A modest contribution is the author's *Einführung in die Frühgeschichte der Slawen* (Neumünster 1970), which gives selected chapters on this topic. Other works in German are devoted exclusively to specific problems or individual Slav regions.

This publication started as a Czech edition (Prague 1977) and was revised and adapted both in text and illustrations. Its aim is to outline in a brief informative survey the beginnings and cultural forms of the Slavs from their ethnogenesis until the emergence of the first states and nations. In view of the considerable progress made by archeological research in recent decades, these finds are given a prominent place but are set in the context of historical development, including other fields of research. Stress is placed on the pictorial documentation, including reconstructions in the form of drawings, which should give a closer insight into the life of the vanished world of the ancient Slavs.

The author wishes to acknowledge his gratitude for the selection and loan of illustrations to these institutions and individuals:
Archeologický ústav Nitra; Arkheologicheski institut i muzey Sofiya; Arheološki muzej Zagreb; Bulharské kulturní středisko Praha; Ermitazh Leningrad; Kreis-Heimatmuseum Brandenburg; Kreis-Heimatmuseum Neuruppin; Landesmuseum für Vorgeschichte Halle; Magyar Nemzeti Múzeum Budapest; Märkisches Museum Berlin; Moravské muzeum Brno; Museum für Ur- und Frühgeschichte Potsdam; Museum für Ur-und Frühgeschichte Schwerin; Muzeum Archeologiczne Poznań; Muzeum Archeologiczne Wrocław; Národné múzeum Bratislava; Národní muzeum Praha; Państwowe Muzeum Archeologiczne Warsawa; Staatliche Museen zu Berlin; Zentralinstitut für Alte Geschichte und Archäologie Berlin; Dr. M. Beranová, Prague; Dr. Z. Čilinská, Nitra; Dr. B. Dostál, Brno; Dr. M. Holeček, Prague; Dr. K. Reichertová, Prague; Prof. Dr. V. Hrubý, Brno; Dr. H. Keiling, Schwerin; Dr. Ľ. Kraskovská, Bratislava, Dr. B. Krüger, Berlin; Dr. B. Nechvátal, Prague; Dr. I. Pleinerová, Prague; A. Popov, Prague; Dr. A. Točík, Nitra; Dr. R. Turek, Prague; Dr. B. Tykva, Prague. The author is especially grateful to Dr. M. Beranová and Dr. R. Turek for very valuable comments on the text.

SEARCHING
FOR THE ORIGIN
OF THE SLAVS

THE OLDEST WRITTEN RECORDS

It is an amazing fact that so little attention has been paid for so long to so large a section of the European population as that represented by the Slavs — roughly every third European is of Slav origin. Not a single mention of the existence of the Slavs can be found in the works of ancient historians and geographers until the time of the migration of nations, yet they described the entire known world of the time and left detailed records of, for example, the Germanic and the Celtic tribes. There are a number of reasons for this. Chief among these is that the Slav ethnogeny took place at a much later date than was the case of the Celts or the Germanic tribes. Furthermore, these processes were taking place beyond the sphere of interest of the ancient world — in the remote regions of Eastern Europe where even the more enterprising traders visited only on rare occasions. They were acquainted mainly with the southern parts of European Russia which they called Scythia or Sarmatia after the peoples living there. Greek colonies were founded along the northern shores of the Black Sea as early as in the seventh and sixth centuries B. C., and it is highly likely that the Greeks ventured further inland along the big rivers in search of trade. But barely any records exist of these early discoveries except a mention in the works of Hecataeus of Miletus.

In the fifth century B.C. Herodotus, the father of Greek historians, visited Scythia. He went no further than the town of Olbia and stayed at the mouth of the Dniester, but he learnt many facts about the nations living further north from local experts; these he recorded in the fourth book of his *History (Historiés apodexis)*. For long centuries his detailed description of Scythia provided the bare facts of what the ancients knew about Eastern Europe. Herodotus was aware that broad steppes lay in the southern parts crossed by a number of rivers and that boundless forests stretched further to the north. He knew the rivers that flow into the Black Sea: the Danube (Istros) with the Siret (Ordessos) and the Prut (Pyretos), the Dniester (Tyres), Bug (Hypanis) and Dnieper (Borysthenes). He was informed about the Don (Tanais) that flows into the Sea of Azov (Maiotis). He described the dramatic but unsuccessful expedition that the Persian King Darius undertook, towards the end of the sixth century, against the Scythians, a militant tribe

The river Vistula played an important role in the emergence of the Slavs as a people. Its river basin was inhabited from the first century B.C. to the early fifth century A.D. by the ethnically mixed Przeworsk culture, which included the Germans and the mysterious Venedi, who are considered the ancestors of the Slavs. The early Slavs emerged here at the end of the fifth century.

9

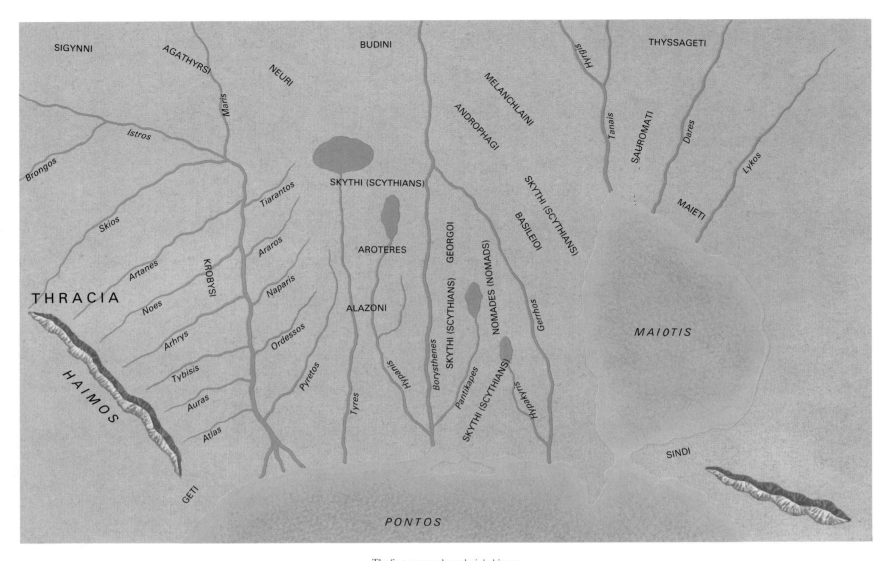

SIGYNNI AGATHYRSI NEURI BUDINI THYSSAGETI

Maris Istros Brongos Skios Artanes KROBYSI Noes THRACIA Arhrys HAIMOS Tybisis Auras Atlas GETI Tiarantos Araros Naparis Ordessos Pyretos SKYTHI (SCYTHIANS) AROTERES ALAZONI Tyres Hypanis Borysthenes GEORGOI SKYTHI (SCYTHIANS) Pantikapes NOMADES (NOMADS) SKYTHI (SCYTHIANS) Hypakyris MELANCHLAINI ANDROPHAGI SKYTHI (SCYTHIANS) BASILEIOI Gerrhos Hyrgis Tanais SAUROMATI Dares MAIETI Lykos MAIOTIS SINDI PONTOS

The first reports about the inhabitants of Eastern Europe were given by the Greek historian Herodotus in the fifth century B.C. His description of Scythia provided the bare facts of what the people of antiquity knew about that part of the European continent.

of Iranian origin. Herodotus also knew of other tribes who had settled to the west, north and east of the Scythians, and helped them in the guerilla war against Darius. To the west were the Agathyrsi, a tribe that was probably of Thracian origin, "loving luxury and gold", which they mined in Romanian Transylvania. To the north, between the upper Dniester and the middle Dnieper, lived the mysterious Neuri. Their name has survived in certain place-names in eastern Poland: the rivers Nura, Nurzec, and Nurland, the name for the entire region. The Neuri are therefore associated with the Slavs. According to Herodotus, they left their former homeland to escape large numbers of snakes. Their customs were similar to those of the Scythians, but at a certain time of the year they all turned into wolves. This report by Herodotus clearly refers to the belief in werewolves, which was widespread in Eastern Europe

until the modern era. Between the middle course of the Dnieper and the Don lay the settlements of the cruel Androphagi (cannibals) and the nomad Melanchlaini, whose name derived from their habit of wearing black garments. To the north of these, probably already in the forests, and as eastern neighbours of the Neuri, lived the teeming nation of fair-haired and blue-eyed Budini, who likewise remain a mystery. They lived mainly by hunting and dressed in furs. They may have been a Finnic tribe, although they are sometimes mentioned in connection with the Slavs, for their name does have a Slavonic sound. Beyond these tribes, further north, Herodotus knew only of uninhabited regions; the tribes living to the east of the Don — the Thyssageti and Sauromati — are outside the scope of this work.

What remains open to discussion is the possible Slav origin of the Ploughmen Scythians (to be distinguished

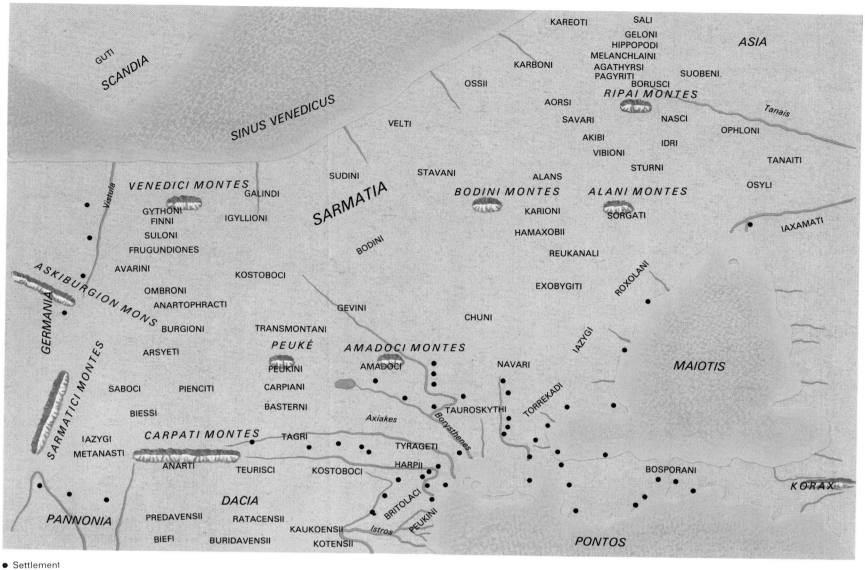

● Settlement

In the first and second centuries A.D. ancient authors knew that the large nation of the Venedi lived on the territory of present-day Poland. They were linked with the emergence of the Slavs as a people. According to Ptolemy, they lived between the Baltic Sea (the Venedian Bay) and the Carpathians (the Venedian Mountains).

from the Royal Scythians and the Nomad Scythians), Neuri and Budini. There is nothing to prove this, and the link between these tribes and the Slavs remains a matter of hypothesis.

This link may apply in the case of the large nation of the Venedi, who lived beyond the Vistula, between the Baltic Sea and the Carpathians. They are mentioned in the works of Roman and Greek writers of the first and second centuries A.D. Records exist in Pliny the Elder's *Naturalis Historia* of *c.* 77 and in the *Germania* by Tacitus of the year 98. They are also mentioned by Ptolemy the geographer, who died in 178.

Tacitus was at a loss as to whether to count the Venedi among the Germanic tribes or the Iranian Sarmatians. But since the Venedi moved on foot, built houses and used shields, in contrast to the nomad Sarmatians, who lived in their wagons, he considered them aligned with the Germanic tribes. This view has never been confirmed.

Valuable facts on the Venedi were supplied by Ptolemy, the outstanding mathematician, astronomer and geographer, who lived in Alexandria in the second century A.D. On his map he placed the Venedi to the east of the Vistula towards the Venedian Bay (probably a bay in the Baltic Sea between the mouths of the Vistula and the Memel), and they were spread as far as the Venedian Mountains (clearly the Carpathians). In view of Ptolemy's records scholars looking for settlements of the ancient Slavs have been concentrating largely on the Venedi. For until the sixth century their name was used for the early Slavs, and it has survived to this day in the German name for the Slavs — *die Wenden*. But it is not entirely clear whether the ancient Venedi can be identified with the Slavs. Their name is not of Slav origin

— it may derive from the Celtic *vindos,* "the white" (and survives, for example, in the ancient name for Vienna *Vindobona*). Or it may come from the Proto-Indo-European *ven'd.* For that reason many scholars are of the opinion that the Venedi may have been part of the Celts or Illyrians, who later migrated further south into the Mediterranean region. (From this we get, for instance, the name of Venice.) Others, on the contrary, believe that the Venedi were an unknown European people, who later merged with the Slavs and gave them their own name.

On Ptolemy's map we can find one other ethnic term which remains a puzzle to historians and ethnographers: the Suobeni, which many believe to mean the Slovene. Unfortunately, Ptolemy reveals only that this tribe lived in northern Scythia by the side of the Alans and Alanorsi. These statements have never been confirmed.

The mystery of the existence and location of the Slavs during Roman times is enhanced by the fact that the

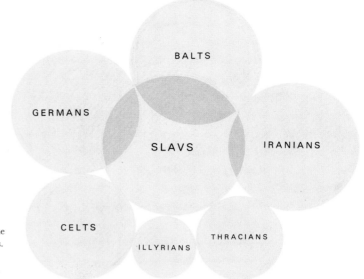

The Slavs had closest linguistic contacts with the Balts, then the Germans and Iranians, followed by the Celts, the Illyrians and the Thracians. These contacts indicate the ethnic setting in which the Slavs developed.

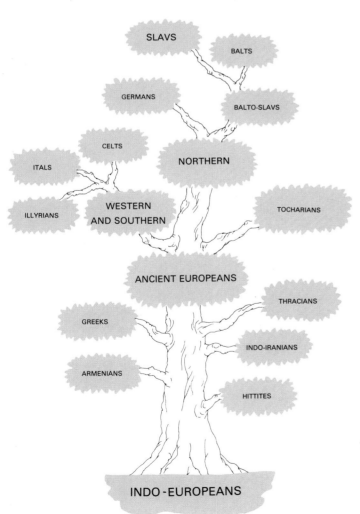

The Slavs belong to the linguistic family of Indo-Europeans. They were the last to split off as an independent unit and are therefore the youngest of all the Indo-European branches.

Romans never came into closer contact with Central and Eastern Europe, although they penetrated to the vicinity of later Slav settlements on several occasions, for example, under Emperor Augustus in 9 B.C., during the reign of Tiberius in the years A.D. 14—16 and at the time of Trajan (A.D. 98—117). The Romans' last successful attempt to break through into Central Europe was an expedition led by Marcus Aurelius (A.D. 161—180) against the Marcomanni and Quadi on the territory of Slovakia today. The Roman Emperor and philosopher sat on the banks of the Slovak river Hron and wrote his *Meditations.* He left an inscription on a rock at Trenčín in Slovakia, which to this day marks the Romans' most northerly inroad into Central Europe. But the Emperor failed to establish the province of Marcomannia, which was to have occupied the territory of present-day Czechoslovakia, or the province of Sarmatia, to cover the eastern parts of present-day Hungary, for he died at Vindobona (Vienna) in A.D. 180. In the following centuries the Roman Empire found itself on the defensive against its northerly neighbours until finally it succumbed to the influx of barbarians at the time of the migration of nations. Only its eastern parts, Byzantium, survived.

And at this point a new factor arrived on the scene — the Slavs, advancing in vast numbers into Central and South-Eastern Europe from the regions beyond the Carpathians. They are mentioned for the first time, and by their own name, by Pseudo-Caesarius Nazianus in his book *Dialogi* dating from the beginning of the sixth century. The main information on the Slavs in the sixth century was, however, provided by Procopius and Jordanes.

The Byzantine historian Procopius of Caesareia took part in the struggle of the Byzantines against the Germanic Goths and wrote a book about it. Among others, he describes the long migration of the Germanic Heruli in 512 from somewhere along the middle course

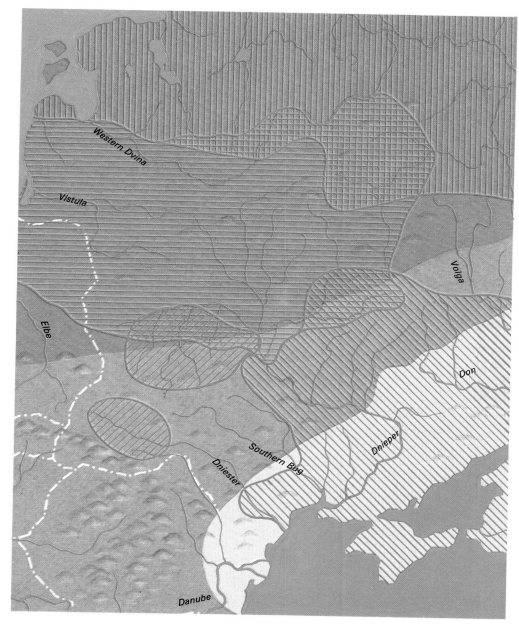

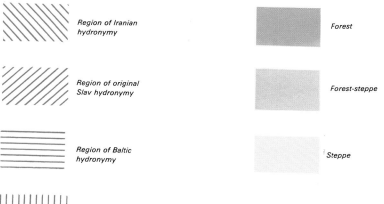

Region of Iranian
hydronymy

Region of original
Slav hydronymy

Region of Baltic
hydronymy

Region of Finno-Ugric
hydronymy

Forest

Forest-steppe

Steppe

The location of the original homeland of
the Slavs can be partly deduced from
the names of Eastern European rivers,
which reveal the original range of
Baltic, Slav, Iranian and Finnic
settlement.

of the Danube "traversing all Slavic nations" and across empty regions to the Varni in the Elbe valley, from where they returned to their original homeland in Scandinavia. Even though the exact route of their migration is not entirely clear, this report confirms that the Slavs were already in Central Europe at that time. But they did not occupy it completely; there were still "empty regions", that is, parts that had not yet been settled. Another report by Procopius relates the adventurous struggles of the Lombard Hildigis, who, in the course of a life full of vicissitudes, often found refuge among the Slavs. Since the Germanic Lombards at that time occupied the Danube valley of today's Austria and Hungary, and their enemies, the Gepids, lived along the river Tisza, we probably have to look for the settlements of Hildigis's Slavonic friends in the northern neighbourhood of the Lombards, that is, somewhere in the region where Slovakia and Moravia extend today. This means that by the first half of the sixth century the Slavs had already arrived there. But the report says nothing about when and from where they had come.

The report by Jordanes is not much more satisfactory either, although he supplies further facts. He also wrote the history of the Goths, whom he knew from personal experience since he was in the services of Gunthigis, King of the Goths. He mentions the Slavs too, whom he calls Venedi or Venethi, as being a numerically large people settled over a vast area and divided into many tribes. The most important, according to him, were the Sclaveni and the Antes. The Sclaveni were living between the Vistula, the Dniester, the town of Novietunum and Lake Mursia. Novietunum can be identified with ancient Noviodunum in the Danube delta on the territory of Romania. What is not clear is the location of Lake Mursia. It might be identified either as Lake Balaton or the confluence of the Tisza and the Danube in Hungary, or possibly as the confluence of the Sava and the Danube in northern Yugoslavia. In any case, Jordanes depicts a moment when the Slavs had set out from their original homeland. The mysterious Antes — possibly an Iranian tribe that later became engulfed by the Slavs — lived somewhere between the Dnieper and the Dniester. In the seventh century they were defeated by the Avars and vanished.

Historical sources, in other words, only reveal that the Slavs entered European history as a unit in the sixth century. At that time they began to spread to their present settlements, but it is not clear where they had lived before and what their previous development had been. The relationship to the ancient Venedi is merely hypothetical. One can certainly not equate the Slavs with the Venedi.

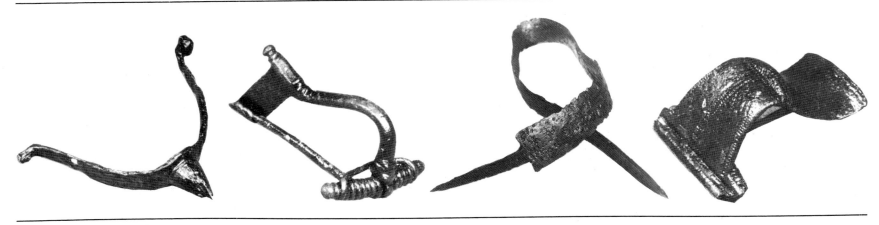

The territory of present-day Poland was dominated, from the first century B.C. on, by the Przeworsk culture. The shape of their pottery, weapons and ornaments, here represented by items from the Spicymierz site, reveals the local origin as well as Germanic influence so that ethnic determination is not entirely clear. There is only a partial cultural link with the early Slavs.

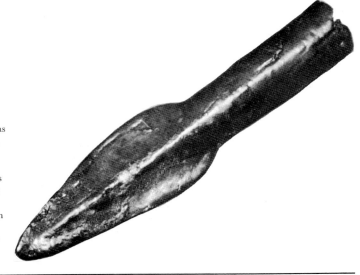

WHAT PHILOLOGY CAN PROVE

Along with the historians the philologists have made great efforts to delve into the secret of the origin of the Slavs. They approach the matter in two ways: the study of linguistic relations to neighbouring ethnic groups and the analysis of local names, especially *hydronymy*, the names of watercourses.

Together with the Balts, Germans, Celts, Romans, Greeks, Albanians, Armenians, Iranians and Indians, the Slavs belong to the vast family of Indo-Europeans. In the past certain other groups had been members, who have since died out, such as the Hittites (Anatolians),

The Dnieper — the Borysthenes of antiquity — was known to Herodotus in the fifth century B.C. The Iranian tribes of the Scythians and Sarmatians lived along its lower reaches in ancient days and the Scandinavian Goths came this far in the second century A.D. The existence of the first Slavs can be proved in the fifth and sixth centuries, and the river became the axis of their settlement and political development.

Thracians, Illyrians and Tokharians. Philologists differ greatly in their views as to how the individual languages gradually developed from the originally almost unified Indo-European language, and individual stages of development are dated in a very relative and approximate manner. It would seem that the first to split off were the Hittites and the Indo-Iranian languages; the next phase saw the independent development of Greek, Armenian and Thracian, and gradually Italic, Celtic, Germanic and Illyrian, and lastly, and most likely, the unified Balto-Slavic, which later divided into Baltic and Slavonic. Views as to the stages of this development are not fully agreed upon, and there is no precise chrono-

In the second century B.C. the Zarubintsy culture arose in the middle reaches of the Dnieper and undoubtedly contributed to the emergence of the Slavs. Simple pottery, bronze fibulae and iron tools suggest certain Celtic influences.

logy. But one thing is clear: the Slavs as an ethnic unit were among the last to develop and are relatively the youngest of all Indo-European branches. For that reason the early Middle Ages knew only one Slavonic language *(lingua slavica)*, which was spoken from the sixth to the ninth or tenth century by all Slavs from the Baltic to the Aegean Sea, and from the Elbe to the

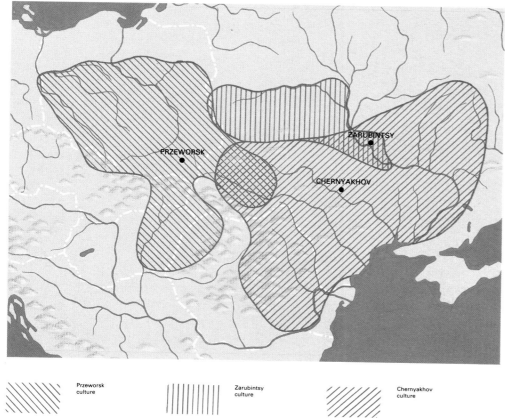

The map shows the distribution of three major cultures — the Zarubintsy, Przeworsk and Chernyakhov — which are characteristic of the development of Eastern Europe between the second century B.C. and the fourth century A.D. It is among these that the archeologists are looking for the roots of the Slav ethnic group.

Dnieper, with only minor dialectal deviations among the Western, Eastern and Southern Slavs.

After the consolidation of new settlements and the establishment of the first Slav states different national tongues began to develop, due to geographical, political and cultural differentiation. These languages are in use to this day. Altogether twelve languages formed, divided into three groups: (1) the Western Slav group: Polish, Lusatian, Polabian (a vanished tongue of the Slav tribes on the territory of East Germany today), Czech and Slovak; (2) the Eastern Slav group: Russian, Ukrainian and Byelorussian; (3) the Southern Slav group: Serbo-Croat, Slovene, Macedonian and Bulgarian. These languages became more differentiated in the twelfth and thirteenth centuries. But even before this happened, there existed a literary language of Church Slavonic — thanks to the mission of Constantine and Methodius, the apostles to the Slavs, in the ninth century. In Eastern Orthodox circles this Church Slavonic is used with local modifications to the present time. It is not known when the three major groups began to split up into separate groups of Eastern, Western and Southern. Some philologists assume there had been dialectal differences between them already in their original homeland. But it seems more likely that the differentiation took place after the Slav tribes had settled in different regions, lost

contact with each other and came into touch with different cultures and languages in their new settlements, which brought about a differentiated development.

The degree of relationship of Slavonic languages to the other Indo-European languages varies. The greatest number of common features can be found with the Baltic languages: Lithuanian, Latvian and the now vanished Prussian and Yatvingian. This leads one to deduce that there had once been a common Balto-Slavic unit. Then there are links with the Germanic and Iranian languages, and certain elements are in common with Celtic, Illyrian and Thracian. In other words, the Slavonic language developed somewhere in between these ethnic units: the Baltic to the north, Germanic to the west, Iranian in the east and Celtic, Thracian and Illyrian in the south.

An analysis of ancient topographical names, especially those of rivers, helps in localization of the development of Slavonic languages. Pure Slavonic names are to be found mainly in the region between the Oder and the middle Dnieper, and linguists are all agreed in stressing the relatively archaic type of the names in the valley of the Oder and the Vistula. The hydronyms on the Pripyat' and Dnieper rivers, by contrast, seem to be of a somewhat later date and provide proof that the Slavs migrated towards the east at a later stage. The problem is how to determine the time at which these local names came into existence as well as dating the oldest language contacts with the neighbouring ethnic groups. The Slavs had closest relations with the Balts, who, once upon a time, occupied a far larger area of Eastern Europe than today. Their heartland lay in the river basin of the Nieman, Pregel, upper Dnieper and Western Dvina. If we are to believe hydronyms, the original Baltic settlements reached much further east to the region between the Volga and the Oka, south-east to the Seim and south as far as the right bank of the Pripyat' — that is, a region that was already firmly in Slav hands in the sixth century A.D. The present-day Baltic nations — the Lithuanians and Latvians — are, in other words, an insignificant fragment of a once large ethnic unit. In this respect their fate resembles that of the Celts. It can further be shown that the Balts had ancient linguistic connections with the Finns, Iranians and Thracians who complete the semi-circle to their north-east, east, and south-east. The Slavs, therefore, must have developed to the south and south-west of the Balts, and their western and northwestern neighbours can only have been Germanic tribes, who were closest to them linguistically after the Balts.

Philological research suggests that before the beginning of migration in the sixth century the Slavs must have occupied a region between the above mentioned ethnic groups, that is, north of the Carpathians, and somewhere between the middle course of the Dnieper and the river basins of the middle and upper Vistula and Oder.

WHAT ARCHEOLOGY HAS REVEALED

Since language provides few concrete facts in regard to the chronology of the oldest period, one must turn to archeology for help. In the last few decades archeologists have managed to trace and work out in increasingly fine detail the cultural development of the assumed Slavic homeland back to the Neolithic period. However, all attempts to prove that the Slavs already existed in the distant past remain a matter of speculation. The

The ethnically mixed Chernyakhov culture developed between the middle reaches of the Dnieper and the Black Sea from the second century A.D. on. Its typical pottery is grey or black with polished patterns and they produced iron tools, metal and glass ornaments, and possessed objects imported from Rome.

archeologists can easily distinguish individual cultural units and map their geographical spread, but they encounter insuperable barriers when trying to stipulate ethnic adherence. This only becomes possible in the developed phase of the Bronze Age. At that time, at the turn of the second to the first millennium B.C., an extensive region of related cultures came into being known as the URNFIELD CULTURE. It stretched from the Baltic to the Mediterranean Sea and from the Rhine and the Rhône as far as the Vistula, the upper Dniester and the middle courses of the Danube. It is highly likely that it was inhabited by an Old European people who were not yet divided up into Celts, Germans, Itals, Illyrians and Balto-Slavs. The LUSATIAN CULTURE on the territory between the rivers Elbe, Oder and Vistula formed a part of this large region, and at one time it was considered as being of Slavic origin. But at that period the forebears of the Slavs were still integrated into that Old European unit in which differentiation began only in the first millennium B.C. The bearers of the Lusatian culture can, therefore, have represented no more than one of its dialectal groups, not yet ethnically de-limited.

A breakthrough in development occurred at the transition from the Bronze to the Iron Age (the eighth to the seventh century B.C.), when the southern Russian steppes were ruled by the Iranian Scythians, who undertook destructive raids far to the west into Central Europe. Their invasion broke up the Lusatian culture, and in the sixth century B.C. it became overlaid by the neighbouring POMERANIAN CULTURE that developed on the south-eastern coast of the Baltic Sea. This must be regarded as the first sign of the differentiation taking

place among the Baltic ethnic units. The merging of the two cultures led to a complex of Bell-Grave burials (the BELL-GRAVE CULTURE); the name was given by Polish archeologists on account of the burial custom in which the urn was covered with a bell-shaped vessel. This new culture existed in the fifth to second centuries B.C., mainly in the river basin of the middle and upper Vistula and Warta, from where it spread west to the middle course of the Oder and east to Volhynia and the Pripyat' Forest. In its neighbourhood, along the lower courses of the Oder and Elbe, developed the JASTORF CULTURE associated with Germanic tribes. A little earlier the Celts had appeared on the scene; they advanced into Central Europe from their original home in southern Germany and northern France around the year 400, and some of them reached the areas related to the Slav ethnogenesis — that is, the southern parts of Poland. Proofs of Slav contacts with the Celts can be found both in the language and in certain cultural relics, among them religious practices.

In the first century B.C. the Bell-Grave culture was replaced by a new cultural unit, the PRZEWORSK CULTURE. In recent years this has been the centre of attention in all efforts to determine Slav ethnogenesis. This culture occupied a somewhat larger domain than its predecessor and spread chiefly south-eastwards

The first archeological traces of the historical Slavs were finds of simple, mostly undecorated pottery. This became known as the Korchak type in the region of western Ukraine.

along the Carpathians to the upper Dniester and the Tisza valley in Hungary. It flourished throughout the Roman period until the early fifth century A.D., and some scholars, especially in Poland, therefore, identify it with the ancient Venedi. They point out the continuous development from the local roots of the Bell-Grave culture and to certain links between the simple shapes of Przeworsk pottery and the pottery of the early Slavs in the sixth century. On the other hand, the strong Germanic contribution to the Przeworsk culture should not be overlooked, especially in burial rites, pottery, weapons and ornaments, which have an undoubted relationship to the neighbouring Germanic regions to the north-west. It is often considered a bi-ethnic culture documenting the co-existence of Slavic and Germanic tribes, with the Germanic element predominant along the Oder to the west, while the Venedi-Slavic may have been supreme to the east along the Vistula. The only thing that is certain is that the Przeworsk culture was ethnically a mixed one; all other conclusions remain in the sphere of hypothesis.

In dealing with Slav origins one must take into account not merely the territory of southern Poland but likewise the western Ukraine, where a complex development was taking place at a period contemporary with the Bell-Grave and the Przeworsk cultures. This can

likewise be traced to the early Slavs in the sixth century. Geographically one might distinguish three zones in the broad plains of Eastern Europe: 1. the steppes to the south, which were the realm of nomadic tribes, in antiquity mainly the Scythians and the Sarmatians; 2. the forests to the north where widely scattered Finno-Ugric peoples lived (in the eastern parts) and Baltic tribes (to the west): 3. the forest-steppe lands in between with the river basins of the middle Dnieper, Pripyat', Bug and part of the Dniester. This central zone lent itself more favourably to agriculture and should be taken into account in the search for the origins of the Slavs.

In the second century B.C. the ZARUBINTSY CULTURE emerged in the Ukrainian forest-steppe land and partly in the forest regions. Certain Soviet and Polish archeologists consider this already Slavic, others regard it as Baltic or even as representing a transition between the Balts and the Slavs. It belonged to an agricultural people who founded settlements on the protected banks of the rivers and lived in small dwellings, a separate one for each family. They had an outstanding mastery of iron production, even making ornaments. Their material culture shows strong Celtic influences especially in the case of fibulae (clasps), tools and pottery. They buried their dead after cremation and placed the ash in urns or straight into the earth — as did the Slavs later.

A direct identification with the Slavs is, however, disproved by the multifarious origin of the Zarubintsy culture (including Baltic, Scythian, Pomeranian and Bell-Grave elements) and by its relatively early disappearance — basically already by the second century A.D. Only in the north, in the remote forest lands along the upper Dnieper, did certain Zarubintsy traditions survive until the fifth century A.D. (known as the LATE ZARUBINTSY CULTURE or KIEV TYPE). But by that time the territory was occupied chiefly by Baltic tribes.

The name "Korchak" comes from an important site where a number of early Slav settlements were excavated, each with typical semi-subterranean dwellings.

In the second century A.D. a new cultural group emerged on the southern part of the territory where the Zarubintsy culture was dying away and far beyond it — in the broad steppes of the Ukrainian plains right to the shores of the Black Sea. This culture has been subjected to intensive studies and a very lively exchange of views. It is the CHERNYAKHOV CULTURE, called after an extensive burial ground at Chernyakhov near Kiev, which was uncovered and studied in 1900. To date hundreds of settlements have been discovered scattered mostly in narrow strips along the rivers — sometimes to a distance of 800 metres (about 815 yards) — and a large number of burial grounds with mixed burial rites, both cremations and inhumations, the latter predominant. What is typical is gray or black pottery with polished patterns and of good craftsmanship, but beside it also cruder, unpolished artifacts have been found. The production of iron tools and metal ornaments was of high standard. There were even imports from the Roman Empire, which are very important for dating: coins, amphoras, buckles, little lamps and fine pottery known as *terra sigillata*.

Most highly debated is the problem of the ethnic membership of the Chernyakhov culture. Since it flourished at a time when the southern Russian steppes were ruled by the Germanic Goths, who penetrated this far from Scandinavia across the south-eastern Baltic regions in the second century A.D., some scholars stress their particular inclusion. Others have pointed out that the basic elements of this culture had already been established before the arrival of the Goths from a local Scythian-Sarmatian base, on whose territory it existed. But it is further possible to distinguish Thracian, Przeworsk, Zarubintsy and eastern Pomeranian (i.e. Gothic) components, which proves that several ethnic groups linked in one economic and political unit, contributed to the formation of an otherwise more or less unified culture. Even if the process of Slav ethnogenesis seems partly connected with the Chernyakhov culture, so far no definite proofs have been presented that confirm ties between the culture of the early Slavs and the Chernyakhov culture. For life came to a sudden stop in the settlements in the whole territory around A.D. 400; many settlements bear signs of a violent end. This seems to reflect the invasion of the nomadic Huns, who at that time made incursions across the Volga and the Don into the Ukrainian steppe, broke up the Gothic tribal units and set up bases for further raids into the Carpathian Basin. The bearers of the Chernyakhov culture were scattered mainly to the west and south. In the fifth century there then occurred a time gap in settlement in their former territory, which is difficult to bridge to the definitely Slav finds of the sixth century, although a number of scholars have tried to do so. To date only very few early Slavic finds have been made in the region of the Prut, the Dniester and the Bug. They may date from the fifth century and show a certain connection to the Chernyakhov culture, which as a unit disappeared

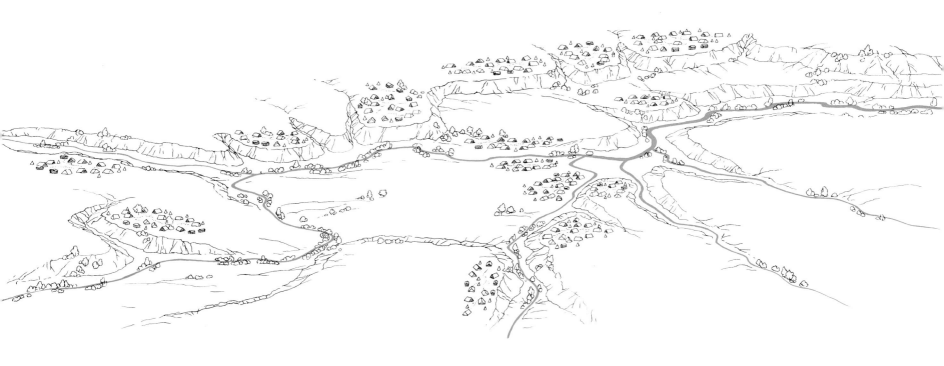

A total of fourteen settlements of Slav peasants gradually grew up along the banks of the river Teterev near Korchak in the sixth and seventh centuries.

just before that time. This link-up is only a partial one and cannot, therefore, be considered proof of direct ethnic continuity, only a reflection of how the remaining Chernyakhov population became assimilated into the newly emerging ethnic group.

We shall now sum up this brief survey of the history, according to the early archeological evidence of the territory where the early Slavs settled from the sixth century on. It is typical of the entire region between the Oder, Vistula, Dniester and Dnieper that by the end of the fourth century and at the latest in the early fifth century all developed cultures with Late Roman traditions vanished: that is, the Chernyakhov, Late Zarubintsy (Kiev type) and the Przeworsk. Instead, after a certain gap in time, a new culture emerged which has partial connections with the preceding ones but does not tie up with any of them directly. On the contrary, it represented quite a novel phenomenon on this territory, where previous cultural elements tended to merge.

Let us take a closer look at the culture of the early Slavs. It differed from that of their predecessors mainly in its simplicity, comprehensible if we take into account that it was formed by a people on the move, in the whirlpool of the big tribal migration, which did not leave time for richer cultural development. It would seem that in its earliest phase it took shape in the lowlands between the eastern Carpathians and the rivers Pripyat' and middle Dnieper, where, in the fifth to seventh centuries, we find the KORCHAK TYPE, called after Ukrainian sites in the Zhitomir region. These finds are concentrated in the river basin of the Pripyat', mainly along its southern tributaries; eastwards they reach as far as the Dnieper, westwards to the Western Bug and south to the Dniester. The relatively small settlements lie along low river

In the dwellings in the settlements at Korchak unusual clay discs, known as *khlebtsy*, were found. They are probably associated with the religious beliefs of the people.

banks. They are often grouped in a nest of three to four settlements in close proximity to each other. Typical semi-subterranean dwellings of a square ground plan (average 4 m × 4 m, about 4.5 yds × 4.5 yds) served as shelters everywhere, each with a stone oven. The dead were cremated and the remains placed in simple hand-made and undecorated urns buried below tumuli or simply in the ground. Finds of the Korchak type can be dated by the weapons and cast bronze or silver ornaments, such as clasps, belt trimmings, pendants and armbands known from the fifth to seventh century southern Russian treasures. Byzantine coins from the sixth century were brought to light in the hill-fort at Zimno.

The western equivalent of the Korchak type is the PRAGUE TYPE, with finds covering the southern parts of Poland and East Germany and the entire area of Czechoslovakia, with occasional finds in the Danube basin of Austria. Of these only the southern part of Poland and perhaps the eastern tip of Slovakia may be counted as the original homeland of the Slavs. The settlement of the rest of the territory already reflects Slav expansion.

At the turn of the fourth to fifth century far-reaching changes were taking place on the territory of the Przeworsk culture in southern and central Poland, caused by the incursions of the Huns into the Carpathian Basin. The settlements and burial grounds of the Przeworsk type disappear, the Roman tradition survived only in isolation into the first half of the fifth century when it merged with Hun influences spreading from the Carpathian Basin. All this vanished when the Hun dominance came to an end in 455. Then the Slavs were able to advance from the east into this region bringing with them their simple, unornamented pottery, semi-subterranean dwellings and burial by cremation. Few aids exist that might help in dating these finds, but there is every reason to suppose that the Slav settlement occurred in the second half of the fifth century.

The third region associated with the process of Slav ethnogenesis lay between the lower Dnieper and the Dniester and in the river basin of the Southern Bug. According to a site found in 1955 the archeologists appended the name PEN'KOVKA TYPE to this group. Excavations brought to light five settlements spread over seven kilometres (about four miles) along the banks of the river Tiasmin. In character, choice of terrain and type of dwellings, they were of a similar type as the settlements of the Korchak group. Likewise the hand-made, unornamented pottery is close to the Korchak group but differs from it by the predominance of bi-conic shapes that are strongly reminiscent of similar finds in the forest regions of the north. Among the numerous metal objects are valuable fibulae which facilitate dating into the sixth to seventh century. But strong links with the preceding Chernyakhov culture, which vanished at the turn of the fourth to the fifth century, point to an earlier origin of the Pen'kovka type. These two types have even been found side by side. The contacts with the remnants of the Chernyakhov population and the assimilation of their culture must have taken place in the fifth century. Some scholars are, therefore, of the opinion

A local type of early Slav pottery, the Pen'kovka type, developed in the region between the Dnieper and the Dniester. It is considered to be the work of the Slav Antes mentioned by the historian Jordanes in the sixth century. Valuable finds of metal objects have been made, e. g. this bronze figure of a lion from the Skibintsy site, which dates from the sixth or seventh century.

that the people who created the Pen'kovka type were survivors of the original Iranian population, probably Sarmatians, who adapted to Slav ways and were called Antes (or Anti) in the historic records of the sixth century. Jordanes, for example, distinguishes them from the Sclaveni, probably pure Slavs, but stresses that they likewise spoke a Slavonic tongue. Their mighty union of tribes succumbed to the Avars in the early seventh century, but the culture survived longer and the spread of finds to the south indicates that these Slavs participated in the expansion to the Balkans.

Archeologists are at a loss in regard to another cultural group that existed in the forest regions of the upper Dnieper, roughly today's Byelorussia and the river basin of the Desna as far almost as Kiev. According to two important finds it is usually called the KOLOCHIN-TUSHEMLYA TYPE. These people lived in small settlements along the river banks, using semi-subterranean dwellings or houses built at ground level supported on posts. They made simple pottery, slightly different in shape from the Korchak-Prague type: conical, bi-conical, gently profiled, etc. The women wore bronze ornaments of the Baltic type inlaid with enamel. Their garments were held together with one fibula, they wore bracelets with widening ends and spun wool with the

aid of bi-conical spindles with a large hole in the centre. The men wore belts with gilt bronze ornaments, and their weapons included bow and arrow and spears. The dead were cremated and the remains were placed in pits, sometimes in urns or below tumuli.

In view of the similarity in features of the general cultural model, scholars have put forward the ideas of a possible connection between the Kolochin-Tushemlya type and the Slavs. They point out that certain elements spread to the south, the area where Pen'kovka type finds associated with the Slav Antes were made. On the other hand, it should not be overlooked that basically the Kolochin-Tushemlya type had its roots in the Baltic Iron Age cultures with some influences of the Zarubintsy culture (shapes of pottery, ornaments with inlaid enamel). It is, furthermore, widely spread over a territory where philologists have found Baltic, names of watercourses; it did not continue to develop but was overlaid, in the eighth to ninth century, by the influx of the colonizing Slavs. They brought a different culture from the south, the area of the Korchak and Pen'kovka types. It is now thought that the inhabitants of the upper Dnieper basin, where the Kolochin-Tushemlya culture grew up in the fifth to eighth century, were most likely Baltic or at best mixed Balto-Slavic in origin.

WHEN DID THE EMERGENCE OF THE SLAVS TAKE PLACE?

We have summed up the archeological findings in the hypothetical homeland of the Slavs, from the first reports by ancient writers to the period of the migration of nations when the foundations of the ethnic map of Europe were laid. Despite the inevitable simplification this brief survey indicates how complicated a process the emergence of the Slavs was. In many regards scholars are still in the dark, even though they have gathered up a considerable quantity of material to uphold their arguments.

The following questions still require clarification: how to decide between mutually contradictory facts, how to make them fit the mighty, historically proven appear-

The largest and most recent settlement of the Pen'kovka type lies on Makarov island. The numerous finds made on the site, dating even from the eighth century, included a cache of iron objects.

ance in the sixth to seventh century of the Slavs, a people who had been completely unknown to the civilized world until that time? How to explain the fact that an ethnic unit for which, in the first half of the first millennium A.D., there was no place historically or archeologically — on which all scholars might agree — managed suddenly to flood a considerable part of the European continent in the course of two or three centuries? How is it possible that such a mighty section of European peoples, who, from the sixth century on, emerged in linguistic and cultural unity, should until then escape the attention of the entire civilized world of the Greeks and Romans, who were otherwise so well informed about far more remote regions? It is equally remarkable that among the large Indo-European branches, such as the Germans, Celts, Illyrians, Thra-

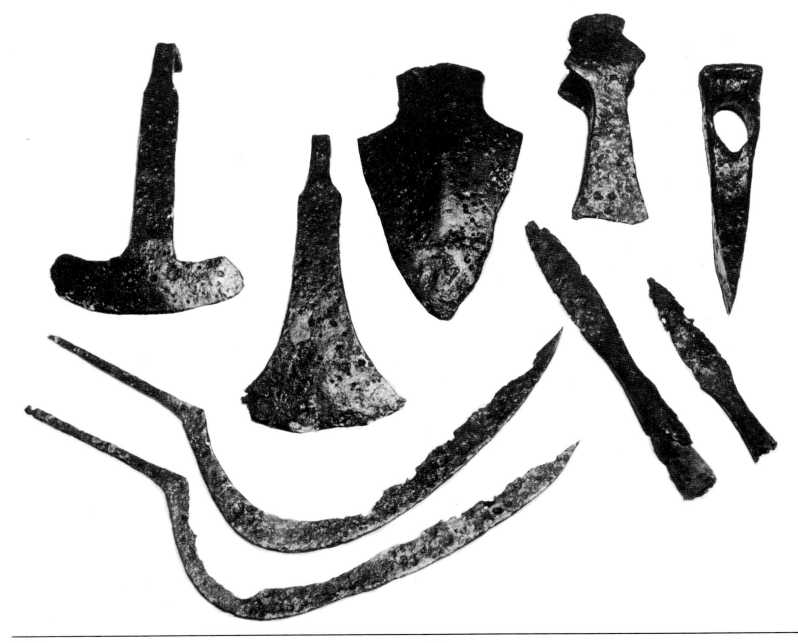

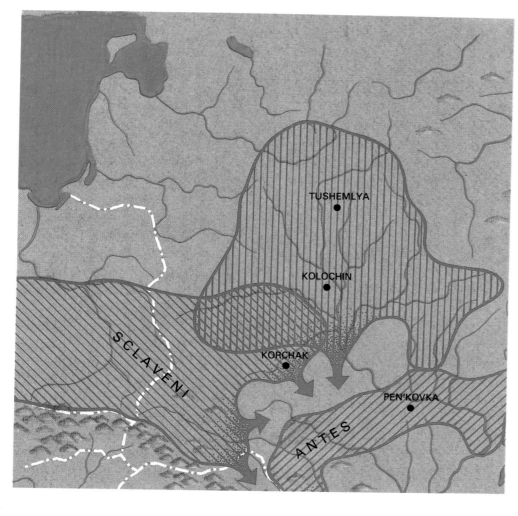

Korchak and Prague type

Kolochin-Tushemlya type

Pen'kovka type

TUSHEMLYA

KOLOCHIN

KORCHAK

PEN'KOVKA

SCLAVENI

ANTES

Map of archeological groups in Eastern Europe in the first half of the first millennium A.D.: The core of the Slavs – Jordanes's "Sclaveni" – is represented by finds of the Prague-Korchak type; the "Antes" – probably Slavicized Iranians – by finds of the Pen'kovka type. The Kolochin-Tushemlya type relates, in all likelihood, to Baltic inhabitants, later also Slavicized.

cians, Dacians, Scythians, Sarmatians, etc., the Slavs were the only ones who were known by name only after the fall of the Roman Empire. The view that a mere change of name, that is, from the Venedi to the Slavs, took place is not satisfactory given the comparative stability of names of the other large ethnic groups. While we can trace archeologically the development of the Germanic tribes, the Balts, Celts and Iranians, far back into antiquity, the Slavs vanish without a trace before the fifth to sixth century. Very little help is rendered by the efforts of certain archeologists who try to show the overlaying of early Slavonic culture upon the cultures of the Roman period. This refers only to marginal features and not to the culture as such. Equally unsatisfactory are propositions as to a change in the cultural model during the critical historic situation of the migration of nations, e.g. from the model of the Przeworsk culture to a deviating model of Early Slavonic. This does not explain the time gap between the disappearance of the old and the birth of the new culture.

There is only one highly likely, if hypothetical, explanation for these contradictory historical, ar-

cheological and linguistic facts: the Slavs as a cultural and ethnic unit, in the form known from the sixth century A.D. on, did not exist in antiquity. They underwent a complex process of ethnogenesis that reached its culmination in the fourth to fifth century and was completed just before the great migration began. This might even be regarded as a sign that the entire process had matured by then. The difficulties that arise in trying to determine ethnically the cultural groups of the Roman period living between the Oder and the middle Dnieper (Przeworsk, Chernyakhov, Zarubintsy) derive from the fact that in marginal areas they all contributed to the birth of a new ethnic unit, a process that the Celts and Germans had undergone long before. Of all the members of the large Indo-European family the Slavs were the last to emerge. And for that reason their arrival in history took place with such youthful strength. Only if that is so can we understand how, all of a sudden, they emerged in the sixth century as a unified linguistic group and how, by contrast to the Germanic groups, who underwent a much longer development, they became differentiated in language relatively late — between the ninth and the thirteenth century. To this day they remain comparatively closer to each other than do the nations of the other Indo-European branches.

The ancient Venedi must have played an important role in this ethnogenetic process even if one cannot place an equation mark between them and the early medieval Slavs. Their ethnical character remains unclear (Illyrians, Celto-Germans, or more likely Balto-Slavs — a transition between the Balts and the Slavs?). In fact, they probably were no more than an organizational component that later merged with its economic substratum and represented therefore a mere developmental pre-stage of the early Slavs. That would help us to understand why Tacitus was at a loss to say whether the Venedi were part of the Germanic tribes or the Sarmatians.

The new ethnic group emerged along the fringes of several large Indo-European groups confirmed in the records. There were the Balts to the north, the Germans to the west, the Iranian Sarmatians to the east and, to a lesser extent, in view of certain linguistic relations, even the Celts, Thracians and perhaps the Illyrians to the south. Closest in language to them were the Balts, whose share in the ethnogenetical process of the Slavs was most pronounced. Recent research has shown that Baltic names of watercourses can be found surprisingly far south and east, even south of the Pripyat', that is, the domain of the Slavic Korchak type of the fifth to seventh centuries. They occur over an infinitely larger area than the river names of definitely Slavonic origin. This fact strongly contrasts with the spread of Slav and Baltic settlements formed, according to archeological evidence, in the eighth to tenth centuries. It indicates the great importance of the Baltic component in the origin of the Slav ethnic group.

The one Slavonic language, documented in records of the sixth to ninth centuries, can be considered an expression of the completion of the process of integration within the region touching on the Balts, Germans and Iranians (with a major Baltic share), which we must seek somewhere between the middle Dnieper, Pripyat', upper Dniester, Vistula and Oder. All linguistic and archeological facts point to that region. Archeologically this is reflected in the content and extent of three adjacent cultures which partly interlinked: the Przeworsk, Chernyakhov and Late Zarubintsy, to which each of these above mentioned ethnic components contributed. Of particular importance in this regard is the eastern part of the Przeworsk, the north-western part of the Chernyakhov and the southern part of the Late Zarubintsy cultures (Kiev type). The disappearance of these cultures in the fourth to fifth century is a sign of the culmination of that ethnic differentiation and cultural and linguistic integration. The actual Slavs (Sclaveni) then made their appearance in the fifth to sixth century, confirmed by finds of the Prague-Korchak type, a unified cultural unit reflecting an integrated ethnic unit. Once the Slav expansion was complete and new settlements had been occupied, a new process of

disintegration set in which led to the emergence of the three main groups of Slavs — Eastern, Western and Southern — and later, in the Middle Ages, to the origin of nations.

In other words, the Slavs are the youngest section of the European peoples. They appear on the scene only after the middle of the first millennium A.D. Without such a conclusion one cannot explain the relative

linguistic unity of the Slav people in the early Middle Ages, whereby they differed strikingly from other, linguistically highly differentiated contemporary ethnic groups (for example, the Germans), and their sudden emergence in history and archeology, from the sixth century on. This could happen only as a consequence of a complex ethnogenetical process, which took place in the first half of the first millennium A.D. It involved a certain section of the Baltic tribes living in inland Eastern Europe, where, until the Roman period, they had formed a Balto-Slavic unit. They then became individualized by closer contacts with the neighbouring Germanic and Iranian regions. The outcome was the early Slavs, who later set out on the march to find new homes in Europe. But that is a story to be told in the next chapter.

The cultural group of Kolochin-Tushemlya was widespread in the wooded regions along the upper Dnieper in the fifth to eighth century. The inhabitants were probably of Baltic or temporary Balto-Slavic origin. One of their main centres was the hill-fort of Tushemlya where there was a pagan shrine. Excavations have enabled the archeologists to attempt its approximate reconstruction.

THE GREAT
EXPANSION
BEGINS

THE SETTLEMENT OF CENTRAL EUROPE

The eastern part of Central Europe, which was taken over by the Slavs during the migration of nations, used to be inhabited by Celtic and Germanic tribes in antiquity. Certain areas of the Czech lands were the original homeland of the Celts, and the mighty tribe of the Celtic Boii gave their name to the country, where it is used to this day (Boiohemum, Bohemia). They lived here for several centuries, and their political and cultural centre lay on Závist hill, south of Prague. At the turn of the era the Germanic Marcomanni and Quadi drove the Boii out of the Czech lands, and later these tribes moved further east, to Slovakia, where the Roman Emperor and philosopher Marcus Aurelius fought against them in the second century A.D. They were followed by other Germanic tribes from the Elbe region, among them chiefly the Lombards, some of whom stayed long enough, together with certain other Germanic inhabitants, to witness the arrival of the Slavs.

Not a single contemporary historian left any record of when and how the Slav tribes moved into Central Europe. There is only the indirect evidence provided by Procopius and Jordanes, mentioned in the previous chapter. It depicts the Slavs in the process of migration in the sixth century, but provides few concrete facts which might give a clearer idea of this event, which had such an important part in shaping the later history of that part of Central Europe. Some of the Slav tribes had their own legends; they were handed on by word of mouth from generation to generation before they were written down and treated as a work of literature by a medieval chronicler. This is what happened to the collection of Czech legends, which were written down and re-composed in the early twelfth century by Prague chronicler Cosmas. He described the beginning of Slav settlement in the Czech lands in the following manner: "...At that time the surface of this land was covered with broad expanses of desolate forests, without a single inhabitant... When men entered these deserted places, whoever they may have been — unknown and accompanied by a few other people — seeking suitable places for human dwellings, their bright eyes saw mountains and dales, plains and hill-slopes, and I believe somewhere around Mount Říp, between two rivers, the Ohře and the Vltava, they first established settlements, built

Mount Říp rises all on its own out of the plain in central Bohemia and is entwined with legends of Old Father Czech, who after long years of wandering from the homeland in eastern regions stood on its summit and identified the new home area of his tribe.

The historic migration of the Slavs was, to a certain extent, an organized process in which entire tribes or certain sections took part. As peasants looking for land and permanent settlements the immigrants brought with them weapons and tools as well as supplies of corn and herds of cattle.

dwellings and joyfully placed upon the ground their gods whom they had carried on their shoulders.''

The restrained words in which Cosmas formulated his story show that he was trying to establish a historical hypothesis in its medieval form. He used certain local traditions that related the origin of the Czechs, and it was clearly linked to a definite place. With its striking outline Mount Říp, in the very centre of the country, offered itself to the idea of ''Old Father Czech'', the leader of the tribe standing on its summit after long years

of wandering and choosing the surrounding land as home for his people just like Moses long before, who from Mount Nebo set eyes on the Israelites'. Promised Land. This distant past was no more than a misty reminiscence, added to and embroidered with great fantasy. Only one thing is real in the chronicler's report — the fact that the ancestors had come to the country. But Cosmas did not know about their Celtic or Germanic precursors — they were only discovered by the sixteenth-century scholars who studied ancient writers — and he was, therefore, of the opinion that Old Father Czech settled in a deserted, forest-clad land that had not been inhabited since the time of the biblical flood. He did not even dare to guess where the multitude of Czechs had come from. He left that to later chroniclers, such as Dalimil in the fourteenth century, who, strangely enough, spoke of Croatia as the original homeland of the Czechs. If that is a reference to an older folk lore, it cannot mean modern Croatia, as Dalimil himself must have assumed, but Great or White Croatia. In the distant past this stretched to the north of the Carpathians, today's southern Poland and western Ukraine, from where the mighty Slav tribe of the Croats spread, some to the south, the Balkans, others to the west as far as eastern Bohemia. The Serbs, who were related to them, split up in the same manner as the Croats and told similar stories about their original homeland, as we can discover from reports by the ninth-century Bavarian Geographer.

The simple vase-shaped pottery, called "Prague type" by the archeologists, reveals the presence of the first Slavs in Central Europe (Březno near Louny, Bohemia, sixth century).

It is thus possible to cull some truth from legends. But they cannot be taken as providing present-day historians with reliable facts. Their efforts largely failed in view of the complete lack of confirmed sources. Reports, or rather fragments of reports with references here and there, which have so far been found and analysed, often produce more questions than answers.

This almost hopeless situation changed greatly when archeologists joined in the discussions of the historians; their discovery of pottery provides concrete proof of the expansion of the Slavs. According to finds in the Prague region the pottery is known, since 1940, as the Prague type. Soon similar finds were made in Moravia, Slovakia, East Germany, and mainly in southern Poland and the western Ukraine (Korchak type), that is, on a territory that belonged to the eastern regions of Slav migration. The connection between these finds and the movements of the Slavs at the time of the migration of nations suddenly became clear.

Archeologists are not only concerned with pottery but with discovering the circumstances in which it is found: the sum total of facts and relationships investigated in the research then provides a better insight into the life style, work, dwellings and the level of culture. In the case of the Prague type it was a matter of finds of graves and of dwellings. In the graves the pottery most often served as urns, that is, to hold the burnt bones and ashes of the dead. Certain objects had been placed in these urns: clasps, knives, blades, combs, glass beads and the like. The urns containing these remains were buried in shallow graves or a barrow was raised above them. Where the dead had not been cremated, which was rare in the very early period, they placed an urn in the grave as a gift. In the dwellings, the remains of pottery vessels, together with other objects, lay scattered on the floor or in infills as waste, or they were left behind when the dwelling was suddenly abandoned or destroyed. The comparison with finds in other sites, with objects of the same, preceding and following periods, and those in neighbouring and more remote regions and then mapping all these finds enables the archeologists to do what the historians could never read in their records: to get an idea of the overall advance of Slav settlement.

Valuable data on the development of pottery of the Prague type were derived, for example, in investigations of the cremation cemeteries at Velatice near Brno, where on the basis of horizontal stratigraphy it became possible to prove a conclusive link between the Prague type and the other well-known Slav pottery. An important find was also made at Přítluky in southern Moravia, where more than four hundred graves were uncovered together with a settlement that occupied an area of roughly one square kilometre (0.4 square mile). The concentration of inhabitants, which this find proves, is quite exceptional since the majority of settlements and burial grounds of the Prague type were on a relatively small scale.

On the basis of the few accompanying objects the

The tumulus at Žuráň near Slavkov (Austerlitz) in Moravia, from which Napoleon commanded the famous battle in 1805. It covered the tomb of a Lombard ruler of the fifth century. But finds of pottery made during the excavations also show the presence of Slavs.

The dwellings uncovered during excavations at Březno all had the typical shape of early Slav semi-subterranean houses.

Moravian finds of the Prague type can be dated roughly to the period from the turn of the fifth to the sixth century into the seventh century. For a historian this fact is remarkable since, until the middle of the sixth century, he has to reckon with Germanic settlements in the southern parts of Moravia where the early Slav finds are concentrated. In the fifth century the Rugi lived here, who had spread this far from the Danube valley in Austria. After their utter defeat by the Goths in 488 the area of the Rugi was taken over by the militant Lombards, who were traced by the archeologists from finds of skeleton burials with tombs of warriors. An exceptional discovery of this type was the tumulus at Žuráň near Brno. In 1805 Napoleon set up his headquarters right on top of it and directed the famous battle of Austerlitz from there. He had no idea that below him were the tombs of other similar conquerors, who had penetrated into Moravia thirteen centuries earlier. It may well be that this is the burial place of a Lombard king and his wife; the rich dowry for the after-life had unfortunately been stolen, except for some small pieces. But what is interesting is that in one of the tombs, sherds have been found of a vessel that is very close to the Prague type. There have been several such cases, and this proves a certain form of Slavo-Germanic co-existence.

These relationships can tell us something about the arrival of the Slavs, about a period for which written records remain silent. A number of settlements and burial sites have been discovered in Slovakia. At the settlement at Výčapy-Opatovce vessels of the Prague type were found side by side with Hun pottery, which cannot be later than from the second half of the fifth century when the nomad empire of the Huns came to an end in the Carpathian Basin after their defeat on the Catalaunian Plains. The finds are concentrated in the fertile regions of south-western Slovakia, along the rivers Morava, Váh, Dudváh, Nitra, Hron and Ipel'. A little before that time Slav tribes moved into eastern Slovakia, where their pottery is found together with sherds of the barbarian Roman culture from the turn of the fourth to the fifth century (known as the PREŠOV TYPE). In this manner it is possible to document the shift of Slav settlement in Central Europe from east to west.

The living conditions in the most westerly regions - that is, the Czech lands and along the middle course of the Elbe (the southern part of today's German Democratic Republic) — are revealed, on two particularly important sites among many others, where archeologists have been concentrating their attention: Březno near Louny and Dessau-Mosigkau in Saxony.

At Březno a settlement from the end of the fifth and the first half of the sixth century has been uncovered. It belonged to the remnants of the Germanic inhabitants who had otherwise left the Czech lands as they moved further to the south-east and south-west. The people lived in huts of a rectangular ground plan, partly dug into the ground, with a wooden construction usually supported by six poles, in which case three of them are placed on each of the narrower sides. Their settlement gradually moved from its original place in an easterly direction to the right bank of a stream that flows into the Ohře. During the first half of the sixth century new

One of the main centres of early Slav settlement in Bohemia was the river Ohře. Archeologists have been investigating a settlement on the banks of the river near Březno, founded by Slav immigrants on the site of an earlier Germanic settlement some time in the second quarter of the sixth century.

immigrants appeared, who, strangely enough, did not behave in a hostile manner, but settled by the side of the original inhabitants. There clearly was no reason for conflict between the peaceful farming people and cattle breeders, pursuits both people followed, in the sparsely inhabited regions of Bohemia where the soil lay fallow and there was suitable ground both for corn growing and pasture. The immigrants were the first Slavs, who did not greatly differ from their Germanic neighbours in their manner of living and level of culture and for that reason merged with them into one unit in the relatively short period of about two generations. They lived likewise in simple dwellings, partly dug into the ground, but of square ground plan with a trodden earth floor and usually a stone oven in the south-western corner, which did not exist in the Germanic huts. Vessels of the Prague type with or without decorations predominated in their households. The co-existence of the two peoples can be traced in mixed types of pottery and dwellings.

The Slav settlement was likewise moved after a time, probably as a consequence of a cyclical, partially migratory agriculture in which certain areas of the tilled land were left to lie fallow after a certain period and the dwellings were moved closer to the fields then under cultivation. Seven to ten houses were grouped in a circle around an open central space (each settlement had roughly forty to sixty inhabitants), and all around were pits for supplies — deep pits of a circular shape that were used for underground grain storage. The corn found here, mainly wheat but also barley, rye, oats, millet and even peas, lentils and hemp, is proof of a more advanced stage of agricultural technique than the original inhabitants possessed.

A similar village with an open central area was excavated in the years 1962—65 on Zoberberg hill near Dessau-Mosigkau in the south of the German Democratic Republic. Here, too, contacts with the original inhabitants were observed in finds of pottery and the construction of dwellings, and here, too, the settlement was gradually moved, in fact in five stages. Many other similarities can be found, with but one difference: everything took place at a slightly later date, the second half of the sixth century.

In this manner the archeological finds of the Prague type document the advance of Slav tribes from the east to the west: first they are to be found in eastern Slovakia (perhaps as early as in the first half of the fifth century); then in south-western Slovakia (second half of the fifth century); in southern Moravia (at the turn of the fifth to sixth century); later in Bohemia (first half of the sixth century) and finally between the Elbe and the Saale (second half of that century). What the contemporaries of this historic process — Procopius and Jordanes — did not reveal was shown by mute evidence in the hands of the archeologists.

Slav settlement in the north-western parts of Central Europe presents a slightly different picture; this is the

The settlement at Březno comprised a group of seven to ten semi-subterranean dwellings, forming a circle round an open space. Corn and other foodstuffs were kept in covered pits which served as stores.

region between the middle and lower courses of the rivers Elbe, Oder and Vistula. This settlement is not recorded in any chronicle and is not even mentioned in legend, and so we have to rely only on the proofs provided by archeological finds, which have not yet given answers to all the questions.

Here, too, Germanic settlements from the time of the late Roman period came to an end basically at the turn of the fourth to the fifth century. But in places enclaves of the pre-Slav inhabitants survived until the second half of the fifth or even the beginning of the sixth century: for example, in central Poland where a late Przeworsk-culture settlement was discovered at Piwonice; the same is true of Polish Pomerania. The territory further to the west was likewise depopulated in the fifth century — the tribes of the Angles and Saxons moved to Britain at that time, while the Lombards migrated to the south — but

traces of Germanic settlement remained in western Pomerania in Mecklenburg and Holstein until the first quarter of the sixth century, in exceptional cases even until the beginning of the seventh century; in Brandenburg and the middle course of the Elbe the Germanic settlement disappeared around the middle of the sixth century.

The migration of the local Germanic tribes made it possible for the Slavs to penetrate by stages, in larger numbers than elsewhere, and here they will have met the last of the Germans to leave. This conditioned the unique features of Slavonic culture, which differs in some respects from the Prague type of the more southerly regions. In their settlements the archeologists have, for instance, found types of houses other than the semi-subterranean dwellings typical of the Prague-Korchak type: the people tended to live in log cabins above

come to the regions between the lower Elbe, Oder and the Baltic Sea, the shores of which the Slav tribes reached in the course of the sixth century if we can believe the records of the Byzantine historian Theophylact Simocatta. The Slav settlement of eastern Germany, confirmed today by the large number of place names of Slav origin, took place from the middle of the sixth to the middle of the seventh century and the people remained here, despite centuries of dramatic struggles, until the Middle Ages, and in certain areas (Lusatia) they have remained to the present day.

The special cultural status of this north-western Slav group in Central Europe shows a corresponding linguistic development, in the framework of which the Lekhitic group of the Slavonic languages later came into being; including Polish, Lusatian—Sorbian, the now vanished Polabian Slavonic and Kashubian. The early Middle Ages saw the first signs of differentiation among the Slavs, who after settling over a vast territory in Europe began to lose their unified language and culture and gradually split up into more or less big groups; and once independent states came into being, this led to the development of national tongues.

The Slav expansion to the west continued in the seventh and eighth centuries when it nearly reached to the mouth of the Elbe, as proved by recent finds of Slav settlements in Hamburg. They crossed the middle courses of the Elbe and Saale and penetrated to Thuringia and northern Bavaria. This remarkable influx of settlers might have gone even further if, at the end of the eighth century, there had not appeared a mighty barrier in the form of the Empire of Charlemagne who began to push in the opposite direction.

A settlement of Slav immigrants was also excavated on Zoberberg hill near Dessau-Mosigkau in the southern parts of the German Democratic Republic. It dates from the second half of the sixth century.

ground, the interior was not dug into the ground, and only irregular trenches served for storage. In the first phase of colonization the local Slavs produced simple, hand-made and undecorated pottery, but of slightly differing shapes (known as the SUKOW-DZIEDZICE TYPE) than those customary on the territory of Czechoslovakia or southern Poland. Very soon more advanced pottery appeared, turned on a wheel, for example, the FELDBERG TYPE, or the bi-conical TORNOW TYPE vessels found mainly in Lower Lusatia, Silesia and in the Oder valley. The original centre of these two types of ornamented pottery — dated into the seventh, in places even the end of the sixth century — is being sought in the region along the upper course of the Oder and in Silesia at the time of the migration of nations, where similar elements appeared within the late Przeworsk setting. It is from there that the main stream of Slavic colonization must have

37

THE ADVANCE INTO THE BALKANS

There exist far better historical sources to document Slav settlement in South-Eastern Europe, for here they were advancing into the civilized world of the time — the cultural sphere of Byzantium. The Byzantine chroniclers recorded the exact year when the Slavs crossed the Danube and began raids into Macedonia, Thessaly and Epirus — that is, the territory where southern Yugoslavia, Albania and northern Greece lie today: it was in the year 517. These raids occurred on numerous occasions during the reign of Emperor Justin (518—527). For a time Justinian the Great (527—565), the outstanding ruler of Byzantium, managed to put a stop to the Slav influx. He permitted some Slav tribes, among them the Antes, to settle on Byzantine territory, and they became allies of the Empire — called *foederati* — as had been the age-old practice in ancient Rome. Nonetheless, the inroads of Slavs continued: in 536 they reached the coast of the Adriatic Sea, in 548 Dyrrhachium, and further raids continued throughout the fifties of the sixth century.

The beginnings of Slav settlement in Mecklenburg are represented by the hill-fort Alte Burg near Sukow, which was probably built already in the seventh century.

Events took a sharper turn when a new factor appeared on the scene: the Avars. These militant nomads of Asian origin, coming from the Eastern European steppes, were attracted by the Carpathian Basin in particular, where before them their relatives, the Huns, had settled and where two hostile Germanic peoples were living in the sixth century — the Lombards and the Gepids. The Avars helped the Lombards destroy the Gepids, and then the Avars occupied their territory, after the Lombards had decided to leave their uncomfortable new neighbours in 568 and move to northern Italy, where they founded a new empire on the ruins of the Roman Empire. The Avars then made the territory of what is Hungary today their centre, and from there they threatened Western and Southern Europe. They were aided in this by several Slav tribes either as allies or vassals. The tribes that remained on the side of Byzantium — e.g. the Antes along the lower Danube — were destroyed by the Avars in a special campaign in the year 602.

In their raids against the Byzantines the Avars — without intending to do so — contributed to further

Slav colonization of the Balkans. There was one great difference between the behaviour of the Avars and that of their Slavic allies in these raids: while the nomads, as was their custom, only looted, laid everything waste and then moved on, the Slav peasants settled for good on the territory they had attacked. In this way they gradually peopled all the former Roman provinces: Dacia, Moesia, Dardania, Macedonia, Dalmatia and Epirus. In 578 the Slavs even reached the Peloponnese, and from 581 on they began to settle on Greek soil to the horror of the Byzantines who found refuge only in the larger towns. We can well imagine the feelings of the inhabitants of the famous cities of antiquity, such as Athens and Thebes, when they observed with what disregard the barbarian intruders made their homes in their vicinity. It was only by a miracle, attributed to St Demetrius, that in 597 Thessalonica escaped destruction after a siege by the Slavs and Avars; while the Avars returned to their camps in the Hungarian Plain, the Slavs remained in the Thessalonican countryside as permanent settlers. Not quite three hundred years later this enabled the men of Thessalonica, Constantine and Methodius, to learn the

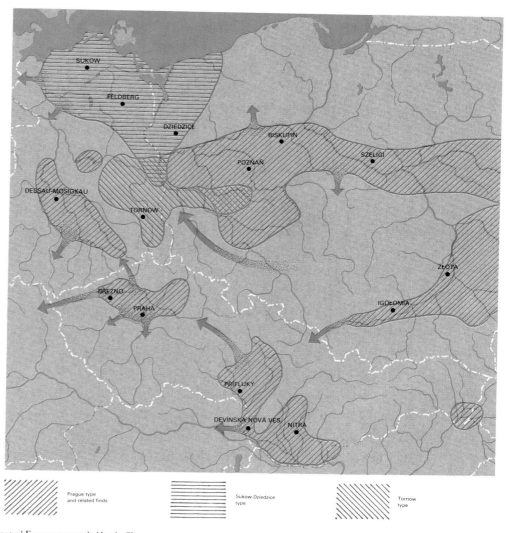

Prague type and related finds

Sukow-Dziedzice type

Tornow type

Central Europe was settled by the Slavs in the sixth to seventh century. They took a number of routes which mainly followed the courses of the bigger rivers.

Slavonic tongue and give it both an alphabet and a literary form.

The Byzantine Empire was in a particularly difficult situation since the eastern border was threatened by the Persians during the reign of Emperor Maurice (582—602). It was only after the dangerous enemy had been defeated that the Byzantines could concentrate their forces on the Balkans again and they beat the Slavs and Avars on several occasions. The Danube once again came to form the border between different centres of power.

At the beginning of the seventh century another wave of Slav settlers came to the Balkans; they penetrated to the west as far as Venice and valleys in the Alps, south across the Peloponnese to the Aegean islands and to Crete and even reached the coast of Asia Minor. Today we have difficulty in imagining the vitality of those invaders, who had been completely unknown until they managed to flood such vast areas in large numbers within a few decades and push a wedge between the Roman west and the Greek east. The local inhabitants heaved sighs of relief only at the beginning of the ninth century, when Nicephorus I managed to defeat the Slavs in the decisive battle near Patras on the Peloponnese and

The hand-made, undecorated pottery of the Sukow type is the Baltic equivalent of early Slav pottery in Central and Eastern Europe.

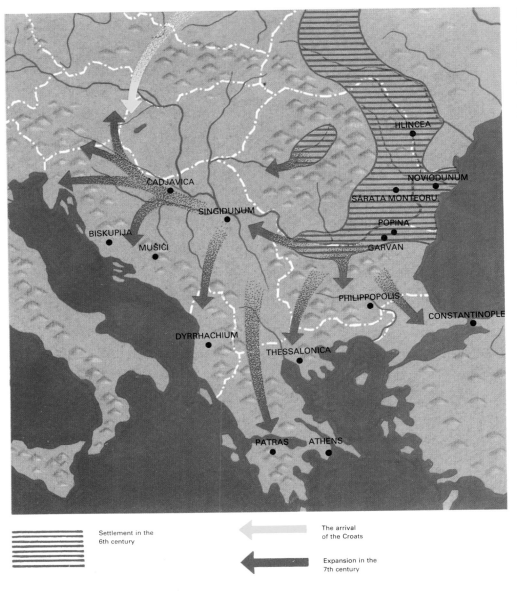

Goths, Turco-Tatar Huns and Avars, and mainly by masses of Slavs; they came to form the core of the local inhabitants from the sixth to the tenth century when, for so far unexplained circumstances, the remnants of the Romanized inhabitants — today's Romanians — began to gain the upper hand both culturally and linguistically. We have mentioned a report by Jordanes from the middle of the sixth century that Slav settlements ranged as far as the town of Novietunum which can be identified as Noviodunum, lying close to the widening delta of the Danube. Even today there is a settlement called Isaccea, where Romanian archeologists have found traces of an old Slav settlement on the ruins of an ancient town.

Until recently little was known about the scope and character of Slav settlement in Romania. Investigations by Romanian archeologists in the last few decades have provided more concrete ideas, even though the explanation of some new discoveries is still hotly discussed.

The oldest Slav finds were made in Moldavia, the northern part of Romania between the rivers Prut and Sereth. This territory lies in close vicinity to the oldest Slav group in the Ukraine, which we met in the Korchak and Pen'kovka types. It is understandable that the bearers of this culture penetrated to Romanian Moldavia already in the second half of the sixth century and left behind settlements with semi-subterranean dwellings and cremation burials of the same kind as Soviet archeologists found in the areas of the Dnieper, Dniester, Pripyat' and Bug. The finds are dated by the ornaments of the MARTYNOVKA TYPE (called after a treasure from the Kiev region) which are a proof of Slav expansion to the Balkans and even by Byzantine coins, with those of the Justinian period dominating, from the second half of the sixth and the early seventh century. The inhabitants of these first settlements often chose boggy terrain surrounded by dense forests, which provided refuge in case of danger. The bearers of the Korchak and Pen'kovka types penetrated, towards the end of the sixth century, not only southwards to the Danube lowlands but across passes in the Carpathians even into Transylvania. These finds include certain elements from the northern areas of the Dnieper, Desna and Berezina, i.e. elements of the Kolochin-Tushemlya type, which clearly belonged to Slavonicized Balts; the migration of the Slavs must have involved tribes from the entire eastern Slavic territory.

Slavic finds from the seventh to ninth centuries are identical in character with contemporary finds to the east, known as the LUKA RAYKOVETSKAYA TYPE, which developed from the early Slavic pottery of the Korchak type. They are proof of permanent relationships with eastern Slav tribes, whose settlements at that time spread over the entire territory of what is now Romania.

The Western Slavs partly shared in the Slav settlement of Romania, when they penetrated from Central Europe to Transylvania. This can be proved by the burial ground with tumuli at Nuşfalău near Oradea with

thus basically put an end to their occupation of Greece. The rest of the Slavs, however, stayed for a relatively long time; in the Taygetus mountains on the Peloponnese tribes of the Erzerites and Milings were still recorded in the fourteenth century, when the Turks arrived there. The territory of Bulgaria today and of Yugoslavia has remained Slav to the present day.

Now let us take a closer look at what archeology can tell us about the process of Slav settlement on the Balkan peninsula. The key area is the territory of present-day Romania, ancient Dacia, for the main stream of Slav colonists moved along the curve of the Carpathians and along the Danube.

At the time of the Roman Empire this was where the Dacians lived, against whom the Romans fought numerous battles, before they incorporated them in their empire at the beginning of the second century A.D. The province of Dacia took up only the western part of present-day Romania, and under Emperor Aurelian in the year 271 the impact of barbarian tribes forced the Romans to retreat across the Danube. The country was flooded by Iranian Sarmatians, Germanic Gepids and

The main flow of Slavs who colonized the Balkan peninsula moved from the Ukraine along the Carpathians and across the Danube. They went as far as the Adriatic Sea, the Peloponnese, the Aegean islands and the coast of Asia Minor.

typical pottery and objects of Slavo-Avar type from the eighth and early ninth centuries.

The Romanian archeologists have tried to trace the process of how the Romanic ethnic group came into existence on the basis of a certain renaissance of provincial shapes of pottery, burial rites and some peculiarities of the ninth-tenth century dwellings, in which they see the first signs of the Romanization of the population. The origins of the Romanians have not yet been satisfactorily explained, but what is certain is that the Slavs must have played a major role in their genesis. This is shown not only by the large number of Slavonic words in the Romanian language and Slavonic place-names all over Romania, but also by archeological clues.

The beginning of Slav settlement in Romania is related to the penetration by the Slavs to the territory of present-day Yugoslavia. Historians and philologists are still engaged in a lively discussion on the share of Western or Eastern Slavs in this expansion, but it seems that those arguments are well founded according to which the main stream of migration arrived from the east across ancient Dacia in the middle of the sixth century. The starting point of a lesser wave of migration were the settlements of Croats north of the Carpathians in the upper Vistula valley, from where smaller tribal groups moved south. This movement was recorded as an old legend by the Byzantine Emperor Constantine Porphyrogenitus in the middle of the tenth century. The fact that the Southern Slav tribes bear the name of that numerically relatively small Western Slav people shows that the Croats and with them the Serbs played an important role in the struggles against the Avars; and the Slavs managed to gather around them tribal groups to which their name was applied.

The picture that archeology provides on this problem is far from complete. But it tends to support the views of historians convinced of the eastern origin of the Southern Slavs rather than the conclusion of scholars who assume a considerable influx of Western Slav tribes to the Balkans. So far no definite find has been made on the territory of Yugoslavia of the Prague type, which would indicate a movement from Central Europe. The finds of early Slav hand-made pottery are very rare in this region and tend to resemble the Romanian, which is of Eastern Slav origin. As an example we can cite investigations carried out in 1966 near the village of Mušići on the banks of the Drina. In the ruins of a Roman villa simple semi-subterranean dwellings of oval shape were dug up with sherds from the sixth to seventh century, revealing an undeniably eastern origin. Beside them there were fragments of a different pottery, which probably did not belong to the Slavs but to the remnants of the local Romanized population, who gradually merged with the new arrivals, the Slavs. Similar signs of symbiosis have been discovered in other places, e.g. at Žabljak near Doboj; they also show the character of a later Slavonic culture combined with a number of elements of ancient local tradition.

Archeological proof of Slav expansion on the Balkans come from finds of the Martynovka type; the name derives from the find of a hoard of treasure in the western Ukraine, dating from the sixth century, which contained typical ray-shaped fibulae, star-shaped earrings, and little human and animal figures.

Strong relations to the southern Russian region are shown by finds of the Martynovka type, ornaments and jewels that are typical of local development in the sixth century on the territory of the western Ukraine. They include, first of all, ray-shaped clasps with masks, star-shaped ear-rings, metal figurines of fantastic animals or human figures, and even matrixes for making those metal ornaments. They are widespread in all places to which the Slavs penetrated in their expansion through the Balkans. In Yugoslavia they are concentrated in the Danube region.

A very important locality that documents Slavonic culture from the time when the Slavs occupied the Balkans is Caričin Grad near Leban in southern Serbia. Originally this was the site of a Byzantine town,

A large burial ground used in the sixth and seventh centuries was excavated at Sărata Monteoru near Bucharest. It contained more than 1,000 cremation graves with early Slav pottery and ornaments of the Martynovka type.

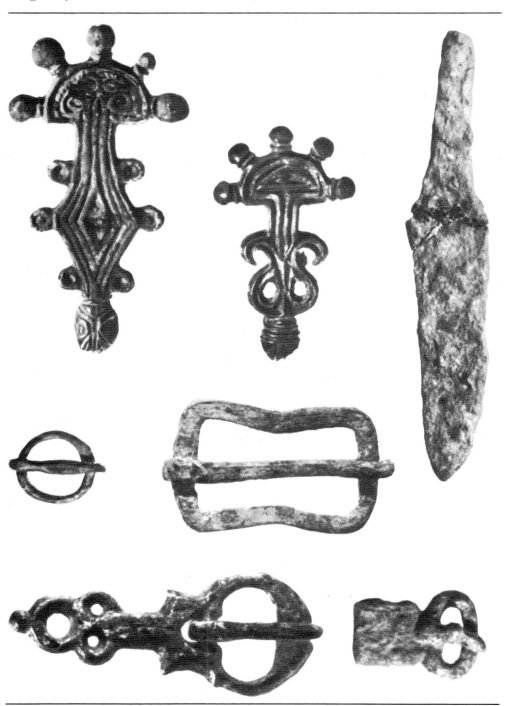

probably Iustiniana Prima, which the Slavs conquered as they advanced, and in its ruins they founded their own settlement. They built the walls of their simple dwellings in the streets and ruins of buildings using brick and stone held together with daub. Most of their houses are single-storeyed, with an irregular square ground plan, trodden earth floors and an open fireplace. Similar examples of early Slav settlement in the ruins of ancient cities have also been found elsewhere, e.g. at Margum, a Roman town at the confluence of the Morava and Danube, at Crkvica in Bosnia-Herzegovina, at Gamzigrad, even in Belgrade itself, the site where once stood the ancient city of Singidunum.

Apart from this, the oldest records of Slavs in Yugoslavia are to be found in monuments of early Avar culture from the sixth to seventh century. Typical features include, apart from nomad weapons, ornaments of pressed metal, mainly of Byzantine origin and related to the Martynovka type. This culture bears signs of an ethnic conglomeration, including, apart from the Avars and Kutrigurs, the remnants of the Romanized population and also, to a large extent, the Slavs, who were the Avars' main allies in their struggle with the Byzantines.

On the territory of Bulgaria the Slavs entered a land with a thousand-year-old cultural tradition. From the Bronze Age this was the home of the Thracians, an Indo-European people close, on the one hand, to the Dacians and, on the other, to the Greeks with whom the Thracians had close contacts. These relations were strongest in the Hellenistic period, when during the reign of Philip II and Alexander the Great the whole of Thracia was under the rule of Macedonia. But influences spread also in the opposite direction: the cult of Orpheus and especially of Dionysus, so popular in the Greek world, is of Thracian origin. When the Romans came, two provinces were established after long and bloody battles under Emperor Tiberius; for long centuries their names became geographical terms: Moesia, to the north of the Balkan Mountains (then called the Haemus) as far as the Danube, and Thracia proper south of the Haemus, which like a backbone runs across the whole country from east to west. Thracia, with the river Hebrus (today Maritsa) as its axis, and Philippopolis (Plovdiv) its capital city, was richer and more densely populated than Moesia; as the latter lay open towards the north into the Danubian lowlands, it was often the target of barbarian raids from the north, who regarded the Roman provinces as full of tempting loot. A milestone in development was the year 395, when, after the split-up of the Roman Empire, the two provinces fell to the Eastern Roman Empire with Constantinople as capital city. But the Byzantines managed only with great effort to keep control over their realms against the constant pressure of the northern barbarians. When in 488 the Ostrogoths led by Theodoric the Great left Moesia and moved to Italy, the land remained deserted. In the sixth century the Slavs

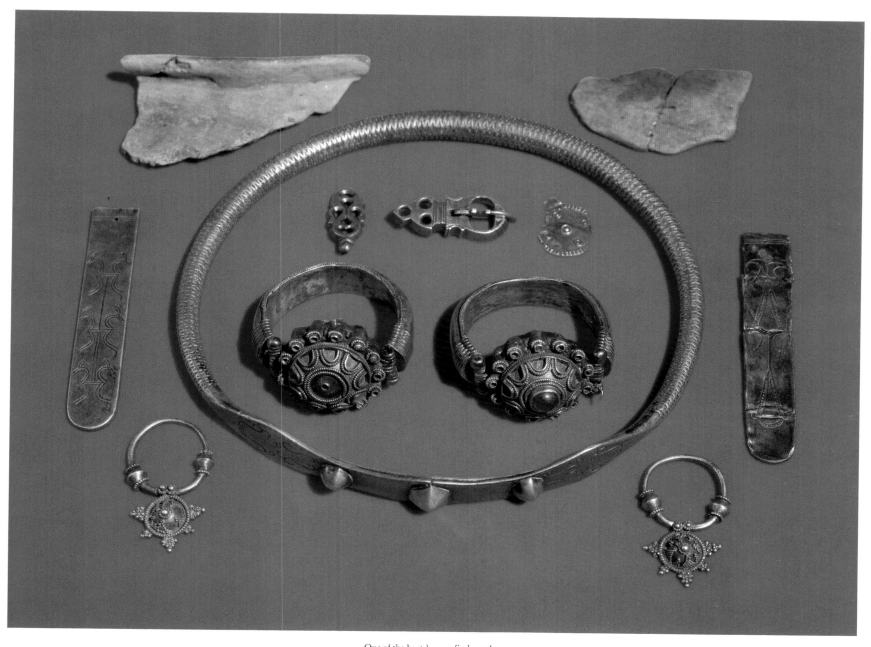

One of the best-known finds on the territory of northern Yugoslavia, indicating links between the Baltic Slavs and the western Ukraine, are silver jewels from a prince's tomb at Čadjavica (seventh century).

penetrated it with ease, and thus gave the subsequent historical development a decisive direction.

In recent decades Bulgarian archeologists have been able to trace the first Slavs who settled in their country from the sixth century on. Most of the sites have so far been discovered in the northern parts of Bulgaria, in ancient Moesia. In southern Bulgaria, formerly Thracia, only isolated finds of pottery have been made.

The oldest Slav settlements in this region also lay along the river, near lakes or in boggy lowlands. The dwellings were simple, as everywhere in the Slav world of those days: semi-subterranean or underground houses with a stone oven in one corner, the floor smoothed with clay. The pottery found in these dwellings is closer to Eastern Slav finds of the Korchak type in its general character than the Prague type of Central Europe. This provides an indication of the origin of the tribes that settled in Bulgaria. Even later, carefully fashioned pottery adorned with wavy or horizontal

grooves is of the same origin, for we can identify it with finds in Romania (HLINCEA TYPE) or in the Ukraine (Luka Raykovetskaya type), which are dated into the seventh or eighth century. Apart from pottery only small objects were found in these huts: iron knives, awls of bone, stone grinding wheels, glass pearls, bronze buttons and the like.

In Bulgaria, too, we find the original Slav custom of cremating the dead. The ashes were placed in urns or simply in circular pits. The modest personal belongings of the dead were placed in the grave, e.g. knives, arrow heads, sickles, scythes, spindles, buttons, rings, bronze coins, ear rings, glass beads, etc. They represent the simple culture of the first Slav settlers on whom the proximity of the Byzantine civilization left its mark only after a certain lapse of time, after the stabilization of their settlements and the founding of their own state in a symbiosis with the Turco-Tatar Bulgarians at the end of the eighth century.

Slav presence in Greek Thessaly during
the sixth and seventh centuries is
confirmed by finds of bronze ornaments
reminiscent of figurines of the
Martynovka type.

SLAV COLONIZATION OF EASTERN EUROPE

The eastern Slav expansion is a chapter unto itself. It was not limited to a short span of time in the sixth and seventh centuries as in the case of the expansion of the Slavs to the west and south. It became an almost continuous process of infiltration into the sparsely settled regions of Eastern Europe and later Asia, lasting throughout the Middle Ages and the new era. At this point, we are interested mainly in the initial stage, the phase of the early Middle Ages.

In contrast to the expansion into the Balkans there exist no written records to reveal anything about this early period. These regions were far too remote for Western European chroniclers of the seventh to ninth centuries, and they possessed but the vaguest ideas about them. Nothing more is to be found either in the works of Byzantine writers, who were geographically far closer. At the beginning they were interested only in the Slavs in the Balkans, with whom Byzantium had direct contacts. What was going on in the vast forest-steppe lands and wooded plains further to the north was none of their concern. The situation changed with the establishment of the Kievan state at the end of the ninth century, when Byzantium made close trade, cultural and military contacts with Eastern Europe. But even then the Byzantine chroniclers were more interested in other things than Slav colonization. There is only indirect evidence from the ninth and tenth centuries: the existence of certain Eastern Slav tribes was mentioned, e.g. in the writings of Emperor Constantine Porphyrogenitus in the tenth century, but they lacked detailed information about settlements. We can cull better knowledge from contemporary Arab sources, e.g. Ibn Khūrdādbih, Mas'ūdī, Ibn Fadhlan and others,

The first evidence of Slav penetration south of the Danube is being unearthed in northern Bulgaria. One of the most important settlements was found at Garvan-Staretsa near Silistra.

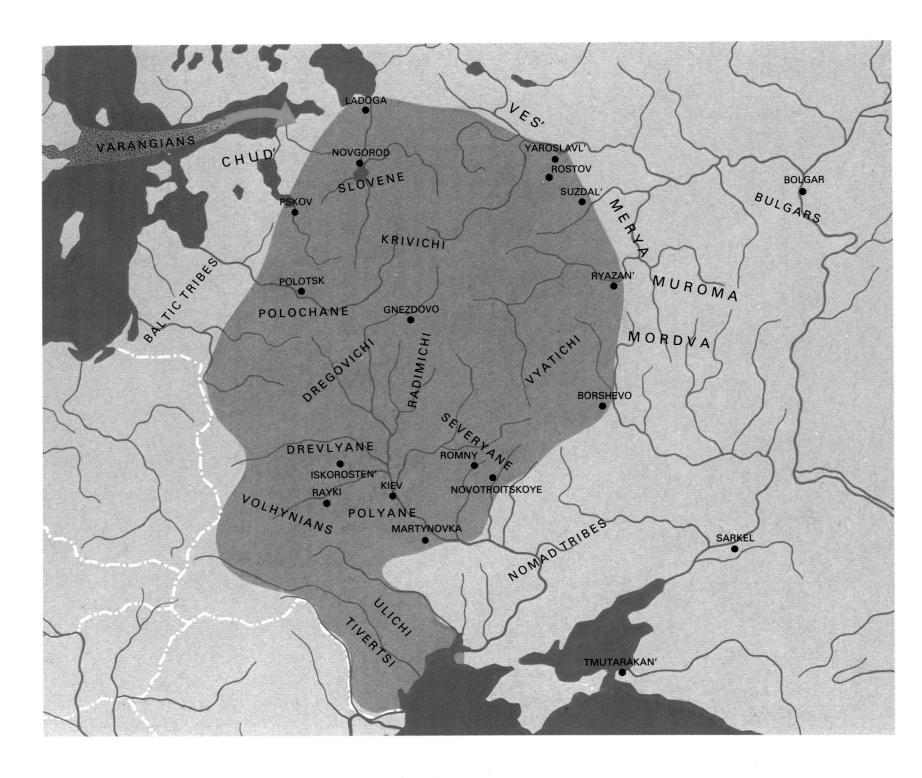

The longest process of resettlement was the Slav migration to Eastern Europe: from the original homeland between the Dnieper, Dniester and Pripyat' settlement gradually spread to the vast forest regions inhabited by scattered Baltic and Finnic tribes and to the steppe lands of the nomad tribes reaching as far as the coast of the Black Sea.

who mentioned the Slav penetration to the Don, Volga and the Sea of Azov in the ninth and tenth centuries.

The largest number of facts can be found in local sources, unfortunately, however, of a relatively late date: in the Old Russian chronicles of the eleventh and the early twelfth centuries. In the spirit of the erudition of the monasteries of the time and following Byzantine patterns the writer deduced the origin of the Slavs from the scattering of the nations during the construction of the biblical Tower of Babel and placed them in the Danube region, from where they spread to their historic settlements. This seems to reflect the knowledge that the

Danube was one of the main axes of migratory movements. According to the chronicles the Eastern Slavs soon split up into tribes. The location of their settlements reveals the range of Eastern Slav migration in the eighth to tenth centuries. One centre was formed by the Polyane in the middle Dniester region around Kiev. To the north-west of these, in the wooded lands along the Dnieper and Pripyat' the Drevlyane lived in towns like Ovruch and Iskorosten'. To the north-east of Kiev, along the rivers Desna, Seim and Sula, were the scattered settlements of the Severyane. The Dregovichi lived between the Pripyat' and the Dvina. Along the

Polot', an upper tributary of the W. Dvina, lay the dwellings of the Polochane, with Polotsk as their centre. They were related to the Krivichi, who by stages came to occupy a vast territory in the river basins of the Dvina, Dnieper and Volga. The region east of the Dnieper was taken over by the Radimichi and Vyatichi tribes, whose original home had been the territory of present-day Poland. Further to the north were the Slovene who had their homes in the vicinity of Lake Il'men' where Novgorod was an important centre. The western fringe was held by the Dulebi, later Buzhani-Volhynians (this may have been one and the same tribe which merely changed its name). The southern end of the Eastern Slav branch was made up of the Ulichi and Tivertsi, who settled along the rivers Dniester and Prut, where the frontier with Romania runs today.

Other important information provided by the chronicler deals with the neighbours of the Slavs — the Finnic tribes of the Ves' in the Byeloozero region, the Merya on the shores of Lakes Rostov and Kleshchino and the Muroma on the confluence of the Oka and Volga. These records lead us to conclude that during the eighth to eleventh centuries the Slavs spread from the original centre between the middle Dnieper, the right bank of the Pripyat' and the Dniester to broader regions between Byeloozero to the north and the Black Sea to the south, between the Bug and Dniester to the west and the river basin of the upper Oka and the left tributaries of the

Dnieper in the east. That is all that can be deduced, though retrospectively, from written records, on the basis of data from the turn of the eleventh to the twelfth century.

Archeologists are able to trace the advance of Slavic settlement in Eastern Europe with more conviction although some of their interpretations remain questionable. What is certain is that the starting point of the expansion lay in the region of the early Slavic Korchak and Pen'kovka types between the middle courses of the Dnieper, Dniester and Pripyat'. As has already been shown, the movements began while these cultural groups were still in existence and not only in a southerly direction to the Balkan peninsula but likewise to the east, i.e. to the left bank of the Dnieper and upstream along its tributaries from the left.

In the eighth century a new cultural group evolved from the Korchak and Pen'kovka type called Luka-Raykovetskaya after the important site at Rayki. There were typical open settlements of an agricultural people with the usual semi-subterranean dwellings and with the burial of cremated dead, as in the preceding period. Certain improvements had been made to pottery, tools and ornaments. The finds of the Luka-Raykovetskaya type were widespread in the forest-steppe lands to the west of the Dnieper, from where they penetrated to Romania and Bulgaria. A slightly different version appeared on the eastern bank of the Dnieper, for which

In the eighth century the early Slav types of Korchak and Pen'kovka grew into a unified culture known as Luka Raykovetskaya with improved production of pottery, tools and ornaments. It spread chiefly in the forest-steppe country to the west of the Dnieper and extended as far as the territory of Romania and Bulgaria.

The usual dwellings at the time of the Slav expansion were semi-subterranean huts with a square ground plan, partly sunk into the ground with a trodden-earth floor and a fireplace of stone, or a clay oven in one corner (reconstruction based on excavations at the Novotroitskoye fort).

At the same time a related type, known as Romny-Borshevo, developed along the left bank of the Dnieper. It is associated with the Severyane and Vyatichi tribes. Typical decorations on vessels include imprints of string, zigzags and comb marks.

the archeologists have coined the name ROMNY-BOR-SHEVO (again after a characteristic site). They distinguish in it the Romny group in the Desna valley, which some scholars attribute to the Severyane tribe, and the Borshevo group living to the north along the upper Oka which they identify with the Vyatichi tribe. The Romny settlements usually consisted of a hill-fort and an open settlement linked to it.

The finds of the Romny-Borshevo type have made it possible for us to trace the gradual Slav colonization south-east towards the upper Don and north-east to the

In the eighth to ninth century one of the main centres of the Severyane tribe was the hill-fort of Novotroitskoye on a steep hill above the river Psyol north-east of Kiev. Excavations have shown that the semi-subterranean dwellings were set quite close to one another.

Volga. During the eighth to ninth century these tribes first moved to the rivers Psiol and Vorskla, then to the upper Don and the Seversky Donets, as revealed by the oldest layers of the Donets hill-fort at Kharkov. In the ninth to tenth century the bearers of the Romny culture reached the lower Don, the Sea of Azov and the Taman'. The Slavs who conquered the Khazar Sarkel in the tenth century brought with them Romny pottery. Later they had to abandon their hill-forts on the Don under the pressure from the Pechenegs.

From the area of the Borshevo variant (Vyatichi tribe) the Slavs penetrated to the Finno-Ugric lands in the forest zone, especially Mordva, where the important Slav centre of Staraya Ryazan' came into being on the site of an old Mordva hill-fort. In the different strata archeologists found typical Vyatichi ornaments, e.g. large ornamental rings with seven rays, rings, round rock-crystal beads, and the like. The Ryazan' land then become the centre of the Vyatichi, while their hill-forts on the upper Don were abandoned in the tenth century.

In the northern parts of Russia relations between ethnic groups underwent a very complex development in the early Middle Ages. The upper Dnieper region was ruled for centuries by Baltic tribes, to which the Kolochin-Tushemlya culture still belonged in the fifth to seventh centuries. In view of strong similarities of their cultural model with that of the contemporary Slav groups of the Korchak and Pen'kovka types, they must have been a part of the Balts that was very close to the Slav ethnic group with which they soon merged. The

actual Slavonic element came to the fore later, mainly in the ninth century. Prior to that (in the seventh to eighth centuries) a further wave of Baltic inhabitants came from the west, from Lithuania and Latvia; they used a special form of burial in "long kurgans", barrows, which grew in length with every fresh burial. These barrows had wrongly been considered typical of the Slav tribe of the Krivichi. In the middle of the ninth century armed bands of Scandinavians came from the north and settled on the confluence of the Dnieper and Svinka and together with the Slavs, Balts and Finns established a trade and cultural centre near Gnezdovo. From here the Old Russian settlements spread along the upper Dnieper, where the foundations were laid for the development of the Byelorussian ethnic group, with Smolensk taking over the role of Gnezdovo.

The north-western part of "Upper Russia" (the Novgorod and Pskov regions) was originally the domain of the Finnic tribe of the Chud'. In the sixth and seventh centuries the "Pre-Kurgan" culture belonged to this, but it has not yet been fully investigated. This was followed by the "sopki", tall tumuli that arose as one burial was placed on top of the other — by contrast to the "long barrows" which grew horizontally and spread to this area from the Baltic region in the eighth century. In the past the archeologists had wrongly linked these "sopki" with the Slovene, but they did not appear here until a little later with another culture, which built characteristic hill-forts, produced hand-made and wheel-turned pottery, possessed imports from the Orient and from Scandinavia, and used smaller circular barrows for burials. The Slovene came here in the eighth and ninth centuries following the river Lovat' and occupied chiefly the southern regions by Lake Il'men'. This came to form the centre of their tribal lands as a starting point for further colonization. The original settlement was mainly of an agricultural character and introduced a higher stage of economic life — tillage-agriculture which was unknown to the original inhabitants. In the ninth century the watercourses grew in importance, facilitating trade contacts with the world at large. This can be shown by numerous finds of treasures of Arabian silver, which were accumulated along the watercourses and in the main centres, such as Novgorod, Ladoga and Pskov. The main stream of colonists to the east, the upper Volga region, and to the north-west set off from Novgorod in the eleventh to thirteenth centuries. During the Middle Ages the ethnically and culturally mixed population of these regions, comprising Finnic, Baltic, Scandinavian and Slav elements, grew into the Old Russian nationality.

The historical development of north-eastern Russia, the Rostov-Suzdal' land, can basically be reconstructed only from archeological sources. Originally three Finnic tribes lived here, the Ves', Merya and Muroma. Their culture with typical ornaments, bone products, bowl-shaped vessels, can be traced by archeologists on burial grounds of the sixth to eleventh centuries. In the ninth

The extensive archeological research at Novotroitskoye has made it possible to reconstruct the original form of an Eastern Slav hill-fort, which was probably destroyed by raiding nomads in the ninth century.

and tenth centuries a wave of settlers arrived from the region of the Il'men' Slovene, and later the Krivichi in the upper Dnieper region, who over the centuries mixed with the local Finno-Ugric population.

The ninth centre must be regarded as a milestone in development. At that time a centre of Slav settlement arose at Yaroslavl' on the Volga. Its early phase is represented chiefly by barrow burial ground from the ninth and tenth centuries. But we also know of fortified settlements, which became the centres of Slav expansion, e.g. Timerevo, which came into existence at the end of the ninth and the early tenth century when colonists appeared from the north-west. It flourished in the tenth century but, in the following century, gave way to the new centre at Yaroslavl'. The Sarskoye hill-fort (on the river Sara) developed similarly; in the tenth century it was a large production and trade centre of the Rostov region, with a mixed Slavo-Finnic population, with the Slavs forming the majority. The feudal city of Rostov then became the successor to the Sarskoye hill-fort. Another important centre was Byeloozero, which from the early ninth century on held the role of the terminal of eastern trade, where the main route turned back from the Volga to the west, to Novgorod and Ladoga. The Slavonic element did not become dominant here until the tenth century. The finds of pottery and ornaments show a mixed Slavic and Finno-Ugric style. This reflects the ethnical process of the birth of the Old Russian and later of the Great Russian peoples. Similarly along the upper Dnieper the Baltic substratum was overlaid by the Byelorussian nationality, while the

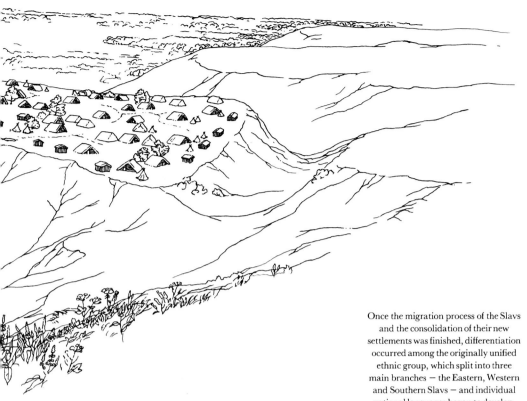

Ukrainian nationality developed in the original middle Dnieper region.

The establishment of the Kievan state at the end of the ninth century gave a decisive impulse to Slav settlement in Eastern Europe.

Once the migration process of the Slavs and the consolidation of their new settlements was finished, differentiation occurred among the originally unified ethnic group, which split into three main branches — the Eastern, Western and Southern Slavs — and individual national languages began to develop.

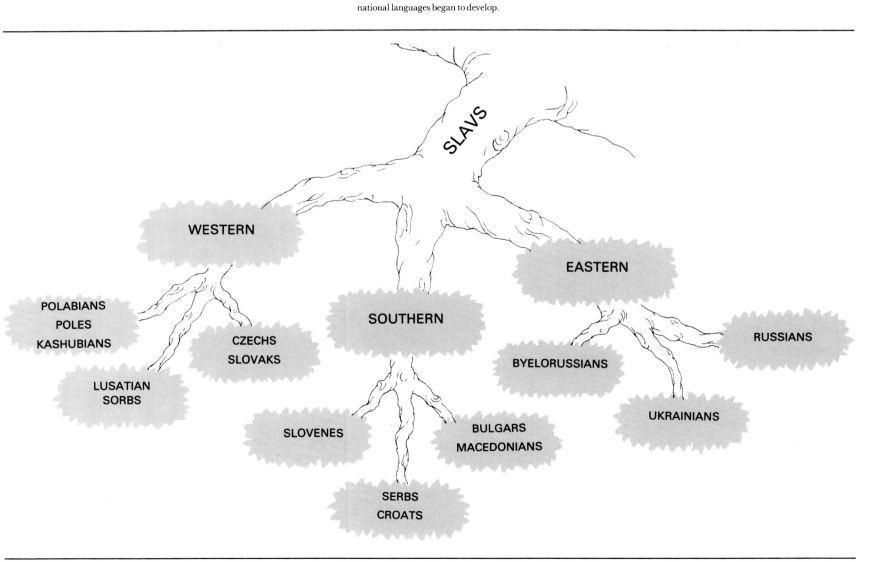

SLAVS

WESTERN

POLABIANS
POLES
KASHUBIANS

CZECHS
SLOVAKS

LUSATIAN
SORBS

SOUTHERN

SLOVENES

BULGARS
MACEDONIANS

SERBS
CROATS

EASTERN

RUSSIANS

BYELORUSSIANS

UKRAINIANS

BETWEEN
THE FRANKISH AND BYZANTINE EMPIRES
AND THE NOMADS

THE SLAVS AND THE NOMAD TRIBES

The broad steppes stretching from the heart of Asia to Eastern Europe and in places as far as the Elbe, the Danube region and the Carpathian Basin have, since time immemorial, served as open spaces for migrating nomads, who from time to time spread like flooding waves in one and the same direction: from east to west. In antiquity there were the Iranian Scythians and Sarmatians, later mainly the Turco-Tatars and Mongolian tribes, in the fourth century the Huns, followed in the sixth century by the Avars, in the seventh by the Bulgars, and towards the end of the ninth by the Magyars (who settled in Hungary). Mongolian raids in the thirteenth century proved a major disaster. All these raiders had one thing in common: they occupied a vast territory for a certain time and founded their large and feared empires there. But none of them lasted long, since the militarily stronger, but otherwise small numbers of unproductive nomads, backward economically and culturally, were soon absorbed by the local population. Only the Magyars kept themselves apart as a unit and survived as a nation and a state up to the present time thanks to having adapted resiliently to European culture. The Bulgars left no more than a name behind — which came to be applied to the Slav tribes with whom they merged.

The oldest migration — that of the Scythians and the Sarmatians — took place at a time when the existence of the Slavs cannot be proved historically or by archeology. Only the Hun raids took place at the time of the Slav ethnogenesis when mutual relations might have been established.

The Huns belong to the militant Turkic tribes, who lived in Central Asia, east of Lake Baykal. From there they raided the frontiers of China not far away. In the first centuries A.D. some of the Huns set out on a westward march: around the year 370 they crossed the Don, and some five years later they destroyed the empire of the Germanic Goths in the Ukraine. The retreat of the Visigoths and Ostrogoths in the face of Hun pressure as far as the Roman provinces began the great migration of peoples on the European continent. Among others, this caused the fall of the western part of the Roman Empire. In the early fifth century the Huns penetrated into Pannonia, which, in the first half of the century, became

The waves of nomad tribes usually came to a stop in the Carpathian Basin where in the valley of the river Tisza they set up a base suitable for further looting and raiding.

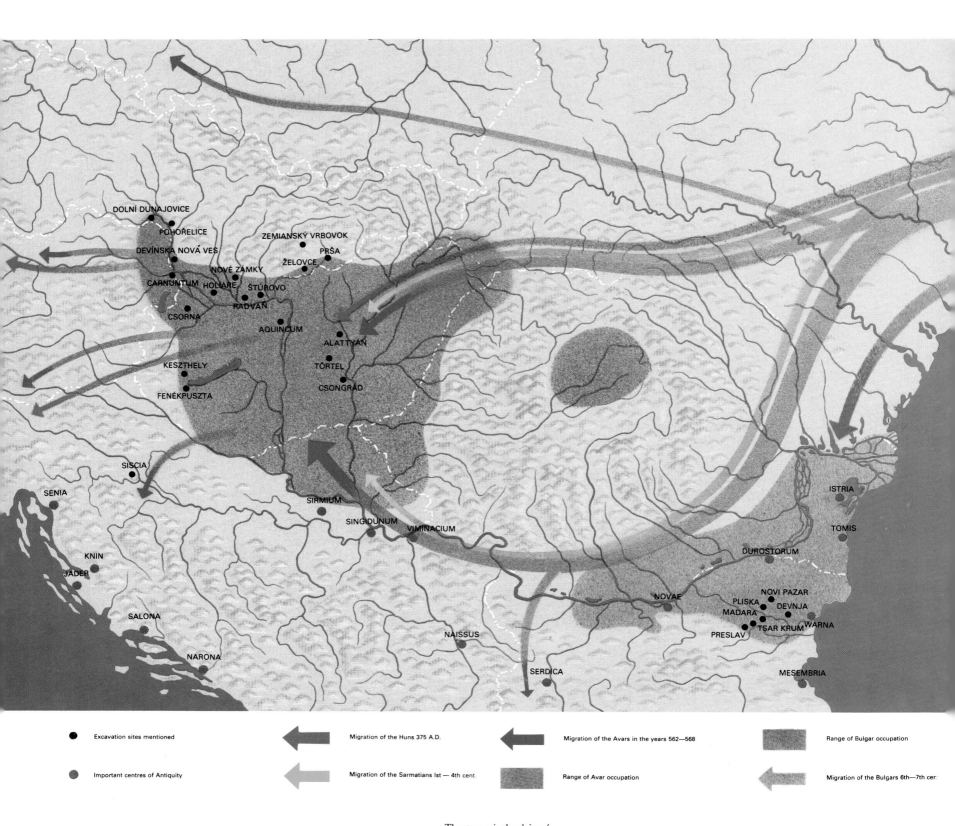

●	Excavation sites mentioned	⬅	Migration of the Huns 375 A.D.	⬅	Migration of the Avars in the years 562—568	Range of Bulgar occupation
●	Important centres of Antiquity	⬅	Migration of the Sarmatians Ist — 4th cent.		Range of Avar occupation	⬅	Migration of the Bulgars 6th—7th cer.

their base for far-reaching expeditions both to the Balkan peninsula against Byzantium and westward to Gaul and Italy. In Gaul they suffered defeat on the Catalaunian Plains near Troyes in the year 451, but only one year later they very nearly conquered Rome; this disaster was prevented only by the skilful diplomacy of Pope Leo I. The Hun empire was doomed after the death of its remarkable leader Attila in 453. The Huns were finally scattered during a successful uprising of the subjected Germanic tribes in 455. The long years of

The steppes in the plains of south-eastern Europe had always been the domain of nomad tribes, who had come from the heart of Asia as far as the Carpathian Basin and the lower reaches of the Danube. The migrations of the Sarmatians, Huns, Avars, Bulgars and other militant nomads basically followed the same direction.

bloody battles between the Germans and the Huns are reflected, among others, in the famous epic *The Song of the Nibelungs*.

The archeologists have found proof of the presence of Huns in the Ukraine and in Central Europe on burial grounds where they found typical graves of people of a Mongoloid type with deformed skulls. This special fashion of deforming the skulls of children to an excessively elongated shape was common among the Huns and some of their Germanic contemporaries, especially the Lombards, Thuringians and Burgundians. Skulls distorted in this manner can be also found beyond the reach of Hun rule — in Bohemia, Moravia, Thuringia and along the Rhineland. The Hun graves, however, differ from the Germanic ones by their offerings, mainly weapons, in which the bow of eastern type with three-edged arrow-heads, double-bladed and short single-bladed swords played a major role. They further included richly adorned saddles with gold or silver mountings, similarly ornamented reins and belts of the warriors. An object that is especially typical of the Huns is a tall slim bronze cauldron. Noble ladies wore gold diadems and used bronze mirrors, as did the Chinese.

The relations between the Huns and the Slavs remain unclear. Usually it is pointed out in this connection that the Huns fought a battle against the Antes in the Ukraine in the third quarter of the fourth century. As we showed above, at that time the Antes must still have been an Iranian tribe, who adapted to Slav ways only at the end of the fifth and in the early sixth century. Two other historical data have likewise not been confirmed. When in 448 messengers from Theodosius II arrived at Attila's court in Pannonia, his historian Priscus recorded that the messengers were given drinks called *medos* and *kamos*. The first can be identified with mead, a favourite drink of the ancient Slavs, and the second with a name that is definitely not Slavonic, referring to some form of beer made of barley. The Goth historian

The Iranian Sarmatians probably played an important role in the life of the first Slavs. Some of them settled in the Carpathian Basin during the Roman period and left behind numerous objects, e. g. an enamelled fibula with an animal motif from Jászmonostor.

Sarmatian pottery had elegant shapes as shown in this mixture of the local tradition and Eastern elements (Csongrád, Hungary).

Jordanes, among others, reveals that a banquet was held over the tomb of Attila, called *strava*, which was a custom and a name given to a similar ceremony among the Slavs. Both *medos* and *strava* are, however, similarly recorded among the Germanic tribes as the two terms can be derived from the language of the Goths with whom the Huns were in historically proven close contact. So that this information cannot necessarily be associated exclusively with the Slavs. Nor does archeology provide a clear picture on this matter. Hun graves from the first half of the fifth century have been discovered on territory that was later inhabited by the Slavs, e.g. in southern Poland, without any further proof that a Slav population lived there already at that time.

While nothing definite can be said about the relations between Slavs and Huns, we are on much safer ground in relation to other eastern nomads — the Avars, who had a far-reaching effect on the life of the Slavs in the Danube region. Archeologists even speak of a Slavo-Avar cultural period; this refers to a period in the seventh to eighth century when characteristic features show a symbiosis of the two ethnical units on the territory of present-day Hungary and neighbouring regions, including south-west Slovakia. It was primarily an economic symbiosis, for from the beginning the Slavs tilled the land while the Avars were nomad pasturalists who lived by cattle breeding and looting. It was, in addition, a political symbiosis in which the Slavs played a varying role from voluntary allies to tribute payers,

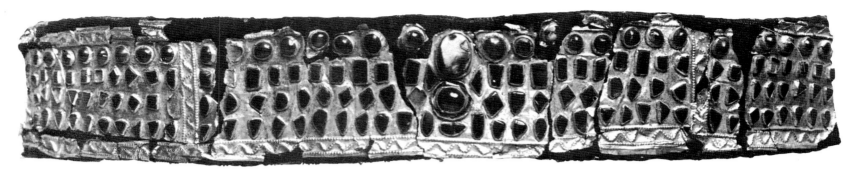

dependent and even serving and exploited tribes. It was even a cultural symbiosis, in which the Slav population, chiefly its nobility, adapted to some extent to the ways of the nomads, especially in dress and certain customs. But they represented a more creative element than the looting nomads, who only amassed objects of value but did not create them. This side of things was entirely overlooked in the past, and therefore literature speaks only of an Avar culture without paying regard to its Slavic component.

The origin of the Avars is wrapped in mystery. Historians have been leading disputes as to whether they were of partly Mongolian, or Turco-Tatar race, whether they belonged to a Central Asian tribal unit whom the Chinese knew as Juan-Juan in the sixth century, or whether they were related to the Hephthalites, known as the White Huns. The last view could be upheld by the names of two Avar tribes — the Uar and the Chunni, recorded in Byzantine sources and in the Caucasian region through which the Avars moved as they advanced towards the west. According to historian Priscus they came there as nomads in the fifth century, appeared, around the year 558, in the steppes to the north of the Sea of Azov and then quickly moved across the territory of the Eastern Slav tribes to the west. In the years 561 to 562 they passed the Carpathian and Sudeten mountains to attack Thuringia, which then belonged to the Frankish Empire, but were driven back. A second attack in the years 566—567 was more successful, since they managed to take King Sigebert prisoner. In the meantime they reached the lower Danube region and moved upstream from there and through the passes in the Carpathians to the middle courses of the Danube and Tisza, where, together with the Lombards, they defeated the Germanic Gepids. They then settled on their territory between the Danube and the Tisza. That was where they had their main *hring* — probably a fortified camp. When in 568 the Lombards moved on to northern Italy, the Avars also took over the region to the west of the Danube — Pannonia. In that way an extensive Avar Empire came into being, which stretched from western Hungary and Slovakia as far as the southern Ukraine and was a major threat to the two great powers of the time — the Frankish Empire in the West and Byzantium in the East.

The lucky star of the Avars set relatively soon, in the first quarter of the seventh century. They received the first blow from the Central European Slavs, who staged a successful uprising under Samo some time in 623—624. At the same time the Croats and Serbs in the south liberated themselves, and in 626 a major disaster occurred in the form of a defeat outside Constantinople. Under the leadership of Kuvrat the Bulgarian tribes of the Kutrigurs and Utigurs split off from the Avars, having until that time belonged to the union of Avar tribes. So gradually the rule of the Avars, limited to the territory of present-day Hungary, fell apart. The fatal blow was struck by Charlemagne in the years 791—799, and the Bulgarian Khan Krum overwhelmed the Avars from the south. From that time on nothing more was heard of them and they vanished completely in the ninth century.

When the Avars reached the Hungarian Plains, they were a great mixture of tribes associated in a tribal union. Their core was formed by two *tümens* of Avars proper, roughly 20,000 people. The second strongest component were the Bulgarian Kutrigurs and Utigurs, the rest smaller tribal groups. These tribes were only loosely related and came under the central power of the Khans only during military campaigns. Apart from these, the Avar community included other ethnic groups, in the first place the Slavs, with whom the Avars had come into contact in their advance towards the west and had taken along to the Carpathian Basin. This gave some scholars the mistaken idea that the entire Slav settlement of Central and Southern Europe was, in fact, due to the Avars. In reality their merit is but secondary or indirect: some tribes came with them as allies, others retreated before them, e.g. the Volhynian Dulebi, groups of whom scattered across Central and Southern Europe after being defeated by the Avars even before the latter reached these regions. Apart from the Slavs the Carpathian Basin was peopled also by remnants of Germanic and Iranian tribes (Sarmatians) and certain sections of the Romanized population, especially in the former province of Pannonia. This has been proved by finds at Fenékpuszta near Lake Balaton, which can probably be identified with the Roman Mogentiana. The presence of the sparse but culturally advanced population of the Roman provinces — so attractive to conquerors — explains the survival of certain ancient traditions in the goldsmith, blacksmith and pottery trades at the time of the Avars and later during the period of the Great Moravian Empire.

The history of the Avars still contains a good deal that has never been explained, for written records about them are but fragmentary and lend themselves to different interpretations. The relatively rich archeological finds both in the Avar territory proper and in neighbouring areas, where Avar influence was strong, are a welcome aid in the search for answers to many of these questions. Finds in graves run into tens of thousands. Here the archeologists distinguish two phases: typical of the older, which covers the sixth and a large part of the seventh century, are ornaments of repoussé gold, silver or bronze plate, while the later graves from the end of the seventh to the end of the eighth century contained cast ornaments of a different style, often in rich settings.

In both cases these ornaments were applied to belts, richly adorned with mounts, attached even to short hip bands. At one end of the belt was a tongue-shaped

Archeologists have traced Hun migration from the heart of Asia to Europe on the basis of finds of large bronze cauldrons with typical ornamentation along the edge (Törtel, Hungary).

strap-end, which was threaded through the buckle at the other end. In the older period the metal mounts were of a variety of shapes: circular, trefoil, lozenge-shaped, escutcheon-like, horseshoe, heart or shield shaped. They were adorned with pearl, lily, trellis or plaited patterns, coloured glass, etc. Far more numerous are the cast mounts of the later period, the seventh and eighth centuries. They include sarmentous, ramified, lily, palmette or trefoil shapes and animal motifs, especially griffins, those legendary beasts of ancient mythology with the body of a lion and the head of an eagle, known in the art of antiquity and the Orient. Apart from these there appeared elements derived from ancient as well as Christian patterns.

The origin of these ornaments and the crafts which produced them is hotly debated by scholars. The older group shows Byzantine-Hellenistic influences which spread to the steppe cultures north of the Black Sea. The Avars came into contact with them during their advance to the west. Far less clear, however, are changes in fashion towards the end of the seventh century, represented by the group with cast bronze ornaments. Patterns for these are being sought in the East, even as far away as in Siberia, and this seems to be an indication that new nomads were arriving from the Kama river area. But there are no historical sources to confirm this. The eastern ornaments occur, moreover, only sporadically among the exceptionally numerous finds in the Carpathian Basin and therefore do not provide proof of their origin. It would seem that these artifacts were made on a large scale in local workshops, where metal-workers adapted influences from Byzantium and the nomads, from Christian art and from provincial tradition, Sassanid Iran and perhaps even from Coptic Egypt. What they produced represented a blend of these individual elements into a unified style, which basically suited the taste of nomads but must certainly have spread also among other ethnic groups in the Avar period — e.g. among the Slavs.

Apart from these objects of distinct style the archeologists have also found weapons and horse saddles and stirrups in the tombs. The Avars were excellent riders and owed their success on the battlefield mainly to fast attacks on horseback. As a result they were often buried with their fully saddled horses. They had typical circular ornaments, called *phaleras*, repoussé or cast, or stirrups, which, in fact, were an Avar invention. The weapons of the Avars were sabres, single-edged swords and bow with bone or horn parts, including triple-edged arrows. The Slavs, on the other hand, as allies of the Avars, fought on foot and their typical weapons include axes, lances, bows and cudgels. But even the Slavs had mounted troops. Their equipment included swords, lances, stirrups and spurs (with counterhooks) which were not used by the Avars, for in the Eastern manner they used little whips to urge on their horses.

Women's graves held bronze, silver and even gold jewels, among them ear-rings of highly varied shapes,

The Fredegar's *Chronicle* of the seventh century gives a lively description of the violence inflicted on certain Slav tribes by the Avars. This scene of a raid on a Slav settlement tries to depict period conditions. There were other cases when the Slavs formed an alliance with the Avars.

often twisted into the hair; in addition bracelets, rings, buckles and glass necklaces have been found. They show the predominant influence of Byzantine goldsmiths but were all made in local workshops, only a few precious pieces being imported. An example is a unique discovery of a silver treasure at Zemiansky Vrbovok near one of the main routes that linked Slovakia with the regions beyond the Carpathians.

Now let us take a look at typical Avar burial grounds which have been systematically examined by Hungarian and Slovak archeologists. Such burial grounds are the most important sources of information on the social structure and cultural level of the time.

Particularly valuable data were produced during excavations of the burial ground near the village of Alattyán in the Szolnok Comitatus in the years 1934 to 1938. A total of 711 graves were opened up, documenting the entire Avar period from their arrival to its very end. The dead were given their personal property to accompany them on their way to the after-life, even food as shown by bones of cattle, pigs, sheep, and fowl, eggshells as well as bowls with liquids. The offerings, burial rites and the location of the graves distinguish

The Slavo-Avar co-existence gave rise to a common fashion in garments, which included richly decorated belt mounts with plant and figural motifs (Pohořelice and Dolní Dunajovice in Moravia, Nové Zámky and Prša in Slovakia).

A belt end with hammered ornaments representing the older phase of ornamentation from the Slavo-Avar period (Holiare, Slovakia).

groups which followed one upon the other in time. Scholars link the two younger groups with the influx of a new population from the East, even though it is very difficult to make any ethnic attribution because even anthropological analysis does not always lead to unambiguous conclusions. The people who were buried at Alattyán are a mixture of Mediterranean, Nordic, Iranian, Pamir and Mongoloid types with the latter, who might have represented the Avars proper, forming only a small percentage. So it would seem that the Avars ruled over a very mixed tribal society formed both of Eastern and local elements.

The burial ground at Devínska Nová Ves, to the west of Bratislava, was excavated in the years 1926—33. It proved of basic importance in trying to solve the complex problem of cultural and ethnic adherence in the Slavo-Avar period. A total of 875 graves were unearthed, dating from the beginning of Slav settlement. In twenty-seven of these the bodies had been cremated; there were ninety-four riders, thirty-five foot soldiers, etc. The analysis of the finds and the burial rites led to the conclusion that the burial ground provided proof of the close co-existence, even the intermingling, of Slavic

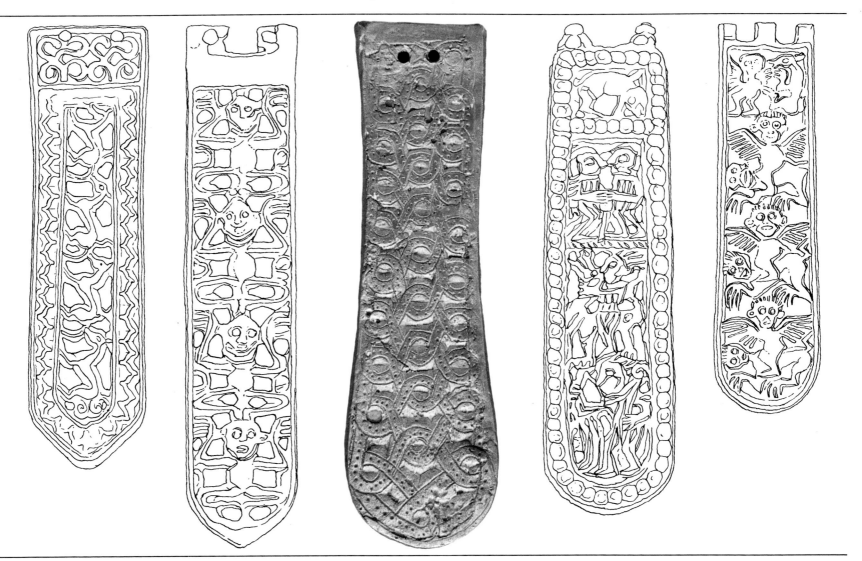

The Avars were excellent horsemen, who were so close to their horses that they often had them buried with them in full harness and armour. This custom was adopted by the Slavs who lived near them (Štúrovo, Slovakia, eighth century).

Štúrovo or Prša, where settlements with semi-subterranean dwellings were found, proof of a settled agricultural population such as the Slavs and not the nomad Avars.

The oldest phase from the end of the sixth and the first half of the seventh century was found in Slovakia only along the Danube, while burial grounds further to the north (e.g. at Nové Zámky) arose slightly later, after the middle of the seventh century.

In this manner archeological sources produce evidence of the strange symbiosis of the nomad cattle-grazers and the settled agricultural tribes in the Carpathian Basin in the sixth to eighth centuries, showing the economic, political and cultural co-existence of different ethnic groups. These grew into the settled Slav peasants and craftsmen led by their newly emerging nobility.

A similar conclusion was reached by the co-existence of the Balkan Slavs and the nomad Bulgars. The latter were tribes of Turco-Tatar origin, whose original home had been the region along the Volga, north of the Caspian Sea and the Sea of Azov. Some of these moved from there in the sixth century together with the Avars advancing across the Ukraine to the lower reaches of the Danube. In the last third of the seventh century they split off from the Avars and, under the leadership of Asparuch, penetrated to ancient Moesia where they formed an alliance with the local Slav tribes in the struggle against their common enemy — the Byzantines.

Archeological finds of these "Proto-Bulgars" — as scholars have called the original Turco-Tatar people to distinguish them from the present-day Slavonized Bulgarians — are centred in north-eastern Bulgaria, the former east Moesia, which in character of landscape best suited their nomadic way of life, with its cattle breeding and looting raids. They settled in *yurts*, the typical dwellings of Eastern herdsmen used widely in Central Asia. They were circular in ground plan, three to four metres (about four yards) in diameter, with the fireplace roughly in the centre. Apart from traces in the ground the appearance of such an ancient Bulgar yurt can be found in a marble model unearthed at Devnya. It depicts the entrance and the roof and a hunting scene is carved on the outer wall, similar to those on stone walls at Pliska or Preslav.

The presence of the original Bulgars is proved by *aouls*, fortified settlements or rather military camps, some of which later developed into towns, e.g. Pliska or Preslav. One of these *aouls* was investigated near the village of Tsar Krum in the vicinity of Shumen; it was probably identical with the *aoul* of Khan Omortag, who cruelly persecuted the first Bulgarian Christians in the first half of the ninth century. It has a gateway with dwellings for the guards, stairs, spacious buildings, which could have been barracks and brick-paved open spaces which must have served as assembly places. The military purpose is further confirmed by finds of weapons and horseshoes.

and Avar elements, as confirmed also in certain written reports, e.g. in Fredegar's *Chronicle*. The Slavic element was evidently numerically in predominance.

Post-war research in Slovakia has greatly complemented and enriched the picture of the whole period. It was shown that the burial grounds of Slavo-Avar type are widespread in south-western Slovakia, and that they were by no means unknown even in the southern parts of central and eastern Slovakia. On some of them, e.g. at Holiare, people were buried throughout the period; in the years 1952—5 seven hundred and seventy-eight graves were uncovered here. There were only slight traces of Avar elements; anthropological analysis showed only four per cent of Mongoloid types. A similar picture was derived at other burial grounds, e.g. at

The burial grounds of the original Bulgars differed greatly until they began to mix with the Slav population. Unlike the Slavs, for whom cremation was characteristic until they adopted Christianity, they buried their dead uncremated, mostly with the head towards the north, sometimes in pits with side chambers. Fear of the dead was typical of the nomad inhabitants of the eastern steppes; they prevented their return by piling up stone mounds above the graves, or the amputation of feet and similar practices, which are known also from ethnographic studies in connection with the belief in vampires.

The first great burial ground of this type was excavated near Novi Pazar close to Pliska, on the banks of the Kriva river. Men, women and children were accompanied by roughly the same offerings: vessels, knives, buckles, ear-rings, beads, and bone needles; in the graves of rich men there were, in addition, weapons, arrows, bone-inlaid quivers, sabres, spears and axes. Some tombs held amulets in the form of eagles' claws, hare or dog bones, connected with the animistic and totemistic beliefs of the Turkic steppe tribes. The bones of other animals prove that the dead were even given food for their journey to the other world. In a number of cases the Bulgars buried the dead with their horses. On many skeletons one can observe artificial deformation of the skulls, which is typical likewise of the practices of the Eastern nomads. Later, under the influence of the Slavs, the Bulgars began to cremate their dead.

The Bulgars brought pottery along from the East, which differs greatly from the Slavonic type both in its dark-grey or dark-brown colour and in its shape and ornament. There are, for instance, round pots with polished linear or trellis patterns and similarly decorated jars (oinochoé), jugs, little amphoras, casks and dishes. Similar items have been found in the entire steppe regions of the Ukraine as far as the Volga and to the northern slopes of the Caucasus, where the Bulgar nomads lived or where they came into contact with the local tribes of the Sarmatians, Alans and Khazars. Soviet archeologists call them the SALTOVO-MAYATS-KAYA CULTURE. Some shapes resemble antique patterns, but not in their contemporary Byzantine form but in older types, which survived among the steppe tribes who had long ago been influenced by the Greek colonies along the Black Sea. The Byzantine influence showed more in the towns, e.g. in the greenish glaze of pottery from Pliska and Preslav. Very soon the Bulgars began to use also Slav pottery, just as the Slavs adopted Bulgar receptacles, and gradually the merger of the two ethnic groups becomes reflected in the change and merger of different types of these common household utensils.

The Slav population of the ninth to eleventh centuries lived in similar settlements and equally simple huts dug into the ground as in the preceding period. Apart from that, however, they also built hill-forts fortified with earthworks, moats and even stone walls. In these hill-forts semi-subterranean dwellings have

The typical outfit of an Avar warrior included a nomad's bow with triple-bladed arrows, a sable, a single-bladed sword, an axe, and the horsemen had stirrups and reins (Holiare, Slovakia).

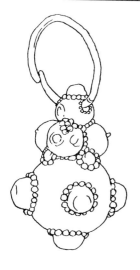
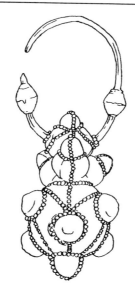

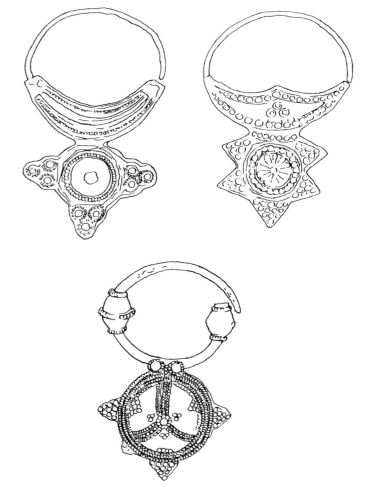

Ear-rings of a great variety of types were found in the graves of women in the Slavo-Avar area. Such rings were often even plaited into the hair. They reflect the influence of Byzantine goldsmiths (Holiare, Želovce, Radvaň, all in Slovakia).

been found as well as houses on the ground, sometimes with stone foundations. The development of craft industries is reflected in finds of wrought metal, glass and pottery workshops with kilns and the respective products. The finds are mainly of pottery, which followed up the preceding early Slavonic period, but is far more perfect in treatment and made of fine, well-washed sand mixed with clay, turned on a potter's wheel and decorated with incised wavy lines and linear strips.

By contrast to the Bulgars the Slavs burnt their dead until they adopted Christianity and placed the ashes in pits or urns; these were sometimes covered by stones or other vessels, even placed in structures made of river boulders or accidentally found Roman bricks. They added gifts to the urns in the form of knives, arrows, stirrups, agricultural tools, jewels, whorls, and also some specific features such as a goldsmith's hammer.

After adopting Christianity in 865 the Slav population began to bury uncremated bodies in graves banked with stone, boulders or flagstone. Most of the offerings are now found in women's graves, where they included parts of garments, or body decorations. Many of these jewels are very similar to decorations of the ninth to tenth century found in Central Europe.

While one can observe the gradual development from cremation to inhumation burials in northern Bulgaria, in the southern parts of the country the latter rite must have existed all the time. The different manner of burial rites and types of ornaments reveal tribal differences. The culture of the southern tribes, primarily the Smolyane, shows the strong influence of Byzantium. This is further upheld by numerous finds of coins, which date the burial grounds into the ninth to eleventh centuries.

The map of archeological sites of Slavonic and Proto-Bulgar cultures has given an interesting picture of the conditions in settlement in the eighth to eleventh cen-

In the later Slavo-Avar period belt ornaments were cast, as shown e.g. by the belt end from Štúrovo decorated with a design of branches (Slovakia).

turies. The settlement and burial grounds of the original Bulgars appear only in the north-eastern parts of the country, i.e. from Varna to the confluence of the Iskar and Danube, from where they extend northward as far as to Romania. Slav finds merge with these, but also appear in other parts of the country, where the Turco-Tatar Bulgars did not settle.

It is clear that such ethnic symbiosis could not take place without being reflected in the cultural sphere. And indeed Bulgarian archeologists are discovering more and more sites — especially in the centre of Bulgaria — which confirm the cultural merger of the two ethnic groups, both in types of dwellings, pottery, ornaments and in burial rites. In a number of settlements Slav semi-subterranean dwellings stood next to Bulgar yurts as an expression of the peaceful co-existence of the population. As the Bulgars went over to the settled life they adopted the Slav type of dwelling, and in certain cases even adopted the cremation rites of burial. The Slavs used Bulgar pottery in their households and in the nomad yurts and in military camps we can, on the other hand, find pottery of a Slav type. A good example of this co-existence is common burial grounds, e.g. in the vicinity of the little town of Devnya, west of Varna. Further to the west the Proto-Bulgar elements disappear. In north-western Bulgaria the Slavs used only their own pottery, in the south of the

The Danube once formed the border between the world of antiquity and the barbarians, and it served as one of the main routes across Europe, attracting Germanic and Slav tribes and the eastern nomads. One of the key points was the confluence with the river Morava, which was guarded by the rocky cliffs of Devín.

Balkan mountains we do not find any Proto-Bulgar artifacts at all.

This process, which took place relatively quickly in the ninth century, led to the Slavonic Bulgarians. What is surprising is the archeologists' discovery that the original Bulgars did not represent a numerically small group, as used to be assumed. Their rapid Slavonization was aided not only by the numerical superiority of the Slavs but also by their economic superiority, for in the framework of the Bulgar state the Proto-Bulgars represented only the military element, while the Slavs formed the economic and administrative component. Of equal importance was their cultural predominance, confirmed by the adoption of the Slavonic form of Christianity and the Slavonic literary tongue. Thus it came about that the terms Bulgar and Slav were identical already in the first half of the tenth century.

The role played in the life of the South-European Slavs by the Turco-Tatar Bulgars and in the development of the Central European Slavs by the Avars was performed in the history of the Eastern Slavs by the Khazars of the seventh to tenth centuries. They were likewise a nomad people of Turkish origin, related to the Bulgars, whose original homes were in Central Asian Daghestan. From there they followed the ancient steppe routes of the nomads at the time of the Hun and Avar migrations to the west. They were first mentioned in the year 627, when they were fighting as allies of Byzantium against the Persian empire of the Sassanids. In the same century they began to rule the Caucasian region, from where their realm gradually spread northwards to the Volga where they founded a new centre at Ityl, close to the delta of the Volga. But they only spent the winter there, for as true nomads they were constantly on the move and preferred life in the steppes. Archeologists have found traces of them in the form of finds of the Saltovo-Mayatskaya culture mentioned in connection with the Bulgars. A peculiarity of their spiritual life was that, under the influence of Jewish traders who came to Ityl, they adopted the Jewish faith. They helped the Slav tribes in the Ukraine to shake off the Avar yoke, but they then occupied the former eastern parts of the Avar Empire; at one time their realm spread from the lower reaches of the Danube to the Volga and further east, from Kiev in the north as far as the Crimea to the south, where they became neighbours of the Byzantines. Their expansion was partly the cause of the migration of the related Bulgars and of the arrival of the Bulgars on the territory of Bulgaria today. The Khazars left a strong influence on the Slavs in the region along the middle reaches of the Dnieper, where later the core of the Kievan state was formed. Its establishment, together with the invasion by other Eastern nomads — the Pechenegs — led to the decline of the political power of the Khazars after the end of the ninth century. The last blow was struck by Prince Svyatoslav of Kiev when he conquered their centre at Ityl between 965 and 969.

THE PRESSURE OF THE GREAT POWERS AND THE FIRST ORGANIZED STATES

The Slavs who settled in Central, South-Eastern and Eastern Europe in the sixth and seventh centuries, did not come into contact only with the nomads, some of whom moved about in their midst. They became involved equally in the struggle between the great powers of the time. To the east there was Byzantium, which grew up on the ruins of the eastern parts of the Roman Empire and brought its influence to bear mainly on the Balkan and Eastern Slavs (and only for a time on those in Central Europe). In the west lay the newly rising Frankish Empire, which laid claims to the heritage of

Pottery was made in the Slavo-Avar area mainly by Slav potters, who also used the ancient traditions handed on by the remnants of the Romanized inhabitants of the vanished Roman provinces (finds from the burial ground at Devínska Nová Ves, Slovakia).

the Roman Empire. The Franks put up a barrier to Slav expansion into Central Europe and the north-western parts of the Balkan peninsula; it was there that the two great powers met face to face, and both were to prove of fundamental importance in the further political and cultural development of the Slavs.

The rise of Frankish power is linked with Clovis (Chlodovech), who adopted Christianity in the year 496. He broke the power of the Visigoths and ruled the former Roman province of Gaul. The Germanic Franks soon merged with the local inhabitants, thus forming the basis of what later became the French nation. The successors to Clovis, members of the Merovingian dynasty, gradually came to rule over further Germanic

The ornaments on horses' harnesses from the Slavo-Avar period sometimes show interesting animal forms of decoration, such as this bronze head of a boar adorned with palm leaves on a punched background (Holiare, Slovakia, eight century). This ornament introduces the beginnings of the subsequent Great Moravian period and the Blatnica—Mikulčice style.

tribes, the Burgundians, Angles, Saxons, Thuringians and Bayuvari and thereby shifted the frontiers of their realm in the direction of the Slavs, who were, at that time, penetrating to the Elbe, the Main and the Danube. In the Danube region the Slavs encountered the Avars, who had occupied the Carpathian Basin and whose power extended as far as the river Ems in Austria.

In this way the Slav settlers in Central Europe found themselves caught between two fires in the second half of the sixth century. But this situation also had positive aspects, as it stirred them in their weak tribal dispersion and provided an impetus for political unification,

and the establishment of the first Slav state, the Empire of Samo.

The first centuries of Slav settlement in Central Europe are veiled in historic darkness and can only be explained on the basis of archeological evidence. But one written record has survived which sheds some light on their fate in the seventh century — the *Chronicle* of Fredegar, an anonymous writer traditionally known by that name. It came into being in Burgundy some time between 640 and 660 as part of a work that was partly compilation, partly original — especially where it talks about Merovingian France at the end of the sixth and in the first half of the seventh century.

This gilt bronze mount of a horse's harness with embossed human faces is an exceptional example of the Late Avar period; it was found at the burial ground at Žitavská Tôň (Slovakia, eighth century).

That is the part that interests us most, for it reveals valuable information about the Slavs, probably learnt from Frankish merchants, who visited the lands of the Slavs in search of trade. One of these merchants was Samo: "In the fortieth year of the rule of Chlothar (i.e. 623—624) a man named Samo, by birth a Frank *de pago Senonago* (today's area of Sens in France) joined a larger group of merchants and set out to the land of the Slavs, called Venedi, to do trade there." In those restless times such a journey required not only business skill but military fitness. Samo travelled at the head of an armed band and reached the Slavs at the very moment when they were rising against the unbearable domination of the Avars. The chronicler describes their undignified serfdom in gloomy words: the Avars demanded tithes, raped their women, and forced them to fight in the front ranks. The uprising was led, he said, mainly by their own sons born of Slavic women. Samo immediately took their side and acted so bravely that the grateful Slavs, after their liberation, chose him as their ruler. He then married twelve Slav women, had twenty-two sons and fifteen daughters and ruled happily for thirty-five years. All other battles that the Slavs waged against the Avars finished in victory for the Slavs. Moreover, the Avars were defeated outside Constantinople in 626, which was a contributory factor in the development of the new state of the Slavs.

But these new conditions irritated their western neighbours, the Franks, whose expansion likewise aimed in that direction. The Frankish King Dagobert (629—638/9) therefore used a local incident, the disgraceful expulsion of his arrogant messenger Sicharius from Samo's court, as an excuse and set off with a large army against Samo. After minor success he suffered a humiliating defeat at the fort at Wogastisburc. The victorious Slavs then attacked the Thuringians by way of revenge and laid waste other parts of the Frankish kingdom. Samo's success made even the Sorbian Prince Derwan acknowledge him as his ruler, having until that time been dependent on the Franks.

The above account is from Fredegar. His story is an attractive one; his knowledge of the conditions in distant lands is certainly remarkable, but they only partly satisfy the inquisitive scholar. For, like all old chroniclers, Fredegar is very sparing in words regarding exact geographical data: he had no idea what difficulties he was preparing for historians, who for two hundred years have vainly been trying to agree where the centre of Samo's rule actually was and where Wogastisburc and its remarkable fort were located.

The Turco-Tatar Bulgars lived in yurts as was the custom of the Eastern nomads. Their appearance is shown on a stone model found at Devnya near Varna with an incised hunting scene.

These can be determined only very roughly. The Slavs in question must have been, on the one side, neighbours of the Avars, on the other, of the Franks. The Franks called their immediate neighbours by the ancient name of the Venedi, used by Fredegar, and before him by Jordanes and other writers in antiquity. The name of the Sorbian Prince Derwan also suggests a location of the Slavo-Germanic borderland — for he was prince of the ancestors of the Lusatian Sorbs.

The fact that a mixed Slavo-Avar population rose against Avar domination points, furthermore, to the borderlands to the west and north-west of the centre of Avar settlement, i.e. the Danube region in Lower Austria, which was then predominantly Slav, and southern Moravia and south-west Slovakia. This conclusion is confirmed by archeological finds, which make it possible to determine the range of Avar and Slav settlement. Accordingly, the area settled by the Avars stretched from present-day Hungary further to the west as far as the Vienna Woods and to the river Dyje in the north; it included parts of Lower Austria. Finds of pottery prove that the Slavonic element left a strong mark on these parts. Westwards of this line, as far as the river Ems and its confluence with the Danube, the area was chiefly dominated by the Slavs. Bavarian colonists penetrated among them, but in the seventh and eighth centuries their compact settlement did not go further than the west bank of the Ems.

We can conclude from the geography of settlement and from archeology that the Slavs, who under the leadership of Samo rose against the Avars in the seventh century, must have lived, in great likelihood, along the north-western borders of their empire, i.e. in Lower Austria, southern Moravia and possibly in south-western Slovakia. These were the regions where the Avar horsemen could most easily penetrate and apply their political influence, which, according to the evidence of the Frankish chroniclers, reached at one time as far as the river Ems. The region further to the north — mountainous northern Slovakia, northern Moravia and the whole of Bohemia — was beyond the reach of the Avars. The Slav tribes who lived there were free and had no reason for resistance, even though they might have come to their assistance. Most closely involved were the immediate neighbours of the Avars, and so it is there that we must seek the centre of the uprising.

To this area Frankish merchants, such as Samo was, might well have come, for the route along the Danube was one of the main routes from West to East, being used not only in war time but also by peaceful caravans of traders. One such caravan was led by Samo, and he found himself unexpectedly in the midst of warring camps. He probably had trade partners among the Slavs, and as he was not loath to engage in adventure he rallied his companions to their aid. So it came about that instead of executing business transactions he founded the first Slav Empire in Central Europe.

Wogastisburc must have stood in the centre of Samo's Empire, somewhere along the rivers Danube, Dyje or Morava. Dagobert will have followed one of the frequented routes along the Danube so that his

The pottery brought to the Balkans by the original Bulgars differs in shape and ornamentation from Slav pottery and recalls similar finds in the steppe region of the Ukraine, along the Volga and in the area north of the Caucasus inhabited by nomads (Novi Pazar, ninth century).

allies — the Lombards and Alamanni living to the
south — could send him additional support without
greater difficulties. The exact location of Wogastisburc
is still unknown. We only know one hill-fort in the assumed centre of Samo's Empire — Mikulčice in southern Moravia, whose foundation goes back to the
seventh century. It cannot be a coincidence that 200
years later one of the main centres of the Great Moravian Empire grew up there. But we have no proof that
either this or any of the other Slav hill-forts, especially
those along the Danube in Lower Austria, was the
elusive Wogastisburc. Archeological research can only

The first Slav state in Central Europe — Samo's Empire — soon after its emergence found itself in conflict with the neighbouring Frankish power. According to Fredegar's *Chronicle* the cause was the insolent behaviour of a Frankish envoy, Sicharius, before Samo which resulted in his ignominious banishment.

give us an idea of how Wogastisburc would have been fortified: it was probably no more than a simple palisade with a moat, or possibly a single wooden wall with earthworks. Something of this kind was found, for instance, on one of the oldest Slav hill-forts in Bohemia, Klučov near Český Brod. At the time of Samo the Slavs were just beginning, so archeological excavations tell us, to build hill-forts as permanent settlements. But the technique of fortification must have been known to them since the time before the great expansion. This is shown by the common term for "fortification" to be found in all Slavonic languages — *hrad, grad, gród, gorod, gard,* etc. At the time of the great tribal migrations there was neither time nor reason for such expensive constructions. Hence no hill-forts are known from the early Slavonic period of the Prague type. They originated only after a certain period of settled life, when the new villages were threatened by dangerous raiders, such as the Avars, the expansion of the mighty Frankish Empire or related neighbouring tribes. The hill-forts served as refuges, but there were also permanent inhabitants who guarded such important sites. In the course of time, they became the ruling class. But this was a lengthy social process, which reached its climax in the ninth to tenth century, even if the initial impulse occurred at the time of Samo. The building of fortified centres reflects the beginning of social organization of the Slav tribes as related in Fredegar's *Chronicle* and confirmed by archeological research.

The Slavs, united under the rule of Samo, could, for a time, keep their independence and resist external pressure. Since the Avar danger did not cease to be acute even after the death of Samo (658), they were soon forced, however, to chose the lesser of two evils and accept support either from the Frankish or the Byzantine Empires, which faced each other across Slav territory. In view of the serious Avar threat both these powers became allies. Under the Frankish King Dagobert (629—638) and the Byzantine Emperor Heraclius (610—641) this friendship was confirmed in a treaty. It was the very time when the Slavs were rising against the Avars. The Byzantines, furthermore, supported the Serbs and the Croats, who drove the Avars out of the north-western parts of the Balkan peninsula, liberating Dalmatia, Illyria, the territory between the Sava and Drava, and Carinthia settled by Slavs. It was a large section of the sphere of interest of the Byzantines, into which the Franks were beginning to penetrate.

This penetration proceeded under the new dynasty of the Carolingians, founded by Pépin in the year 752. His successor, Charlemagne (771—814), dealt a mortal blow to the Avars, who at that point completely vanished from history. He ruled over the Slavs living on the territory of ancient Noricum and Pannonia, i.e. in Styria, Carinthia and the land between the Sava and the Danube. He even reached the Istrian peninsula on the Adriatic and founded what became known as the Friulian Mark. This was to be the springboard for Frankish expansion into the Balkans. After heavy battles the Franks occupied Croatian Dalmatia, whose coastal towns had until that time been the domain of Byzantium. The regions inhabited by Slavs along the coast of the Adriatic Sea thus became the point where the two great European powers of the time met head on in the eighth and ninth centuries.

Further penetration of the Franks into the Balkans was put a stop to by the uprising of the Pannonian Croats under Ljudevit (819—833), who was the first to try, though unsuccessfully, to unify the Slav tribes on

A relief of a horseman found on a stone at Hornhausen near Halle, which gives an idea of a Germanic warrior from the time around 700. It probably comes from a tomb, though some regard it as a depiction of the god Wotan.

the territory of Yugoslavia. Another factor was the newly rising empire of the Bulgars, whose power under Khan Krum (803—814) spread into Serbia and along the Tisza in Hungary, once the Avars were defeated. Krum's successor, Omortag (814—831), invaded Pannonian Croatia and ruled over it for a time. Though later only Slavonia and the territory around Sirmium remained under the Bulgars, their expansion put an end to the ambitions of the Franks in this part of Europe.

Charlemagne put forward the idea of a new universal empire, which was to be an heir to the Roman Empire, at least its western parts, now under Christian influence. The realization of this idea was naturally linked with armed expansion aimed against the independent Germanic tribes such as the Saxons, and against the Slavs, who, at that time, were spreading further west from the Elbe, the Saale and the Bohemian Forest. This advance was stopped by the establishment of Marks. The Ostmark was aimed mainly against the Moravian and Bohemian Slavs — and later developed into the dukedom of Austria. The Thuringian Mark *(Limes Sorabicus)* was aimed against the Sorbian tribes; some lesser Marks on the Elbe against the Veletians (Liutizi) and the Saxon Mark *(Limes Saxonicus)* against the Obodrites. The borders of these Marks ran along the river Elbe. The Slavs on its left bank became, in fact, Frankish subjects, while the tribes on the right bank retained their independence for many years. But they were under constant pressure which intensified after the tenth century.

Bohemia became a major centre of Frankish interest; it had long been on the fringe of development, hidden behind its girdle of border mountains and sunk deep in the mythical period of its history. The road to Bohemia opened up before the Franks, once they gained control over the Slav tribes along the upper Main, Rednitz and Pegnitz rivers in north-eastern Bavaria. The first onslaught came via the Cheb region and along the valley of the Ohře. In 805 the Frankish army reached the mighty hill-fort at Canburg above the Kokořín valley but had to retreat without achieving its aim. Later mutual relations improved, since in 822 representatives of the Czechs and Moravians appeared at the Imperial Assembly of Louis the Pious at Frankfurt. In 845 there is a record of the baptism of fourteen Bohemian princes at Regensburg. This report shows how scattered the Czechs were in their tribal princedoms, which still had a long way to go towards some degree of state organization. Frankish Christianity, with mainly political aims in mind, had not sunk roots in Bohemia when, several decades later, the first historical ruler of the country, Bořivoj, had to be baptised anew.

In the meantime, Moravia under Prince Mojmír

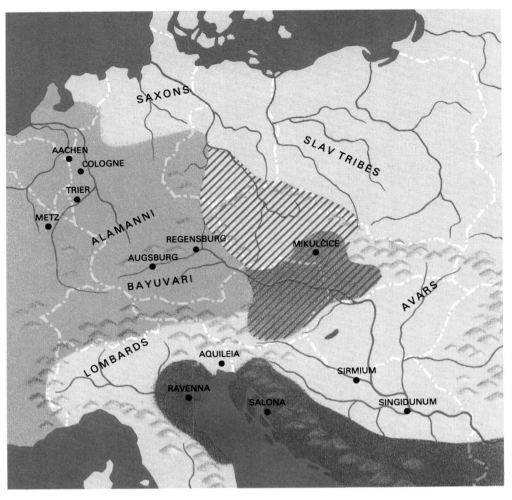

Frankish empire

Byzantine empire

Samo's empire

Core of Samo's empire

Samo's Empire emerged after a major uprising against the Avars in the twenties of the seventh century along the north-western borders of the Avar lands. In view of lack of information we can get no more than an approximate idea of its size.

grew in political importance. The local tribes unified before those in Bohemia, and Mojmír, furthermore, had managed to add the Slovakian Nitra area to his realm, from where he expelled Prince Pribina. The Frankish Empire did not interfere in Moravian affairs until Louis the German, who aided Mojmír's nephew Rastislav to become ruler. But on his return home he was defeated by the Bohemians who then attacked the Frankish territory themselves. A new Frankish expedition in 849 ended in catastrophe. This enabled the Czechs and Moravians to gain greater independence. Another expedition in the years 856/7 was only of limited importance, altering merely local conditions. The Franks drove from a castle belonging to Wiztrach his son Slavitah and put in his place the brother, who obviously had made an alliance with them. Attacks continued from both sides. During one of these the

Charlemagne played a significant role in the history of the Central European Slavs so that his name has become the title of a king in the Slavonic languages. The statue of Charlemagne is part of the cathedral treasure at Metz.

74

Franks got hold of the rich dowry of an unknown Bohemian bride, whose wedding procession was going to Moravia. It may have been the bride of Svatopluk, the successor to Rastislav, who fought constant battles with the Franks. In the year 872 Carloman undertook a large but unsuccessful expedition against him. Success was reached only by troops under the leadership of Archbishop Luitbert, who came to Bohemia and defeated five Bohemian princes: Světislav, Vitislav, Heřman, Spytimír and Mojslav. It is not known where these princes were rulers, but the smaller number of names indicates that, at that time, the process of unification of the Bohemian tribes had advanced, probably under the pressure from the Franks. Then the first historical prince, Bořivoj, appeared on the scene. Some time in 869—870 he adopted Christianity in Moravia where the Byzantine missionaries Constantine and

The centre of the empire of Charlemagne was Aachen. The model of Charles' palatinate there evokes the period appearance of his residence with a palace and a church.

Methodius were then working. This cultural and political orientation of the Bohemians and Moravians towards Byzantium was not of long duration. No more than one year after Svatopluk's death (895) the Czech princes once again acknowledged Frankish sovereignty at an assembly in Regensburg. The orientation towards the Latin West determined the further development of the Central European Slavs.

While the Western Slav tribes were exposed to the pressure of the Frankish Empire, the Slavs on the Balkans were exposed primarily to Byzantine influences, which, for a time, reached as far as Central Europe but affected to a far greater extent the economic, political and cultural development of the Eastern Slavs. This influence formed a kind of countercurrent to Slav expansion towards the south, which, for more than two centuries, threatened the core of Byzan-

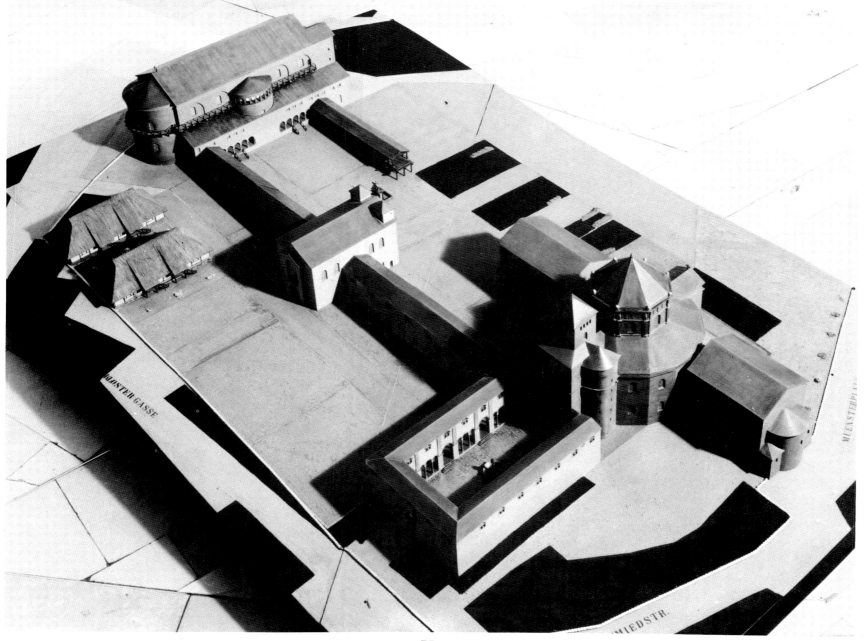

75

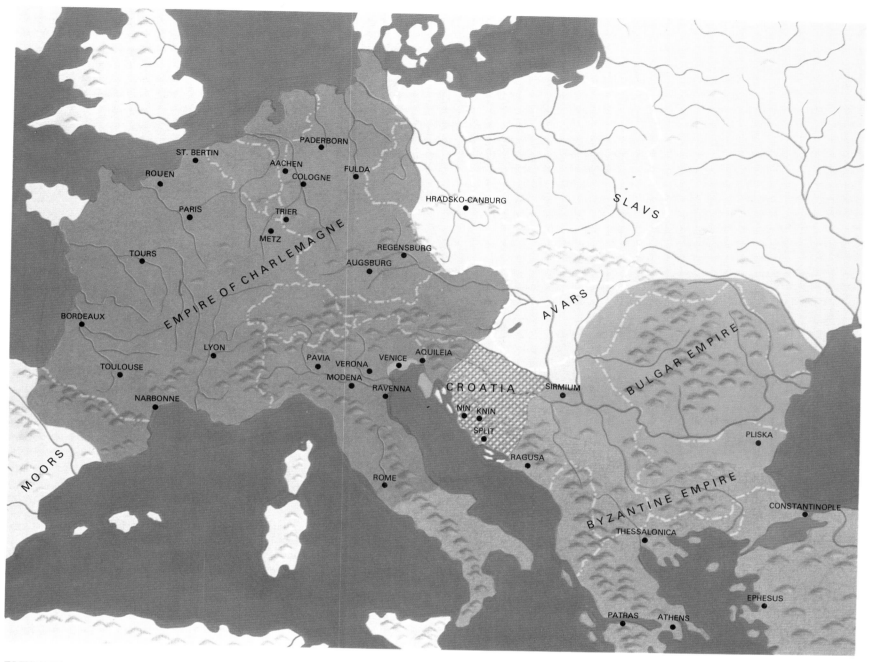

Meeting of Byzantine and Frankish spheres of interest

The Slavs who settled in Central and South-Eastern Europe soon found themselves drawn into the power struggle between the two great empires of the day: the Byzantine Empire to the east and that of the Franks in the west, the latter growing particularly under Charlemagne (771–814).

tium by their occupation of Greece, until, in the end, the Slavs succumbed to their culturally stronger opponent. The relatively speedy assimilation of the Greek Slavs was facilitated by the fact that they were not politically organized, as had been case with Samo's Empire, the Bulgars, Serbs and Croats. They often lent their services to the Byzantine army where they adopted Greek ways and even reached leading positions. The founder of the Macedonian dynasty Basil I (867–886) may himself have been of Slav origin.

The Franks undertook their first onslaught against the Czech Slavs in 805. But they did not achieve much success although their army advanced as far as castle Canburg, which, excavations confirm, can be identified in great likelihood with the hill-fort Hradsko-Kanina near Mělnik in central Bohemia.

The relations between Byzantium and the Balkan Slavs were varied. As we have shown, the Croats were partly under Byzantine and partly under Frankish influence. Byzantine influences spread mainly from the coastal towns of Dalmatia. In the tenth century the Croats became vassals to Byzantium, but from the second half of the eleventh century Western influences again dominated, which can be found in the distinct culture of the Croats to this day. On the other hand, the Serbs acknowledged Byzantine sovereignty almost con-

An iron helmet lost by an unknown warrior at Hradsko-Kanina, which might be evidence of the battle of the Czechs against the Franks.

tinuously until the twelfth century, when they became independent but retained cultural links. The same is true of the Bulgars, who defended their political independence in numerous battles against the Byzantines until the early eleventh century. Tsar Boris I (852—889) even intended to adopt the Latin form of Christianity as a cultural counterbalance to Byzantium. In the end he availed himself of a different means of achieving this end: he gave asylum to disciples of Methodius, who had been expelled from Moravia by Svatopluk and were seeking refuge in Bulgaria, where they introduced Christianity in its new, Slavonic form. This suited the endeavours of the Bulgarian rulers in their quest for independence. This form of Christianity, however, brought them culturally closer to the Byzantines.

The contacts between Byzantium and the more remote Eastern Slavs were, at first, in the form of wars or trade. Military encounters played an important part especially among the militant Scandinavian Varangians, who settled in Russia after the ninth century. Most of them were unsuccessful on the Slav side. But trade contacts, secured even in the form of treaties, developed very intensively. The famous route from the Varangians to the Greeks led along the rivers Volkhov, Dvina, Dnieper, and the Black Sea — and furs, amber, honey, wax, resin and slaves were moved down it. In the opposite direction metal objects, precious materials and spices were transported. When in 989 Prince Vladimir adopted Christianity, a new stage in profound cultural penetration began and it found its reflection in architecture, literature, and in religious and legal life.

The Byzantine influences on Slavonic culture showed most clearly in architecture — ecclesiastical and secular. This is exemplified in numerous churches all over the Balkans and in Eastern Europe, e.g. the palaces of the Bulgarian rulers at Pliska, Preslav and Madara, adorned with mosaics, marble and glazed tiles. And in craftsmanship, the work of goldsmiths and potters. Byzantine jewels and pottery enjoyed great popularity not only among the Slavs who came into direct contact with Byzantium, but all over Central Europe where they were one of the main influences in the goldsmiths' work of the Great Moravian Empire in the ninth century.

Contacts between Central Europe and
Byzantium are confirmed by a hoard of
silver jewelry, vessels, coins and sherds
from the seventh century, found at
Zemiansky Vrbovok in Slovakia.

The battle of Patras in 805 put an end to Slav rule on the Peloponnese and began a new phase of Slavo-Byzantine contacts. Legends has it that the besieged town was saved by a false sign given by a spy that help was at hand. The defeat of the Slav army could not be warded off even with the support of the Saracenes.

GODS,
DEMONS
AND SHRINES

Arkona — symbol of defiance and the doom of Slavonic paganism. The place where the famous Svantovit temple once stood has been washed away by the waves of the Baltic Sea.

THE RELIGIOUS IDEAS OF THE SLAVS

Slav paganism grew out of the common Indo-European core and therefore has certain features identical to those of the ancient Indians, Iranians, Greeks, Romans, Celts, Germans and Balts. This is true of certain basic terms such as *div, diva, divý* to indicate a spirit of nature; these correspond to the old Indian *deva*, the Iranian *div, daeva*, the Latin *divus, deus, dea*, the Lithuanian *devas*, etc. Similarly the expression for "god" *bůh*, or *bog* corresponds to the old Indian *bhága* (master), the Iranian *baga, bag* or the Armenian *bagin*. Certain Indo-European groups held the god of thunder in the greatest respect. In the sixth century the Byzantine writer Procopius mentioned that the Slav Perun corresponds to the Greek Zeus and Roman Jupiter, and the Germanic Thor. Apart from these similarities, or alien influences, the Slavs had beliefs of their own: there even were differences between individual groups and tribes.

On the whole, we possess far less information about the spiritual life of the pagan Slavs than about the religious ideas of other ancient Europeans. This does not mean that their life was poorer in this respect, but they entered the stage of history and the awareness of the cultured nations at a relatively late period, so that they had no Caesar or Tacitus, who might have related their history with unbiased objectivity as was the case of the Celts and the Germans. When they did appear on the scene, civilized Europe was already Christian and was not greatly interested in or showed an understanding of the spiritual life of barbarians, whom they viewed with condescension and with the sole aim of bringing them at the earliest possible date into the Christian community. Contemporary evidence is not always of equal value; apart from reliable reports by eyewitnesses there is often second- or third-hand information with various degrees of distortion. Later chroniclers, remote in time and thought from the pre-Christian period, added many facts, and even invented them when they misunderstood popular customs. The legends of the first Czech saints from the tenth and eleventh centuries and the Czech chronicler Cosmas from the early twelfth century speak of gods, idols, shrines, sacrificial altars, burial rites, magic practices, and so on, but do not cite any god by name (at most they are compared with the gods of antiquity) and the general characteristic of paganism reveals very little that is concrete. In the Czech lands the expulsion of witches and Church prohibitions of pagan rites in the eleventh and twelfth centuries show that there must have been a hidden stratum of ancient beliefs beneath the cover of Christianity.

This is true of all the countries where the ancient beliefs were fairly soon overlaid by Christianity, i.e. Central and Southern Europe. Apart from survivals in folklore there exists today hardly anything of the original religious ideas of the Czechs, Slovaks, Poles and Yugoslavs. Some reports about the more remote Eastern Slavs have survived in local sources, mainly the *Kiev Chronicle* of the eleventh century, and in Oriental (that is chiefly Arab) reports. We know relatively more about the religion of the Baltic and Polabian Slavs, who have died out. Until the twelfth century it served them as an ideological weapon in the fight for independence, for Christianity introduced by Western missionaries meant only serfdom for them and the gradual loss of national identity.

In recent decades our knowledge of Slavonic religious beliefs has been enlarged by archeology, both by excavations of shrines and places of sacrifice and the finds of idols and cult objects. Objects — weapons, tools, ornaments, vessels with food and drink — were placed in the graves. The burial rites themselves developed from the original practice of cremation, when the ashes of the deceased were placed in urns, to the inhumation of uncremated bodies; this increased under the influence of Christianity. Certain objects in the graves expressed special symbolism, e.g. eggs were symbols of life (painted Eastern eggs were known among the Slavs as early as in the tenth century) and coins placed in the mouth or hands of the dead served as payment for the ferryman to the Underworld — a custom known also among the ancient Greeks and Romans. Historically and archeologically we have con-

The Slav custom of painting Easter eggs goes back to an ancient pre-Christian tradition. As early as in the tenth century clay eggs, *pisanki*, were painted in Kiev.

84

An Arabian traveller, Ibn Fadhlan, visited Russia in 922 and among his many experiences he witnessed the burial of a Russian noble. His colourful and dramatic description of the entire ceremony points to a mixture of Norman and Slav customs: the corpse was burnt on a ship together with numerous offerings and a sacrificed female slave.

firmation of the belief in vampires — dead persons who suck human blood and who have to be rendered powerless by the deformation of the dead body. In the same way the Slavs practised the burning of widows, a custom that survived in India until not so long ago. Even objects of daily use — weapons, tools, ornaments, pots — were marked with well-known ancient symbols such as the swastika, cross, sun-wheel, pentagram, etc., which through magic were supposed to ensure success in the relevant activity.

The marks on the bottom of Slav vessels all take the form of old, generally used symbols and were originally associated with magic ideas before they became the trade marks of the potters.

A stone with the relief of a male figure holding a mighty horn is set in a wall of the church at Altenkirchen on the island of Rügen. It is believed to be one depiction of the god Svantovit.

A similar stone can be found in the wall of the church at Bergen on Rügen.

Many old pagan rites live to this day in folk customs, for example carols, which relate to the festival of the winter solstice; "death" being carried outside in spring, which is a survival of the folk sacrifice to the gods of nature; the midsummer bonfire, which is all that is left of the celebration of the summer solstice.

The core of religious life was the respect for the gods and cults associated with this. Like other Indo-Europeans the Slavs, too, had their Olympus. Some gods were held in common or at least enjoyed a broader significance. This applies mainly to PERUN, the god of storms or of thunder and lightning, worshipped mainly in Russia, where in the tenth century his idols stood near Kiev and at Peryn' near Novgorod. There is proof that his cult also existed in Poland and among the Polabian Slavs, where Thursday was consecrated to him as *peründan*. ("Thursday" as such derives from the ancient Germanic god Thor; *jeudi* — *dies Iovis* comes from the Roman Jove). In the Czech lands Perun occurred only as a name, and in Slovakia he has survived in curses, for example, *parom do teba* — "May Perun strike you", and *Do paroma* — "By Perun".

The Eastern and Western Slavs knew a SVAROG or DAZHBOG, the god of the Bright Sun, and his son SVAROZHICH was worshipped e.g. in Obodrite Rethra. Svarog's name is probably connected with the Old Indian *svarga* (sky), the second name Dazhbog probably meant "god-the-donor", that is, the donor of warmth and light as conditions of life. Svarozhich was the personification of fire, understood as the son on earth of the sun. In the Czech region proof of the cult of the sun was found in symbols, e.g. a cross in a circle incised on a clay disk found at Libušín.

The third god of broader significance was VELES, called Volos in the east, the protector of herds and farming. In the Czech lands traces of his cult survive only in old folk idioms, such as *u velesa* (meaning "the deuce") or *ký veles ti to našeptal?* ("What devil put you up to it?").

The majority of gods, however, were only of regional or entirely local importance. In Russia they worshipped, for example, STRIBOG, the god of the winds, the goddess MOKOSH, perhaps of Finnish origin, CHORS and SEMARGL, who came from the Orient, and TROJAN, who cannot have been anybody other than the deified Roman Emperor Trajan, introduced to the Slavs possibly by the Dacians.

The Olympus of the Polabian and Baltic Slavs was particularly crowded. They clung firmly to their paganism and therefore roused the lively interest of the chroniclers of the neighbouring Christian lands. A renowned site of worship was Rethra, the centre of the Obodrite tribe of the Retharii and the famous oracle that foretold the future, especially harvests or the outcome of warfare, with the aid of the sacred horse of Svarozhich. This god was also known by the names of RADOGOST, Radigost or Radegast, which often appear as local names.

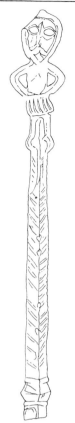

This small wooden statue found at Novgorod probably depicts Perun.
←

This wooden figurine found at Wolin probably represents the god Triglav, who was worshipped at Stettin and in the surrounding countryside.
←

→
Similarly associated with Svantovit is an idol almost three-metre (ten-feet) high with the god depicted in relief on all four sides. It was raised from the bottom of the river Zbrucz near Husyatin in southern Poland.

Another god to enjoy great fame was SVANTOVIT, whose temple stood at Arkona on the island of Rügen on the Baltic coast until the year 1168. He had four heads and held a drinking-horn filled with wine in his right hand, from the level of which he foretold the prospects for future harvests. Last century a stone idol almost three metres (about ten feet) high was discovered on the river Zbrucz in southern Poland; as it had four faces and a drinking-horn, it was immediately assumed to be a depiction of Svantovit. But that is not certain since other Slavonic gods, too, were many-headed. In Stettin (Szczecin) for instance a three-headed TRIGLAV was worshipped, at Korenica on Rügen a four-headed PORENUTIUS, a five-headed POREVIT, and even RUGIEVIT with seven heads. In Europe this phenomemon is relatively rare among, for example, the Celts or the Romans, but it recalls the old Indian gods, which to this day have such appearances. We cannot, therefore, eliminate some connections with the Old Indo-European culture, of which survivals can also be traced in other aspects of Slavonic paganism, e.g. in burial rites. Many-headedness must have symbolized the multiple power of the relevant god.

A pagan shrine was discovered at hill-fort Schlossberg near Feldberg, but it dates from an older period (seventh to ninth century) than legendary Rethra, with which it was once mistakenly identified.

88

South of Novgorod at the point where the
Volkhov flows out of Lake Il'men' they used
to worship the god of thunder and lightning,
Perun. His shrine in the form of three
circular moats with the idol in the centre
was discovered in the grounds of the
monastery at Peryn'. Long after Patriarch
Akim of Novgorod had the shrine
demolished, passing boatmen would offer
coins to Perun.

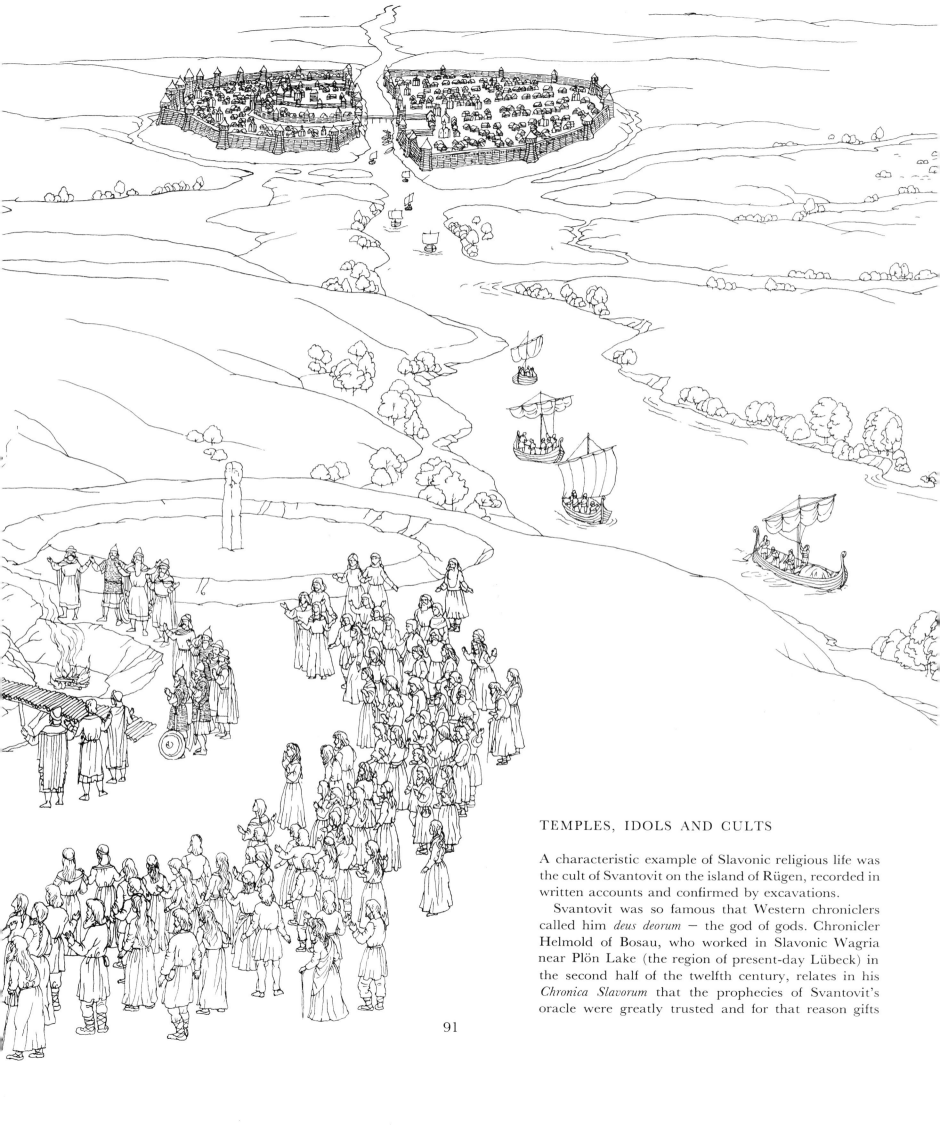

TEMPLES, IDOLS AND CULTS

A characteristic example of Slavonic religious life was
the cult of Svantovit on the island of Rügen, recorded in
written accounts and confirmed by excavations.

Svantovit was so famous that Western chroniclers
called him *deus deorum* — the god of gods. Chronicler
Helmold of Bosau, who worked in Slavonic Wagria
near Plön Lake (the region of present-day Lübeck) in
the second half of the twelfth century, relates in his
Chronica Slavorum that the prophecies of Svantovit's
oracle were greatly trusted and for that reason gifts

91

were sent to him from all Slav lands, even from the non-Slavonic neighbours, as proved by a precious cup, the gift of the Danish King Sweyn. Every year human sacrifices were made to Svantovit's idol from among the Christian prisoners. The inhabitants of Rügen had a reputation as being the most obdurate pagans, and of all the Slavs they held out the longest against the adoption of Christianity.

Similar evidence about the cult of Svantovit and its disappearance was recorded by the Danish priest Saxo Grammaticus, who died at the beginning of the thirteenth century. He gave a vivid description of the temple built on a mound in the centre of the fortified town of Arkona in the most northerly corner of the island. The temple was surrounded by a wall, adorned with carefully executed carvings and crudely painted motifs. Only one gate led into the shrine itself. The temple proper had an outer wooden wall, supporting a red roof, and inner walls of magnificent rugs, hung on four pillars. Inside stood the wooden idol, larger than life-size, with four heads, two of which were turned to the front and two to the back. In his right hand he held a metal horn, which the priest in attendance filled with wine every year and from its level estimated the harvest in the coming year. By the side of the idol lay a bridle, saddle and numerous insignia, among which greatest admiration was roused by a gigantic sword with a beautiful hammered silver handle and sheath. Furthermore a white horse was consecrated to Svantovit, on which only the priest was allowed to ride. They believed that Svantovit used it to go out fighting at night, because in the morning the horse was found sweating and muddy, as if it had returned from a long

A site associated with the cult was discovered at Pohansko near Břeclav, a hill-fort from the time of the Great Moravian Empire. Eight post holes laid out in a circle around nine others in the centre and traces of a fence indicate that a group of idols must have stood here in the ninth century.

At the Old Kouřim hill-fort in Bohemia archeologists have unearthed a shrine from the ninth century surrounded by a symbolic moat. The place was considered sacred even after the adoption of Christianity.

journey. With the aid of the horse they foretold the success or failure of military expeditions being planned: if the horse stepped over a number of lances placed in front of the temple right leg first, it was a favourable sign; in the opposite case, they would abandon such an expedition. Only one priest was permitted to enter the temple and did so holding his breath — each time he needed to breathe he had to run back to the door. Sacrifices were made in the form of wine and a large round honey bun. The ceremony was followed by a lively banquet at which none was allowed to remain sober. Svantovit's sanctuary was guarded by a company of three hundred riders, who also saw to the enlargement of the temple treasure. With his attributes Svantovit most closely resembled the Roman god of war Mars, even though, as the ceremony with the horn shows, he also had other functions.

Since the location of Arkona is well known — remains of its mighty ramparts to this day stand up to the waves of the Baltic Sea on the chalk cliffs of Arkona Point — it is not surprising that it attracted the interest of archeologists. This culminated in 1921 in excavations by one of the leading German archeologists Carl Schuchhardt. Following Saxo's descriptions he concentrated on a slightly raised plateau in what he assumed to have been the centre of the town, now largely swallowed up by the sea. Schuchhardt managed to find the foundations of a square structure with four posts inside and marks of the stone base of the idol. Without hesitation he declared this to be the temple he had been looking for. The scientific world on the whole accepted his interpretation, though doubts began to arise after the Second World War, by which time techniques of research and documentation had greatly improved.

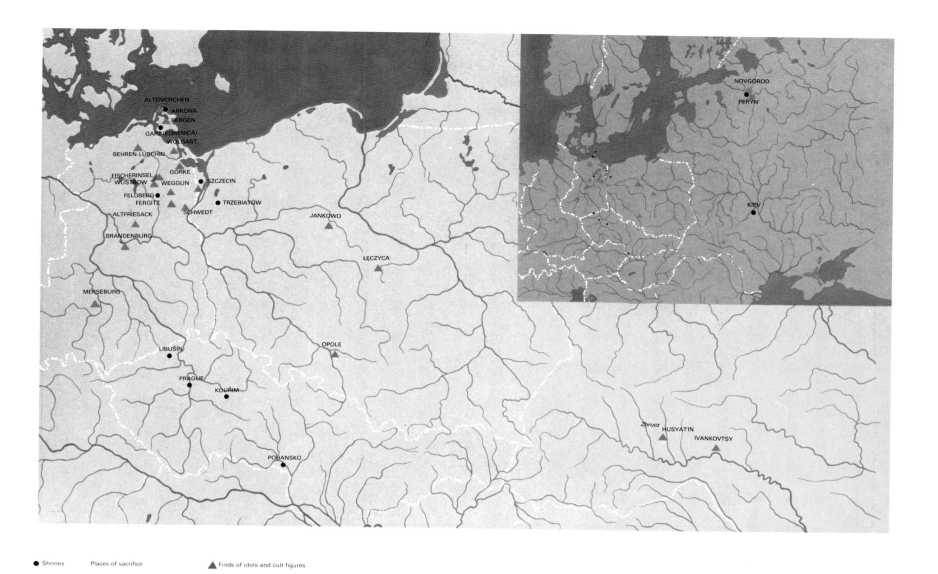

● Shrines   Places of sacrifice   ▲ Finds of idols and cult figures

According to today's standards of archeology Carl Schuchhardt did not carry out his excavations in too exact a manner — he cut only narrow trenches instead of opening up a larger area, which would have given an overall picture of the site. Divergencies from the description provided by Saxo Grammaticus, both in size

The map shows the sites of the most important archeological finds of Slavonic pagan shrines and idols.

A clay disc with an incised symbol of the sun was connected with a certain cult or magical practices (Libušín, Bohemia, sixth to seventh century).

and the technique of building, led the Danish archeologist E. Dyggve to the conclusion that the object discovered by Schuchhardt might at best have been the remnant of a Danish mission church built on the site of the pagan sanctuary, as was the customary practice of the Church. The final development in this dispute was

reached when H. Berlekamp carried out new excavations in the place where Schuchhardt had dug and found nothing but the remnants of internal fortifications. The shrine itself must have stood further to the east, where today everything is beneath the waves of the Baltic Sea. We shall never know its precise location and must rest content with the description given by the Danish chronicler.

Schuchhardt's assumed discovery of the second most important temple of the Baltic Slavs — Rethra — met a similar fate. This main temple of the Retharii tribe was first described by Bishop Thietmar of Merseburg, who died in 1018. He related that in the centre of a sacred grove there stood a magnificently decorated temple made of timber, built upon animal horns; it contained a number of idols fully dressed in armour. The most important among them was dedicated to Svarozhich, who was thought to be the son of the sun-god Svarog, known too as a member of the pantheon of the Eastern Slavs. He was worshipped together with Svantovit by all the Slavs in the north, and human sacrifices were made to him, e.g. in 1066 Bishop Johann of Marienburg. A sacred horse was consecrated to Svarozhich and was used by the priests in their prophecies. The temple was finally pulled down in 1068 and Bishop Burchard rode back to Halberstadt on this horse to humiliate the pagans.

Thietmar relates somewhat obscurely that the town of Rethra was triangular *(tricornis)* and had three gates. In view of the large number of similarly built castles surviving in the north, the archeologists looked for Rethra in at least twenty places. Generally they accepted the view put forward by Carl Schuchhardt, who in 1922 undertook a minor excavation on the fortified Schlossberg near Feldberg on the shores of Lake Feldberg. He declared this to be the site of the Rethra that they had been looking for and explained its "three-cornered" appearance by the fact that there were three gates with towers.

The imposing location of Schlossberg in a dense beech-wood makes this hypothesis highly plausible and attracted modern archeologists who sought to put it to

Two stone idols have survived near the Ukrainian village of Ivankovtsy on the left bank of the Dniester; they relate to a pagan cult. The standing idol has a human face in relief on three sides and is reminiscent of the find in the river Zbrucz.

This wooden idol found at Altfriesack (GDR) is probably related to a fertility cult. Radiocarbon tests have dated it to the second half of the sixth century, i.e. the beginning of Slav settlement.

→
This wooden figure attached to the wall of a building at the hill-fort at Behren-Lübchin (GDR, eleventh to twelfth century) is also connected with the cult.

the test. Excavations by J. Herrmann in 1967 indeed confirmed that this had been an important tribal centre, in which, to judge by the density of dwellings, some six to twelve hundred inhabitants had lived permanently. He even discovered the temple, but not at the top of the hill-fort, as Schuchhardt had assumed, but on a spur projecting above the lake, on a site surrounded by a moat. But his finds showed clearly that the hill-fort at Feldberg had been used in the seventh to ninth centuries, while there was not a trace of settlement at the time when Rethra enjoyed its greatest fame as historically recorded, i.e. in the tenth

On Fischerinsel in Lake Tollense near Neubrandenburg (GDR) archeologists recently found a two-headed wooden idol with a mighty moustache standing on a square column (eleventh to twelfth century).

and eleventh centuries. This case, too, still remains open — at least for the time being — and the search needs to be continued. Thietmar's description does not fit the Feldberg temple, which was a simple rectangular building divided into several parts and separated from the hill-fort itself by a moat.

Archeologists have managed to form some impression of the anonymous cult places consecrated to local gods, which are known to have existed in large numbers. In western Pomerania two such places were discovered at Trzebiatów (Gryfice district) in 1931—3. There were two moats of oval ground plan, 65 m or 70 yds apart, whose shallow depth (0.5—1 m or about 2.5 ft) and width (1—1.5 m or about 4 ft) provided no more than symbolic protection. In the midst of the smaller oval (8 × 10 m or 26 × 33 ft) traces were found of a single fire that must have burnt there. Inside the larger oval (10 × 13 m or 33 × 43 ft) there were two hearths and three wooden idols, of which only three post holes survive. Sacrificial fires burnt likewise in the moats, to judge by charcoal found there. These two cult places were related to a settlement dated by finds into the ninth to tenth centuries.

Soviet archeologists discovered a similar cult place belonging to the Eastern Slavs at Peryn' near Novgorod. The *Novgorod Chronicles* reveal that the local Slavs resolutely refused to adopt Christianity and were forced to submit to baptism only after heavy battles. Akim, the first Patriarch of Novgorod, had the Perun idol cast into the river Volkhov. This idol had been set up in the tenth century by Dobrynya, uncle of Vladimir, the first Christian ruler of Russia. An old tradition relates that this place was in the village of Peryn', lying near Novgorod at the point where the Volkhov flows out of Lake Il'men'. While philologists regarded the derivation of Peryn' from Perun with reservations, the Moscow archeologist V. V. Sedov managed to uncover remnants of a pagan temple in the premises of Peryn' Monastery (1948, 1951—2). It had a circular ditch with eight shallow niches, in which ceremonial fires burnt. In the centre of the circle stood the idol, of which only the pit is left today. Traces of other similar circles, clearly to be associated with idols of minor gods, were later discovered along the sides.

Written records exist which show that temples were built similarly in Bohemia: shrines were set up and

A wooden head of a man with a shaped beard came from a lake near Jankowo in Poland; it was probably originally attached to a pole. It is similar to idols found in the regions of the Polabian and Baltic Slavs.

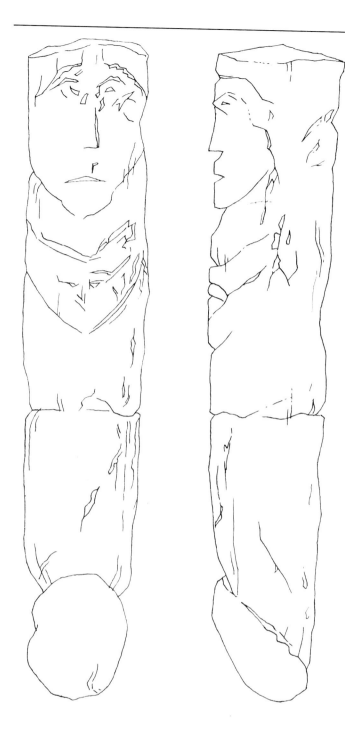

found. Similarly in Loretto Square (Loretánské náměstí) near Prague Castle there was a pit with six skulls of cattle and a large number of animal bones next to a shrine surrounded by stones. Traces of other shrines were discovered near ninth- and tenth-century burial grounds.

A typical example is the enclosed sacred precinct near the prince's burial ground at the hill-fort in Kouřim, in the ninth and early tenth centuries the centre of the Zličané tribe. It included a little lake called Libušinka, with a spring filled by rainwater running down the underlying rocks into a ravine between the inner and outer earthworks of the hill-fort. The inhabitants dug a pond 40 × 70 m (130 × 230 ft) in size, its walls strengthened with wooden posts and laid out good access to the water. The importance of the shrine is shown by the fact that it was symbolically

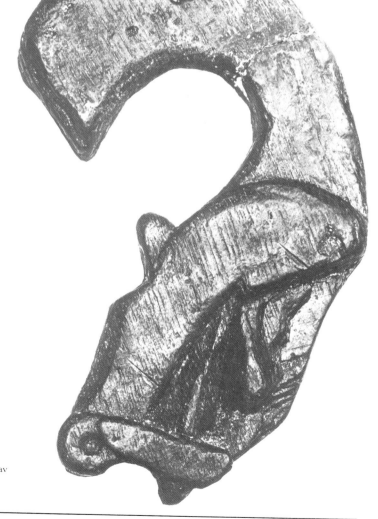

idols of gods and the figures of ancestors *dědci* were worshipped. The first Slav settlers of the country brought these with them if we are to believe the legends about Old Father Czech. St Vitus's Cathedral at Prague Castle, for instance, was built on the site of an ancient pagan shrine called Žiži. The name suggests ceremonial fires that burnt here in honour of we do not know what gods. Some shrines can be recognized by the big piles of bones of sacrifical animals, mostly in the vicinity of burial grounds, the remnants of funeral feasts, a custom that was widespread among the Slavs. This was the case at the former Church of Our Lady at Prague Castle, where entire young wild boars were

This wooden head of an animal, possibly a horse or a dragon, once decorated an unknown object at Behren-Lübchin. It bears out the reports by the chroniclers that the Slav temples were richly decorated with carvings.

97

A lead amulet in the shape of a fish, which was to ensure the person who wore it a rich catch (Neubrandenburg, Fischerinsel, eleventh century).

surrounded by a ditch, which enclosed the area on the north-western banks of the little lake. Ceremonial fires in honour of the god of the spring burnt in a number of pits in the ground between it and the lake. The level of the lake might well have served as an oracle, as was the case, for example, among the Polabian Slavs. It is interesting that this place retained its function as a sacred precinct even after the adoption of Christianity. The little lake, its fence fortified with a stone wall, served as a natural font for baptism, in which adults were christened by submersion. On its banks, on the south-western end of the burial ground, stood a small wooden Christian chapel.

Mountains were also held to be sacred. In Bohemia this must have applied to Mount Říp, worshipped for its striking shape and location in the Central Bohemian Plain even before the arrival of the Czech Slavs. According to legend, their ancestor, Old Father Czech, stood on the mount and decided there and then that his people should settle in this land. There are archeological finds to prove that other hills were likewise worship-

ped: for instance on the summit of Milešovka, the highest mountain in the Central Bohemian Massif, ninth-century sherds have been found, which cannot have come from any settlement, and, furthermore, a little disk of horn with the symbol of the sun incised upon it.

Convincing archeological proofs of Slavonic paganism are finds of idols in wood, stone and metal. Wooden gods survived only in favourable soil conditions as, for instance, in the region of the Polabian and Baltic Slavs. Among older finds there is, first of all, an idol that came from the southern shores of Lake Ruppin, close to the Slav hill-fort of Altfriesack. To begin with it was not certain whether the idol was of Slav origin, but archeologists turned to the physicists for help. Using radio-carbon tests (1967) they dated the statue to the second half of the sixth century, i.e. the very beginning of the Slavic settlement in those parts. One cannot help thinking of the old Czech legends written down by Chronicler Cosmas, where he speaks of the gods that the forefathers of the Czechs brought along on their shoulders when they came to settle in the land. The idol of Altfriesack is carved in oak and represents a slim male figure with an opening for the phallus, which was separately attached, clearly as a symbol of the god of fertility. Similar idols have been found near the hill-fort at Behren-Lübchin and at Braak (Eutin district). The phallic cult of fertility, which is mentioned in written records, e.g. among the Eastern Slavs, was confirmed by the discovery of an oaken phallus at Łęczyca near Łódź in Poland.

Idols were also made of other materials. There is, for instance, a Svantovit stone walled into the church at Altenkirchen near Arkona, depicting in relief a male figure holding a mighty drinking horn — the symbol of Svantovit. A similar stone — likewise set into a church wall — can be found at Bergen on the island of Rügen.

The Gerovit (Jarovit) stone with a primitive picture of the local god holding a cudgel in his hand as a symbol of his function as a god of war exists at Wolgast.

Apart from these large figures smaller statues likewise related to the cult, for example a lead figurine found in a grave near Weggun (Prenzlau district), a bronze figure of a man in the hill-fort at Schwedt in the Oder region, a little head of bone at Merseburg, etc. There were also cult animals e.g. lead fish amulets at Wustrow on Lake Tollense and at Fergitz near Prenzlau, also a serpent carved from a stag horn, found at Görke near Anklam, and particularly figures of horses — the attributes of gods of war such as the little lead horse unearthed at Brandenburg.

A recent find of two oak idols in a fortified settlement on the Fischerinsel in Lake Tollense south of Neubran-

The little head of a man from Merseburg (GDR) carved in horn must likewise have depicted some unknown god.

denburg caused great excitement. The settlement dates from the eleventh to the twelfth century. One of the idols, 165 cm (65 in) tall, represents a female goddess; the head is roughly hewn, and stress is placed on the features showing her sex. It is interesting that it was carved to be seen at a slanting angle from the front so that it must have stood as a secondary goddess in the corner of the temple. The other idol depicts a two-headed male god, 170 cm (67 in) tall, standing on a square post. Both his heads sit on one shoulder and the most characteristic features are mighty drooping moustaches.

The extinction of the original religion of the Slavs was caused primarily by an internal crisis due to social changes. To them the culturally more advanced Christian civilization, which introduced the feudal system of society, better corresponded. This transition did not take place without resistance. In the Czech lands, for instance, there was a pagan uprising by Strojmír against the first Christian prince, Bořivoj, in the last quarter of the ninth century, and in the eleventh century it was still necessary for decrees to be published against pagan customs. In Bulgaria, too, there was a pagan reaction under Boris's heir Vladimir. Instead of him Boris gave the throne to his younger son Symeon, who completed Boris's work of Christianization.

This process progressed slowly among the Eastern Slavs, where pagans were still living in the remote areas of medieval Russia during the fifteenth century. Very great resistance was also put up by the Polabian and Baltic tribes.

It is clear that the presence of determined pagans in the heart of Europe was considered an anomaly in Western Christendom in the eleventh and twelfth centuries to be eliminated as soon as possible. Hence the persistent efforts over the centuries to use force to cast out this scandalous religion. In the year 1147 a major crusade was undertaken against the Obodrites and Liutizi instead of to the Holy Land following an appeal issued by St Bernard of Clairvaux. Under the leadership of Henry the Lion, Albert the Bear, the archbishops of Magdeburg and Bremen, the papal legate Anselm and other famous princes, it was composed of the armies of Saxony, Denmark (including its fleet), Bohemia and Poland. The undertaking was not very successful from a military point of view, but by laying the country waste and decimating the population it broke the strength of the Baltic tribes to such an extent that within a few decades they succumbed completely. Their pagan ideology in its decadent and atavistic form could not stand up to the more advanced Christian civilization.

The horse was the attribute of a god of war; in some temples (Arkona, Rethra) horses were kept as sacred animals. Equal importance can be attributed to a small wooden horse from Opole in Poland with an incised symbol of a slanting cross on its chest.

100

Small figurines, e.g. the lead figure of
a horse from Brandenburg (GDR),
were related to this cult.

The year 1168 brought catastrophe to
Slavonic paganism on the Baltic Sea.
Its last bastion — the famous Svantovit
temple at Arkona on the island of
Rügen — was destroyed by King
Waldemar of Denmark.

A MAJOR
MILESTONE
IN DEVELOPMENT

The masses of Slav people who flooded a large part of Europe in the sixth to eighth centuries represented a mighty and ethnically almost unified group, but politically they were split up and therefore could hardly resist the militarily well organized nomads or the ambitious great powers such as the Franks in the West and Byzantium — the remains of the Roman Empire — in the East. Samo's Empire was only a temporary phenomenon, which came into being during the resistance to Avar oppression and disintegrated soon after the death of the man who had brought it into existence. It would seem that in the first few centuries of their history when the process of settlement was in progress, the Slavs did not have the conditions or the need for a permanent state organization. At most they established unions of tribes according to the local situation, which broke up naturally when those particular conditions no longer existed. Not until the ninth century did the time become ripe for basic changes in this respect — clearly since the colonization of the new territory had been basically finished by then, economic life was entering a new phase, and the settled area needed to be effectively defended against pressure from outside. For that reason the first Slavonic states emerged at that time in quick succession in Central, South-Eastern and Eastern Europe, and they showed themselves capable of more permanent existence.

THE GREAT MORAVIAN EMPIRE
AND ITS CENTRES

In Central Europe there was a state whose core lay in present-day Moravia, but its sphere of influence went far beyond that territory, from which it derives its name — the Great Moravian Empire. It developed in the first half of the ninth century, soon after the Avars had been routed by Charlemagne, and it put up a barrier to Frankish expansion, which aimed at the lands beyond the Danube in the direction of the Carpathians. It soon became the centre of attention of Western chroniclers, such as the authors of the *Annales Regni Francorum*, *Annales Fuldenses*, and others, the writers of Church records, e.g. papal epistles or the manuscript on the conversion of the Bavarians and Carinthians, *De conversione Bagoariorum et Carantanorum*. The interest of Byzan-

"Rastislav's ineffable fort", mentioned in the *Fulda Annals* for the year 869, has been excavated for several decades at hill-fort Valy near Mikulčice in southern Moravia. This complex settlement covering 200 hectares (about 80 acres) lay on an island formed by the river Morava.

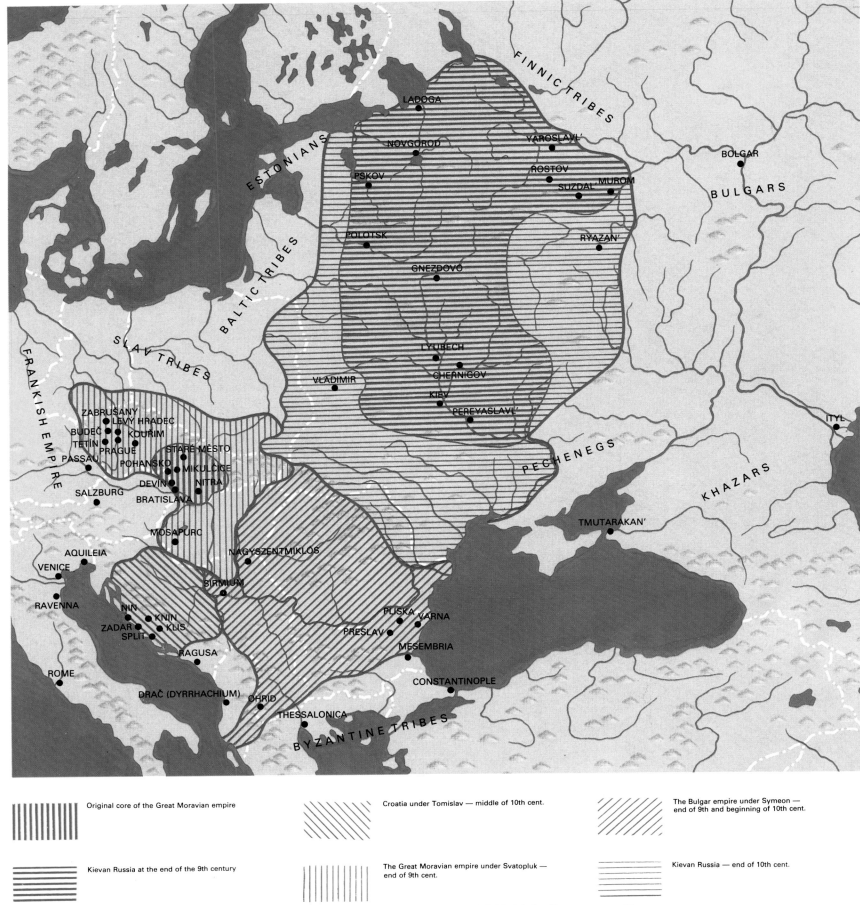

| | Original core of the Great Moravian empire | | Croatia under Tomislav — middle of 10th cent. | | The Bulgar empire under Symeon — end of 9th and beginning of 10th cent. |

| | Kievan Russia at the end of the 9th century | | The Great Moravian empire under Svatopluk — end of 9th cent. | | Kievan Russia — end of 10th cent. |

When the process of colonization of new territories was basically finished the first Slav states appeared in the pages of history in the ninth century. The greatest of these were the Great Moravian Empire in Central Europe, the Bulgarian Empire in the Balkans, and Kievan Russia in Eastern Europe.

tine historians was no less great. The very term Great Moravia was invented by the Emperor and author Constantine Porphyrogenitus. Until not long ago these works were the only sources of information about the state that achieved such great political significance in the ninth century and became a centre of culture with an influence that spread over a large area to the other Slavs. In the last few decades, thanks to intensive excavations, another important source has been added, which not only complemented existing historical knowledge but considerably revised it in many respects.

The first figure to rise out of the darkness of history was Mojmír, the true founder of the Moravian state, who in the years 830—833 added the princedom of Nitra (today's south-western Slovakia) to his estate in Moravia; he expelled its ruler Pribina, an ally of the Franks, from there. By that time Christianity had come to Moravia through the Frankish missionaries, whose centre must have been the bishopric of Passau. The Moravian rulers soon realized the political danger of Christian conversion from that side, accompanied by the threat of loss of independence. For that reason Mojmír's successor, Rastislav (846—869), expelled the Frankish missionaries from his country and aimed at setting up an independent Moravian diocese. Since Pope Nicholas I did not approve his petition, he appealed to the Byzantine Emperor Michael III with the same supplication in 862. He was seeking support against both the Franks and the expanding Bulgarian Empire, whose frontiers ran alongside his own on the river Tisza. This was a brilliant diplomatic move, which was to have far-reaching cultural effects, for Rastislav requested that missionaries be sent who would be able to proclaim Christianity in the Slavonic tongue.

Emperor Michael and Patriarch Photius sent him the brothers Constantine and Methodius, sons of a high officer in Thessalonica. Both possessed a good command of the Slavonic tongue, for the population around Greek Thessalonica was predominantly Slav. The older, Methodius, entered a monastery after working as a clerk and became abbot at Polychronos. The younger, Constantine (later known by his monastic name of Cyril), was Photius's favourite disciple, and worked as teacher of philosophy at the patriarchal school attached to the Cathedral of the Holy Apostles. Both had experiences in diplomacy: Constantine had once accompanied Photius as ambassador to Caliph Mutawakkil. In 860 both brothers travelled with an important political and religious mission to the Khazars on the Crimea, where they gained respect, among others, by finding the relics of Pope St Clement. They made thorough preparation for their mission to Moravia. Constantine invented Glagolitic, a special Slavonic script, able to express the phonetic sounds of the Slavonic language, which considerably differed from the Greek. (Cyrillic, which to this day is used by the Serbs, Bulgarians and Russians, came into exist-

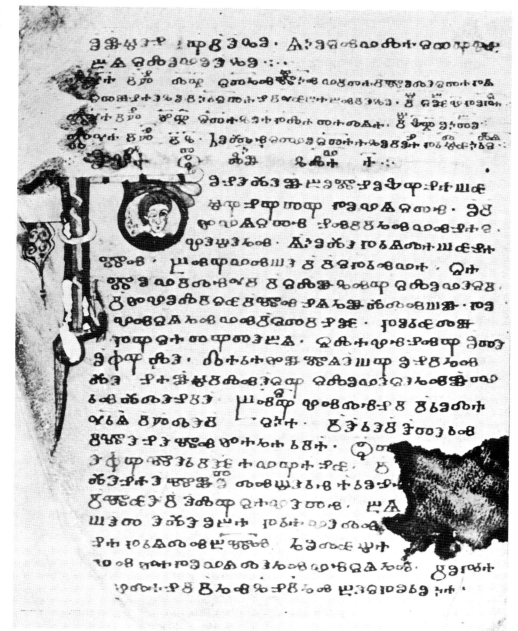

As part of his work as a missionary in Moravia Constantine created the original form of the Slavonic alphabet, Glagolitic. This example is taken from the *Codex Assemianus*.

ence slightly later in the circle of Methodius's disciples in Bulgaria.) Liturgical books were translated into Slavonic, and divine service was held in the Slavonic tongue. At the time that was a dramatic innovation, since throughout Europe only the Latin or the Greek rites and texts were used — with the exception of England under Alfred the Great and Moravia under Rastislav and Svatopluk. This development, which was later approved even by the Pope, met with great success among the Slav population and soon drove the efforts of Frankish missionaries into the background. This naturally caused concern among the Frankish bishops, who after the death of Constantine in Rome (869) for a time abducted Methodius and unlawfully imprisoned him. Their action fits into the political context which was marked by constant Moravian-Frankish conflicts, with varying success on both sides.

The Moravian state reached the height of its power under Rastislav's successor Svatopluk (870–894), with whom the Franks were forced to conclude a peace treaty in 874, in which they acknowledged the independence of Moravia. At that time the Moravian estates stretched from the Elbe and Saale in the west as far as the upper Bug and Styr in the east and to the Danube and Tisza in the south. Decline, however, was soon to set in: a tragic conflict broke out between Methodius, who had been appointed Archbishop of Moravia, and Svatopluk. It came to a head after the death of Methodius (885), when his disciples were expelled from Moravia and the Slavonic liturgy was no longer permitted. The Slavonic priests, thereupon, continued their work in Bulgaria. With the death of

The summoning of the Byzantine missionaries Constantine and Methodius by the Moravian Prince Rastislav in 862 was to have far-reaching consequences for the cultural life of the Slavs: it led to the origin of the Slavonic alphabet, a literary language and literature as such.

109

Svatopluk the decline of the Moravian state continued, and it was given its death stroke when the Hungarians invaded in the early tenth century.

The most important archeological contribution to the problem of Great Moravia was made by excavations carried out at its very centre. In written sources there exist only vague clues, which did not make it possible to identify its precise extent. The *Annals* of Fulda Abbey, one of the important ninth-century sources, relate that in 869 the youngest son of the Frankish King Louis the German, Charles, "came with the troops he had been put in charge of to that ineffable fort of Rastislav's, so unlike all old ones". The writer does not mention whether Charles managed to capture the fort, whose mightiness amazed the Franks and the Alamanni. It is more likely that he was driven off and resorted to ravaging the surrounding countryside, which was regarded as victory. Two years later Rastislav's nephew, Svatopluk, set free from Frankish imprisonment, returned to Moravia at the head of the army of Louis' eldest son, Carloman, allegedly to put down the rebellious Moravians. But when they entered "Rasti-

Gold and silver jewelry testifies to the high level of craftsmanship in the Great Moravian Empire. Highly individual forms were applied to belt mounts and strap ends (Staré Město).

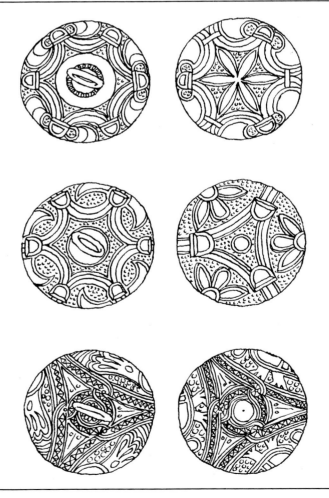

Typical of Great Moravian jewelry are these gilt buttons used to fasten coats. They had rich ornamentation with plant, geometrical and animal motifs.

Great Moravian ear-rings had a wide range of shapes and are examples of perfect craftsmanship (Staré Město).

slav's old town" — as the Fulda annalist called the unknown castle — he turned on the Bavarians with the aid of the Moravians and completely overwhelmed them.

These are two important records of the existence of centres of the Great Moravian Empire. To them might be added one other older report, from the year 864, when Louis the German "besieged Rastislav in some town, which in the tongue of that people is known as Dowina". It must have been Devín, on the confluence of the Morava and Danube, where archeological excavations have, in fact, brought to light fortifications from the period of the Great Moravian Empire. But where was that "ineffable fort" and "Rastislav's old town"? Historians have long held discussions but matters did not become clear until modern excavations produced a better idea of that first political unification of the Slav tribes on the territory of Czechoslovakia.

The search for the "ineffable fort" takes us to the meadows and woods along the river Morava, where close to Hodonín the hill-fort of Valy near Mikulčice spread over an area of about 200 hectares (about 490

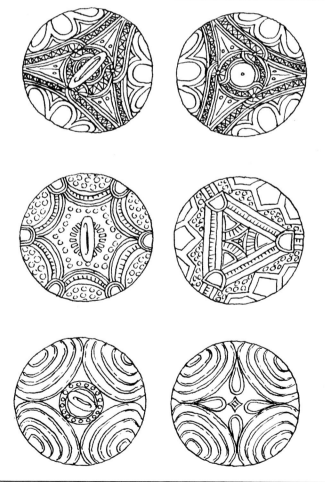

acres). Today it is a Czech National Cultural Monument visited by large numbers of tourists. The complex was formed by the castle itself surrounded by a group of fortified settlements all lying on an island formed by the river. It had undergone a long development, at the beginning of which stood a simple village with pottery of the Prague type, which in the seventh and eighth centuries was replaced by a group of settlements with a castle fortified by a palisade. It was the seat of the prince and his retinue; their presence is proved by numerous finds of ancient iron and bronze spurs with hooks. At that time the inhabited area encompassed 50 hectares (125 acres), which for its period was quite an exceptional concentration of dwellings. The population lived in log cabins with trodden earth floors, occasionally also in semi-subterranean dwellings. In the earlier period they used pottery with a smooth black surface and polished patterns; later pots were made on the wheel and decorated with wavy lines. Apart from spurs, dating is made easier by finds of cast bronze trimmings with plant and animal motifs as well as other bronze jewelry, which are typical of the Slavo-Avar culture that flourished in the seventh and eighth centuries in the Carpathian Basin. These artifacts were not imported to Mikulčice but were produced on the spot, as shown by finds of small crucibles in stone ovens. A whole workshop has even been found with indications that copper, iron and gold were once smelted and worked there.

At the turn of the eighth to ninth century, when Charlemagne destroyed the power of the Avars, the hill-fort underwent far-reaching changes. It was surrounded by a stone wall, supported by a structure of timbered compartments, strengthened with stones and clay. For the first time here appeared a type of earthworks that developed in the Czech lands throughout the entire early Middle Ages. The surrounding settlements and seats of chieftains were similarly fortified, and this gave rise to the enormous fortified area, which in the Slavonic world can only be compared to Staré Město in Moravia and others at Pliska and Preslav, the main towns of the first Bulgar Empire.

Until excavations were carried out at the Great Moravian centre at Mikulčice and Staré Město experts had been convinced that the first Great Moravian churches were made only of timber and that building began only in connection with the mission of Constantine (Cyril) and Methodius. The discovery of the first stone church at Staré Město was, therefore, taken to be an exception. But when such discoveries increased in number, it became necessary to make a new assessment as to the origin of stone architecture in the Czech lands. This was particularly necessary in view of the find of twelve churches at Mikulčice alone. They survived mostly only in negative (removed) foundations, but it became possible to reconstruct not only the ground plan but to a large extent also the original appearance of these buildings. They had a variety of forms: apart from longitudinal buildings mostly with a rectangular presbytery, there was also a square structure with a semicirclular apse, rotundas with one, two and even four apses or conches, and, furthermore, a basilica with nave and aisles, an elongated apse, a narthex and an atrium. Five stone tombs had been sunk into the mortar floor, but all had been robbed. The few remnants of gold, gilt and or silver jewelry and weapons help one imagine the original wealth of offerings. The hope of discovering the tomb of Methodius, who, according to an old Slavonic legend, was buried "in the apostolic church", did not materialize, but there are indications that the basilica was a bishop's church; in its vicinity a baptistery was discovered — a christening chapel with a font.

There were graves all around the church, often with rich offerings of ornaments and weapons, as proof of the high cultural level of the Great Moravian craftsmen, mainly goldsmiths. In its earlier phase, called the BLATNICA-MIKULČICE GROUP, which developed in the first half of the ninth century, it linked late Avar tradition with western Carolingian influences in a creative manner. In the later phase, the influence of Byzantine worksmanship became stronger as a result of the contacts that Rastislav established. But in their workshops the Old Moravians re-worked all these foreign stimuli into a style of their own, which combined influences from South-Eastern and Western Europe.

A lively discussion arose about the origin of the Mikulčice churches, and no conclusion has so far been arrived at. Views have been expressed about the types with rectangular presbyteries having a connection with the Irish and the Bavarian missions. It has also been claimed that their southern origin from the Adriatic region, the land of the patriarchate of Aquileia and the Dalmatian coast is reflected in the basilica and the rotundas. There was talk about Byzantine influences — the tetrakonchos, basilica, etc. It would seem that all these three areas left their mark upon the appearance of this architecture; this is in conformity with Rastislav's epistle to the Byzantine Emperor Michael III, in which he writes that missionaries from "Italy, Greece and Germany" keep coming to Moravia. The variety of building styles is a significant proof of this. These influences, however, were modified, so that the Moravian architecture is only an approximation of the foreign patterns. Nowhere are there any identical types of buildings.

Stone was used to build not only churches but even palaces. So far only one has been unearthed in the inner fort near the basilica — it is a long building divided into sections with a mortar floor, stone fireplace and wooden posts. It must have served as residence for the prince, for the other inhabitants lived in log cabins with trodden earth floors, laid out in irregular rows along narrow streets. The total number of inhabitants of the entire settlement at Mikulčice has been estimated at two thousand, of whom more than three hundred lived in the fort proper. This will have been the residence of Mojmír and of Rastislav, which, with its density of population, stone walls and the number of fortified dwellings linked into one unit with the prince's castle, fully corresponds to that "ineffable fort" of Rastislav's in the *Fulda Annals*. It continued to play a role until the end of the Great Moravian period, when a wave of destructive Magyar invaders fell upon it, and left behind nothing but ruins. On these, at the end of the tenth or more likely during the eleventh century, there grew up an unimportant village, which did not exist for long.

The second important centre of the Great Moravian Empire was Staré Město, which became known much earlier than Mikulčice. This was largerly because of the Church tradition linking neighbouring Velehrad with the beginnings of the work of the Slavonic missionaries Constantine (Cyril) and Methodius; and it roused the interest of archeologists, who, in the nineteenth century, found traces of an ancient cultural development. Sys-

The foundations of church buildings were first discovered at Mikulčice close to the gateways into the inner fort. They represent one of the many types of Great Moravian architecture from the early ninth century.

tematic excavations did not begin until 1948. It was found that the centre of settlement lay on two parallel tongues of land projecting into the confluence of the Salaška and the river Morava. The first to be settled was the northern one, known as Na valách, where, at the period of the Prague type, a village of farmers came into being; it lay on the sides of the spur above the swampy lands along the Morava. In the eighth century this village was turned into a hill-fort with moats and wooden walls, which remained the centre of the Staré Město settlement throughout the period of the Great Moravian Empire. It included a burial ground with a great wealth of finds and in the centre stood a church with an oblong nave and an elongated semicircular apse — the first find of a Great Moravian church ever made (1949). According to finds in the graves it must have come into existence before the middle of the ninth century, and in its layout was probably linked to

113

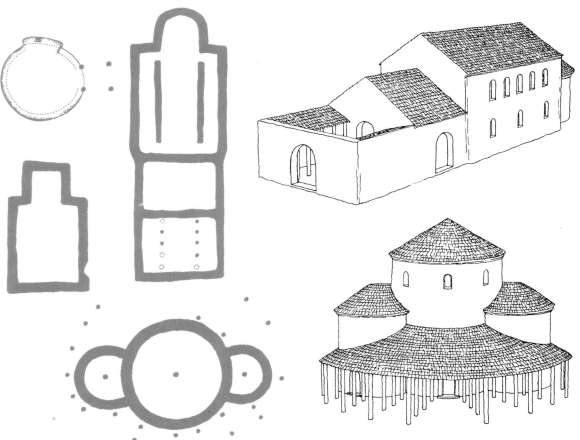

a mission that came from the south-eastern Danube region.

The second Staré Město spur, called Na špitálkách location, lies further to the south; it, too, underwent a long development, during which several smaller villages gradually merged into a hill-fort covering thirty-two hectares (eighty acres), fortified with a palisaded wall on the western approaches. Apart from a number of sites that served as dwellings and workshops, archeologists discovered a cemetery with a church, which had a long nave with pillars, a shorter apse and a narthex on the western side, added at a slightly later date. Graves with gold and silver jewelry, which surrounded the edifice, date from the second half of the ninth century.

Other churches were discovered in the close vicinity of Staré Město. In the first place, a church of elongated ground plan with four internal pillars and a long rectangular presbytery in the village of Modrá, about four kilometres (about two and a half miles) to the north-west of Staré Město. Its style aroused great interest, as it is reminiscent of churches from the time when the Irish missions were active in Europe. Such a style might have been introduced by missionaries from Bavaria, where the building traditions from the period of the Irish missions in southern Germany were kept alive. According to finds in the graves it must have already existed in the first third of the ninth century.

The most important ecclesiastical building that has so far been discovered in the area stands on a hill near the

The discovery of Great Moravian churches at Mikulčice and Staré Město provides proof of the merging and subsequent adaptation of influences from Western and South-Eastern Europe.

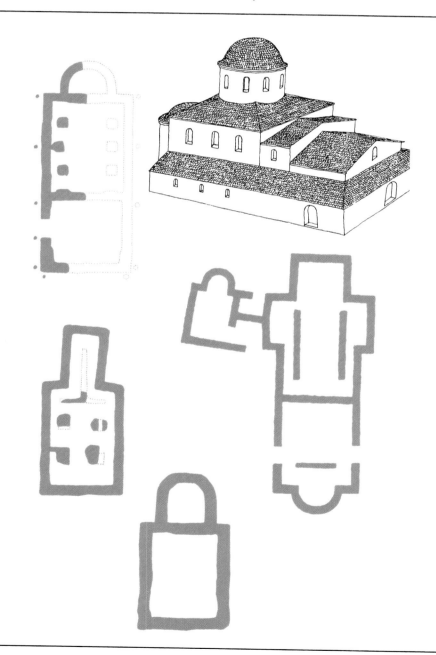

village of Sady, some four kilometres (about two and a half miles) south-east of Staré Město. The church originally had a ground plan in the shape of an isosceles cross with a rectangular presbytery, and later a western nave was added with a semicircular apse (— perhaps evidence of a catechist school). In the final phase a funeral chapel was added to the northern wall of the transept with an elongated horseshoe-shaped apse. At that same time, a circular baptistery was built in the vicinity of the church. This entire building development took place between the end of the eighth and the last third of the ninth century. The oldest graves near the church contained weapons and jewels of Western origin, which is in accordance with the early Carolingian character of the original building. It may well be that it was founded by a bishop or was a monastery. This would be supported by the remains, close by, of wooden buildings with paved streets, a well and a wooden fence and finds of iron and bone writing tools, which were used to engrave wax tablets, or the find of a pewter cross with a Greek inscription.

There was also a rotunda in the Staré Město region, now below St Michael's Church in the area of Na dědině. It was of a different type from the one in Mikulčice (with a semicircular apse), but must relate to the missions that came "from Italy or Greece" even before the Slavonic missionaries.

The fortified town of Staré Město was surrounded by several villages in which craftsmen, such as metal-workers, smiths, founders, tanners and others, worked. The whole complex of settlements covered up to 250 hectares (over 600 acres), had a broad agricultural hinterland and well-developed forms of production specializing in luxury articles: gold and silver jewelry or fine pottery of

Staré Město was an important centre of the Great Moravian Empire. It is likely to have been associated with the Byzantine mission of Constantine and Methodius. At the time of its greatest development (ninth century) the local settlement agglomeration covered an area of almost 250 hectares (about 620 acres).

traditional shapes. The first indication of social distinctions appeared in the offerings in graves, in differentiated types of dwellings, and remains of ecclesiastical buildings in stone. These suggest that this centre must have played a leading role in the political and cultural life of the Great Moravian Empire. It is, therefore, highly likely that the brothers from Thessalonica devoted special care to the area of Staré Město, and Methodius may have been in residence here at the time when he quarrelled with Svatopluk. This is upheld also by the above-mentioned tradition of Velehrad, which, though of a later date, may have had ancient roots.

The Moravian princes must have had many other residences and centres on which their power was based. A number of these have been investigated by archeologists, even though they are on a smaller scale than Mikulčice or Staré Město. One is Pohansko near Břeclav, a hill-fort at the confluence of the Dyje and the Morava, where a homestead was discovered surrounded by a palisade, with dwellings on stone foundations and a church of elongated ground plan with a semicircular apse; in its surroundings was a cemetery with weapons and jewels of the Staré Město type. Higher up the Dyje, near Nejdek, there is another hill-fort with the name of Pohansko, where ninth-century dwellings have been unearthed. And even further upstream, in the village of Hradiště near Znojmo, further mighty fortifications were excavated, whose beginnings date from the eighth century. The grouping of these and other similar hill-forts suggests that the political and cultural centre of the Great Moravian Empire lay along the central and lower regions of the Morava. From there its influence spread in all directions, including the territory of today's Slovakia and western Hungary, ancient Pannonia.

The complex foundations at Sady must be regarded as one of the important discoveries of church buildings at Staré Město. This may have been a bishop's church or part of a monastery (first half of the ninth century).

A church and cemetery formed part of
the fortified seat of a nobleman at
Pohansko near Břeclav (southern
Moravia, ninth century).

PRIBINA'S PRINCIPALITY
AT NITRA AND MOSAPURC

An interesting development occurred in this area after the end of the Avar domination in the first half of the ninth century. A principality came into being with its centre at Nitra, whose first known ruler was Pribina. He worshipped pagan gods, but permitted Frankish missions since he had friendly relations with the Frankish Empire. When the Archbishop of Salzburg, Adalram, accompanied Louis the German on his expedition against the Bulgars, whose empire under Khans Krum and Omortag stretched as far as the Hungarian Tisza region, he visited Nitra on the way, since it belonged to the missionary sphere of the Salzburg metropolis, and he consecrated the first church there. This must have happened in the year 828 and it proves that Christianity existed among the Slav population of the Nitra region. This Christian core might well have been formed by small colonies of Frankish merchants. Pribina himself was not converted by Adalram.

That must have been the reason why the Franks did not come to Pribina's aid when Mojmír, the Christian prince of Moravia, attacked him after 830. He managed to expel Pribina, completed the unification of the Slav tribes on the territory of Moravia and Slovakia and thus set up a strong state. Pribina found refuge with Ratbod, the administrator of the Ostmark, where on order of Louis the German he was baptised. With Ratbod's aid, in about 840, he was given part of Pannonia around Lake Balaton as fiefdom by Louis the German. Here he built castle Mosapurc (*urbs Paludarum*, perhaps derived from the original Blatengrad) and eagerly devoted himself to the spread of Christianity — until 860, when he was killed during a Moravian invasion. He was succeeded by his son Kocel.

Even as part of the Great Moravian Empire the Nitra principality retained a certain measure of independence. During the reign of Rastislav it was administered by his nephew and successor Svatopluk, under whom Nitra in 880 became the seat of a bishop. According to an Epistle by Pope John VIII, this office was given to Viching, Svatopluk's confidant and an obdurate enemy of Methodius. There are no further written reports on the subsequent fate of Nitra, and so we are once again forced to turn to archeology for further evidence.

Systematic research into Pribina's seat at Nitra was started only in 1957. The seat comprises not only the area of today's town but also its surroundings, for it was shown that here was not only one castle, but a whole set of hill-forts, a system of fortifications protecting the entire Nitra countryside. The actual centre has not so far been definitely ascertained. It is not certain whether it was the hill-fort on St Martin's Hill on the slopes of Mount Zobor, which rises above Nitra, or a hill-fort in the centre of the town, where there are today modern buildings.

The hill-fort on St Martin's Hill, fortified with stone walls and a moat with mighty double palisades, encloses an area of twenty hectares (about fifty acres) and came into being in the period before the Great Moravian Empire — as shown by a cemetery with tombs of warriors from the eighth century, discovered below the hill-fort. Within the fort lived peasants and craftsmen, whose dwellings and workshops bordered a broad paved street. Beneath the former Romanesque church of St Martin on the hill-fort an older church was found with an elongated nave and three apses, two of which extended from the sides so that the resulting ground plan was that of a cross. Finds of coins of Charles the Bald date this architecture into the ninth century. But it cannot be said with certainty whether it is identical with that church which Adalram consecrated or whether this is a different one, not mentioned in the records.

The second hill-fort, in the town of Nitra itself, stood on a rocky height above the river Nitra, which provided natural protection with its flood meadows. Otherwise the hill-fort was protected by double earthworks, palisades and a deep moat. Recent construction work destroyed most of the remains of the fort but a ninth-century cemetery was found with silver and gilded jewels and iron tools of the Great Moravian type. From the large number of graves it can be assumed that there must have been a church in the western part of the hill-fort.

A whole series of hill-forts have been discovered in the surroundings of Nitra, which must have served as refuges for the neighbouring population and simultaneously protected the approach routes to the centre proper. The importance of the Nitra region is confirmed

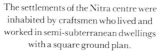

The settlements of the Nitra centre were inhabited by craftsmen who lived and worked in semi-subterranean dwellings with a square ground plan.

not only by this remarkable grouping of hill-forts but by the concentration of unfortified peasant and craftsmen villages, twelve of which were discovered in the surroundings of Nitra alone. Beyond the Nitra region the princely power was based on an entire network of hill-forts strategically located throughout the whole of south-western Slovakia. In the middle Váh region this includes e.g. Pobedim, where swamps and strong fortifications protected a market and crafts centre with the seat of a feudal lord and another less well fortified settlement. A special role was attributed to a group of hill-forts in the vicinity of the Bratislava Gate, with its important crossings of the Danube, mainly the hill-fort at Devín, and one on the site of where Bratislava Castle now stands. Ancient Devín, at the confluence of the Morava and the Danube, served primarily military aims and is probably identical with that Dowina mentioned in the *Fulda Annals* in 864 as the place where Svatopluk's army managed to sink Frankish ships. Bratislava Castle is referred to in the Salzburg *Annals* as Brezalauspurc, and in 907 a decisive battle was fought below it between the Bavarians and the Hungarians. Excavations have uncovered fortifications of timber and earth, dwellings with stone foundations and the remains of a basilica with nave and aisles from the last third of the ninth century. The basilica stood on the highest spot of the hill-fort and indicates that Bratislava Castle was then of greater importance and not merely a frontier outpost.

Prince Pribina, as we have seen, founded Castle Mosapurc near Lake Balaton during his exile from Nitra. From there he ruled over Pannonia in dependence on the Frankish Empire. After his death his son Kocel succeeded him. Kocel played an important role in the missionary work of Constantine and Methodius and in the spread of the Slavonic liturgy and Slavonic literature. Kocel was a fervent Christian. His state comprised some thirty churches which fell under the jurisdiction of the Archbishop of Salzburg. Kocel was enthusiastic about the Slavonic script and the Slavonic cult and therefore received the two brothers from Thessalonica in very friendly manner when they set out from Moravia on their way to Rome; he detained them in his castle and had them teach fifty disciples. His aim was to establish an independent church province in Pannonia. Hence, after the death of Constantine in Rome, he requested the return of Methodius. He was sent to him by Pope Adrian II in 869 as his Legate and Archbishop of Pannonia and Moravia with residence in the ancient ecclesiastical centre of Srem (ancient Sirmium) in northern Yugoslavia. This roused the ill-will of the bishops of Bavaria, who imprisoned Methodius in the years 870—873. Kocel himself fell in the battle against the Croats in 876. His estate was later taken over by the Moravian Prince Svatopluk, who thus enlarged the frontiers of his Empire as far as the river Drava.

The centre of all these events was Pribina's Mosapurc in the swampy regions along the river Zala. The long years of effort on the parts of historians and archeologists were crowned with success when they identified a hill-fort near the village of Zalavár, some nine kilometres (about six miles) south-west of Lake Balaton, as Mosapurc.

The location of Pribina and Kocel's residence was very well protected by the many forks of the swampy river Zala, in which were islands suitable for habitation. The largest was called Vársziget ("Castle Island"), and another island inhabited in the ninth century was Récéskút. Archeologists concentrated on both places. They investigated the village of Zalavár, where they discovered a settlement with a cemetery from the tenth to eleventh century, i.e. the period when the land was occupied by the Magyars.

Excavations on Vársziget were impeded by the fact that the island had been inhabited until the seventeenth century, and consequently part of the oldest strata of settlement had been disturbed. But it was possible to distinguish remains of timber-fortified earthworks together with a gate on the eastern side. The gate was protected inside by a bastion of the same construction as those found in contemporary Bohemian hill-forts, with the one difference that no stone was used at Mosapurc. The dwellings were made of timber. They were semi-subterranean or on the surface, and probably made of logs, of which only post holes or pits with charcoal and ash survive. On the fringe a cemetery with Great Moravian jewelry was found. Its centre must have been further to the west, where Pribina's Church of Our Lady once stood, as written records reveal. Since the most easterly graves were dug into the ruins of burnt dwellings a fire must have occurred in the ninth century, probably during one of the Moravian attacks.

The most important discovery on Récéskút island was the foundations of a basilica with nave and side aisles and a three-conch presbytery, a square baptistery, added to the south-western corner of the church. This stone structure, built in the eleventh century, covered an older wooden church, where two phases were distinguished — the older from the turn of the eighth to ninth century, probably related to Western missionaries, and the younger, with a timber and stone construction, which must be identified with Pribina's Church of St John the Baptist. A cemetery lay adjacent to this church of the same type as the one found at Vársziget.

Mosapurc-Zalavár retained its importance as centre of Pannonia until the end of the ninth century, when new invaders appeared on the steppes of the Hungarian Plain: the nomad Hungarians. Like all previous nomads they came from the Ukrainian steppes through passes in the Carpathians and set up a base for devastating raids in the Carpathian Basin itself, mainly its eastern part. From there they attacked the whole of Central Europe as far as southern Germany and northern Italy. The Great Moravian Empire, torn by vehement disputes among Svatopluk's successors, was broken up; all the mighty and rich centres mentioned above fell into decay. What is remarkable, however, is that the one-time residence of

The residence of the exiled Nitra Prince Pribina and his son Kocel stood, in the ninth century, in the marshlands along the Zala near Zalavár not far from Lake Balaton in Hungary. It was known as Mosapurc.

Pribina and Kocel in the swamps of the Zala remained basically untouched by the Magyar raids. Excavations have shown that the Slav population did not abandon the site, even when they grew much poorer under the changed circumstances. Anthropologically and culturally they survived until the eleventh century, although elsewhere an intermingling of Magyar and Slavonic elements occurred, whose archeological expression is the BIJELO BRDO CULTURE. The local church also continued to fulfil its function; Christianity became cruder and certain pagan customs re-emerged in burial rites. When the Hungarian state began to form after the raids were over at the end of the tenth century, by which time the nomads had settled and adopted Christianity from the Slavs, a fortified monastery was built on Vársziget at Mosapurc under King St Stephen. Remains of this were found during excavations. Furthermore, they unearthed a cemetery chapel, whose simple, elongated ground plan and semicircular apse follows the older Danube and Great Moravian tradition. Thus for two hundred years after the death of its founder Pribina's Mosapurc remained an important ecclesiastical and political centre, which contributed a Slav element to the cultural development of the Hungarian nation.

A basilica with nave and aisles stood in the eleventh century on Récéskút island, which formed part of Mosapurc. Below it the remains of a wooden church from the time of Pribina have been found.
→

Pribina and Kocel's residence at Mosapurc was fortified by a wooden wall, the remains of which were unearthed by Hungarian archeologists.

The spheres of interest of the Frankish and the Byzantine Empires overlapped on the Dalmatian coast, inhabited largely by Slavs, in the ninth century. The Byzantine cities on the coast made a considerable cultural impact upon the local Slavs even if Dalmatia and Croatia ultimately became part of the cultural sphere of the West.

THE CROATS AND SERBS, THEIR POLITICAL AND CULTURAL EMERGENCE

From the end of the eighth century on, the struggle for power between the Frankish and the Byzantine Empires took place on the territory of those Slav tribes which came to form the nations of present-day Yugoslavia. Until that time Byzantine influence had been predominant, interrupted only temporarily by the Avar invasion. But in the seventh century, under Emperor Heraclius (610—641), the Croats, with the help of the Serbs and the support of Byzantium, drove the Avars from the whole of north-western Yugoslavia and southern Austria, where the Slovenes then established themselves. Under Charlemagne (771—814) the Franks came to this area. The Croats living in Pannonia, led by Prince Vojnomir, helped them destroy the Avars, but then had to acknowledge Frankish sovereignty, as did Višeslav, prince of the Dalmatian Croats. The Franks then ruled over the whole of Istria and Dalmatia with the exception of the coastal towns and islands, which remained in Byzantine hands.

The Pannonian Croats rebelled against Frankish domination in 819. They were led by Ljudevit, who tried to rally other tribes to his side, including the Carinthian and Styrian Slovenes and the Dalmatian Croats, whose Prince Borna he defeated. The centre of this ephemeral state was Sisak near Zagreb. After several expeditions under Louis the Pious Frankish power was re-established, and Ljudevit, who had had to flee to the Serbs and Dalmatia in 823, was murdered. The Dalmatian Croats continued to have their local ruler, with his seat at Nin, where an independent Croatian bishopric came into being. For Christianity had already spread throughout this region in the seventh century under the influence of the coastal towns. The Byzantine towns along the Adriatic proved greatly attractive to the Dalmatian Croats and were of far greater significance than the nominal Frankish domination. The Dalmatian princes maintained friendly relations with the Byzantines and for that reason transferred their seat to Klis in the vicinity of Split, which was already the seat of an archbishop and the centre of Byzantine power on the Dalmatian coast.

No change occurred until 864 when Domagoj became ruler in Dalmatia and drove out Zdeslav, who was friendly with the Byzantines. Domagoj then rebelled against Carloman, the successor of Louis the German, whose army was defeated by the Croats in 876, at the very battle in which the Pannonian Kocel met his death while helping the Franks. Byzantium made use of the weakness of their Frankish opponents in 878 to realize its aims in Croatian Dalmatia, using the services of the exiled Zdeslav. But in the following year Zdeslav was defeated by Branimir (879—892), who, with Bishop Theodosius of Nin, led the anti-Byzantine opposition. The fate of Croatia was decided at this time — its adherence to the sphere of Western culture, in which it remained throughout its further history, although the Slavonic liturgy penetrated here from Pannonia and has survived as a rarity to this day. A unified state linking Dalmatian and Pannonian Croatia was established by the Croats only in the first third of the tenth century — thanks to the decline of the eastern Frankish Empire and the ability of their ruler Tomislav (910—928), who became the first king of Croatia.

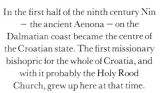

The small statue of a Croatian warrior comes from Biskupija (eleventh century).

In the first half of the ninth century Nin — the ancient Aenona — on the Dalmatian coast became the centre of the Croatian state. The first missionary bishopric for the whole of Croatia, and with it probably the Holy Rood Church, grew up here at that time.

The influence of the Adriatic coastal region spread as far as Central Europe and left a mark on the development of Great Moravian architecture. The precursor of the rotundas can perhaps be traced to St Donatus's Church at Zadar from the early ninth century.
→

In the region of the Serbian tribes, then known by the name of Raška (Rascia), there was a different development. From the end of the eighth century on the dynasty of *župans* (regional administrative officers) ruled, which had been founded by Višeslav. It included names like Vlastimir, Mutimir, Strojimir, Gojnik and others. Throughout the ninth century these tribes, which later developed into the Serbian nation, acknowledged the sovereignty of Byzantium. The only exceptions were the militant Narentans who settled in the delta of the river Neretva and ruled over the adjacent islands (Brač, Hvar, Korčula, Vis, Mljet) and from there threatened the important sea-link between Venice and Byzantium. The Venetians therefore curried their favour, and in 830 they managed to persuade some of the Narentans to adopt Christianity. Mutual conflicts, however, did not stop. Not until 870 were the Narentans subdued by the Byzantine army which was fighting on the coast of Dalmatian Croatia at the time. At the end of the ninth century dynastic disputes arose in the Serbian region, in which both Byzantium and the rising Bulgarian Empire became involved, and it ended with the complete occupation of Serbia by the Bulgarian Tsar Symeon (893—927). Only the tiny princedom of Hum (Zachlumje), on the territory of what is today Hercegovina, remained to some extent autonomous. The other Serbian tribes regained their independence with the aid of the Byzantines and Croats under Česlav (931—960). But they remained under Byzantine

A hoard of twenty-three gold vessels
was found at Nagyszentmiklós (modern
Sannicolăulmare in Romania). They
were covered with antique and oriental
ornamental designs and Greek and Old
Turkish inscriptions. They date from
the period when this territory was part
of the first Bulgarian Empire (first half
of ninth century).

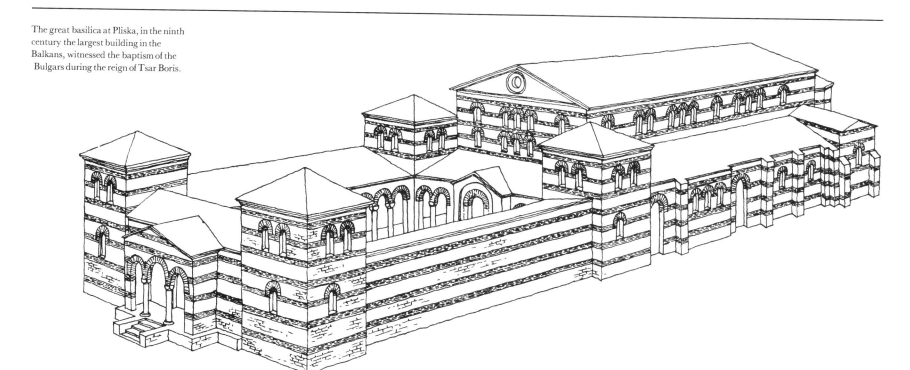

The great basilica at Pliska, in the ninth century the largest building in the Balkans, witnessed the baptism of the Bulgars during the reign of Tsar Boris.

sovereignty, in the cultural sphere of the East, and remained distinct from the Croats.

Certain features of this development can also be traced archeologically. In the ninth century local cultural groups formed, in which one might see proof of how the Croatian and Slovenian elements became

In the early ninth century Pliska became the first centre of the Bulgarian Empire. Originally it had been a military camp and was changed into a town of stone houses under Khans Krum and Omortag. In the very centre stood the Throne Palace – a monumental basilica reminiscent of the Magnaura Palace in Constantinople.

distinct. Both groups grew out of these local developments, in which features of Slavo-Avar, Carolingian and Byzantine origin intermingled, including the traditions of the local Romanized population. The Old Croatian culture developed mainly in Dalmatia, where it achieved a high level e.g. in goldsmith work, and in the

fine arts and architecture, whose influences extended as far as the Great Moravian region. In seeking the pattern for the Great Moravian rotundas reference is often made to the Church of St Donatus at Zadar.

The Serbian region is not sufficiently known in this respect. But Slovenian culture from the ninth and tenth centuries is quite striking; it is called the KÖTTLACH CULTURE, after Austrian finds at Köttlach, or CARINTHIAN. Typical features are jewels adorned with geometrical, plant and animal motifs in multicoloured enamel. The centre of this culture was the region of the eastern Alps of Austria and Slovenia, from which it spread south to Istria and Friuli, and northwards to southern Moravia, where it is documented in the burial ground at Dolní Věstonice. Its influences can also be traced along the Danube as far as north-eastern Bavaria, settled by Slav tribes at that time.

In the tenth century there arose by the side of these two cultures, in the northern parts of Yugoslavia, an independent style called the Bijelo Brdo culture (to

which we have already referred) after the most important Croatian site. Here elements of Slavo-Avar, Old Croatian, and Köttlach origin merged with others from the Great Moravian Empire, and even from the Eastern Slavonic area into a new culture. Its development was aided by a historically new factor in the Carpathian Basin, the Magyars, who after heavy defeats had to come to terms with their Slav neighbours after the second half of the tenth century. Hence the whole of Hungary belongs to the sphere of the Bijelo Brdo culture, as do Slovakia and part of Romanian Transylvania, and its influence even extended to the neighbouring Slav regions. Typical features include necklaces and bracelets of twisted bronze wire, bi-partite metal pendants, bracelets with serpent heads, S-shaped ear-rings, and rings and ear-rings of every conceivable type. The traditional style of these Bijelo Brdo jewels survived on the territory of Yugoslavia into the late Middle Ages, and some features still exist in national folk art.

Towards the end of the ninth century Preslav took over the role of Pliska. It was a town of richly adorned palaces and churches, and Slavonic literature flourished here in the tenth century. The pride of Preslav architecture was Tsar Symeon's "golden church", a rotunda with twelve semicircular apses.

130

Out of a remarkable symbiosis of two entirely different ethnical groups on the territory of ancient Moesia and Thracia — the Turco-Tatar Bulgars and the Slavs — there arose at the end of the seventh century, under Asparuch, a state which throughout the eighth century was to cause the rulers of Byzantium great troubles. But it became a serious danger only in the early ninth century when the feared Krum (803—814) became Bulgarian Khan. He strengthened the organization of his state and laid the foundations of the Bulgarian Empire proper, which successfully competed with the two great powers of the time — the Franks and the Byzantines. In 811 he defeated Nicephorus, and later used the skull of the defeated Byzantine Emperor as a drinking cup when he feasted with his warriors. He subdued both Thracia and Macedonia, and the frontiers of his state extended to present-day Serbia and Hungary as far as the river Tisza. Krum's successor Omortag (814—831), like the later Malamir (831—852), put a stop to Frankish penetration of the Balkans and occupied part of Pannonian Croatia, including ancient Sirmium.

Under Boris (852—889) there was a strong cultural approach to the Byzantines. To curb the excessive influence of Byzantium in church affairs, Boris established contacts with Rome. His Empire became a source of conflict between the Eastern and the Western Churches until Boris, with the aid of the disciples of Methodius, found a compromise solution in the form of the Slavonic Church, which thereby became a permanent basis of the cultural development not only of the Bulgarians but of the Serbs, Romanians and Russians.

The pottery icon of St Theodore was made in the famous workshops of the Preslav monastery of Patleyna in the tenth century.

The owner of this beautiful silver goblet adorned with ancient plant motifs was the Preslav district administrator Sivin, as the Greek inscription reveals.

Boris's work was carried through to great effect by Symeon (892—927), who used his Greek education and knowledge of Byzantine diplomacy to strengthen his empire and turn it into a greater power, which began to overshadow even Byzantium itself. The Byzantine rulers vainly tried to limit his power, but even with the aid of the Magyars, Pechenegs, Serbs or Croats, their army suffered a number of humiliating defeats and Symeon very nearly achieved his aim of becoming Byzantine emperor himself. He at least managed to have himself crowned as Basileus and co-Emperor with Constantine Porphyrogenitus — then still a minor. The ceremony took place at Constantinople in 913. His plans for the future were foiled by Constantine's mother Zoë, who became regent, and by his death, which occurred before he could set out to conquer Constantinople. Nevertheless, in 926, he succeeded in bringing about an important ecclesiastical and political development — the foundation of an independent Bulgarian patriarchy. Under his rule Bulgarian culture and Slavonic literature flourished, but none of Symeon's successors reached the same heights. The power of the Bulgarian state gradually weakened until, by 1018, the once feared Empire was no more than a Byzantine province.

The development of the first Bulgarian Empire is closely connected with two important centres, which for many decades have been the centre of intensive archeological work — Pliska and Preslav.

According to an eleventh-century apocryphal manuscript *The Vision of the Prophet Isaiah*, Pliska was founded by Asparuch himself. But it would seem that originally only a large fortified military camp stood here, which was later turned into a proper town with the Slavonic name of Pliska. It must already have been in existence under Khan Krum (803—814). In 811 Pliska was destroyed by the Byzantine Emperor Nicephorus, but it soon rose again in new beauty, especially under Krum's successor Omortag (816—831). Throughout the ninth century Pliska had no rival, and when, under Tsar Symeon in 893, its role was taken over by Preslav, it still remained an important town until the end of the fourteenth century, when Bulgaria was occupied by the

→
St Naum's Monastery was founded south of Ohrid at the end of the ninth century, and the relics of this important disciple of Methodius are kept here.

After being expelled from Moravia Methodius's disciples Clement and Naum worked in Macedonian Ohrid when it was part of the Bulgarian Empire. The local school of literature used Glagolitic script, while in Preslav Cyrillic was adopted, which became the basis for the Russian alphabet. The picture shows the thirteenth-century St Clement's Church.

Turks. The town was laid waste and became a wilderness, and its site was occupied only by a small village called Aboba. In 1886 the Czech scholar Konstantin Jireček recognized in the ruins around the village the remains of the first capital city of Bulgaria, and another Czech, Karel Škorpil, undertook the first excavations in the years 1899—1900. Surprising discoveries came to light of monumental architecture, showing an advanced building technology and such ostentation as was known at that time only in Byzantine towns. Excavations continued in the subsequent decades and assumed a large scale after 1944; they continue to this day.

The very size of Pliska, which lies close to the town of Shumen in north-eastern Bulgaria, is quite exceptional. With the outer wards forming an extended trapezoid ground plan, the longer sides 7 kilometres (4.4 miles) in length and the shorter 3.9 and 2.7 kilometres (2.4 and 1.7 miles), the town covered a total area of 23 square kilometres (9 square miles). This area was protected by simpler outer ramparts in the form of earthworks with a moat, such as nomad tribes used to fortify their military camps. Roughly in the centre lay the inner town with a stone wall, likewise trapezoid in ground plan, and in its centre stood the citadel surrounded by a strong brick wall. The walls were fortified with numerous towers — round at the corners, pentagonal in the centre. Furthermore the gates that led into the town from all four directions were each protected with four square towers. The greatest importance was attributed to the eastern gate, through which a wide street led to the palace. The walls were built of ashlar, laid alternately lengthwise and across, a technique known as *opus implectum*. This involved the stone blocks being used to face the outer and inner sides, while the interior of the walls was filled in with rubble and stones. On the other hand, the towers and gates were built entirely of ashlars, this style being called *opus quadratum*. This building technique was already familiar in Bulgaria in the Hellenistic period, so it must be assumed that its tradition was maintained by the Greek — and later Roman — influenced Thracian population.

Craftsmen and peasants lived in the outer town in simple huts or semi-subterranean dwellings, as known from the open villages in the Slav areas. There existed potters' workshops, metal founding, glass-making, goldsmithry, bone-carving, metal casting, all dependent on the ruling classes. With their poverty and low standard of living these people did not greatly differ from the inhabitants of the countryside.

But the inner town was a different world. Here stood the ostentatious homes of the nobility, the tsar and his boyars. First of all there was the big Throne Palace, a monumental building of two floors 52 metres (57 yards) long and 26.5 metres (29 yards) wide. It was built, according to a pattern from antiquity (it resembled the Magnaura Palace in Constantinople), as a basilica with a northern apse, and the tsar's throne stood on the upper floor. The Audience Room, inlaid with marble tablets, was reached by a stone stairway that led off the southern entrance hall. The walls were made of mighty limestone blocks, among which Roman tombstones can be found. The ceilings would have been vaulted in brick. The palace probably dates from the time of Omortag, since beneath its foundations the archeologists found an older, even larger building 74 × 59.5 metres (80 × 65 yards) in size, divided into sixty-four square sectors and with four towers. It had been destroyed by fire, and so we have every reason to suppose that it was Krum's old palace, which burnt down during Nicephorus's invasion in 811.

While the Throne Palace played a representative role, the dwellings of the rulers of Pliska lay inside the citadel. There stood a smaller palace made up of two almost identical buildings, baths heated by a hypocaust as in the Roman period, another building, barracks for the castle guard, and a water reservoir. A peculiarity were secret passages, one of which linked the small palace with Krum's palace while the other led from the small palace into the outer town. In the pagan period a temple stood near the small palace, of which only the foundations in the form of two concentric rectangles survive. Another shrine was built outside the citadel, west of the Throne Palace; after the adoption of Christianity a basilica with nave and aisles took its place, and was known as the palace church.

In the outer town a total of thirty churches have so far been excavated, associated with the smaller boroughs, feudal mansions and monasteries. They are of two types: either basilicas characteristic of Pliska, or single-naved buildings in the shape of a cross. Most of them date from the eleventh to the fourteenth century. The oldest is known as the Great Basilica; it is 99 metres (108 yards) in length and 30 metres (33 yards) in width and is the largest building of its kind in the whole of the Balkans. It is associated with the baptism of the Bulgars, for it was erected under Tsar Boris I at a time when he was intending, in opposition to Constantinople, to adopt the Latin form of Christianity. Hence this monumental basilican shape, for which a predecessor must be sought in Rome (e.g. the Basilica of S. Giovanni in Laterano) rather than in Constantinople. The church was part of a monastery, which is probably the one to which Tsar Boris retired towards the end of reign.

Apart from the foundations of buildings archeologists found a rich selection of smaller objects in Pliska, mainly of glazed pottery; and apart from traditional Slavonic and Proto-Bulgar artifacts, there were also finds of weapons, iron tools, jewelry, statuary, engravings, and dozens of Greek inscriptions, mostly from the time of Khans Omortag and Malamir. All bear witness to the high level of culture of the inhabitants of Pliska.

A typical feature of the early Bulgarian towns is the scattered layout of buildings over a wide area, differing from contemporary Byzantine or Roman towns with houses close to one another along little streets. This is true not only of Pliska but of its successor in the role of capital city — Preslav.

Preslav assumed this role under Tsar Symeon soon after 893, who — legends tell us — built this town in twenty-eight years. In reality it must have been a matter of reconstruction, since excavations have shown the existence of a fortified palace (aoul) on this site a whole century earlier. This leaves aside the traces of settlement in antiquity, which included, among others, an early Christian basilica from the fifth century on Deli Dushka Height. The reason for the transfer of the capital city must have been Symeon's consistent Christian orientation, which was opposed by some of the boyars in Pliska. This came to a head after Boris entered a monastery and handed over the throne to his older son Vladimir, who stood at the head of the pagan reaction. His behaviour forced Boris to reassume the rule, remove Vladimir and place his younger son Symeon on the throne, who took his father's intentions upon himself and brought his work to a culmination. For, as we saw above, Boris, after hesitating between Rome and Constantinople, took advantage of the fateful opportunity that occurred when Methodius's disciples were expelled from Moravia by Prince

Svatopluk. In this manner he saw the fulfilment on Bulgarian soil of the wishes of Prince Rastislav who had anticipated support for the political independence of the Great Moravian state from the Slavonic inclinations of Cyril and Methodius's mission. But Svatopluk foiled the attainment of this goal. Methodius's disciples Clement, Naum, and Angelarius fled and with the others found a possibility to develop their missionary and literary work fully under Boris, thereby laying the foundations of the Eastern Orthodox Church. Clement was active in Macedonian Ohrid, then part of the Bulgarian state. The second most important centre of Slavonic literature came into existence in Preslav, where, under Symeon, the Slavonic language became the tongue of state and Church. Constantine created the Cyrillic script, a simpler type of writing than the Glagolitic alphabet of Constantine-Cyril, which the Ohrid School continued to use. Cyrillic became the basis of the Russian alphabet and the script of all Orthodox Slavs in the Balkans and in Eastern Europe.

In the tenth century Preslav became the centre of the Golden Age of Bulgarian literature. Apart from Constantine, later Bishop of Preslav, John the Exarch was working here, one of the most profile writers of his time, who, apart from his own works, devoted himself to numerous translations from the Greek. A monk named Khrabr became famous for his *Concerning Slavonic Letters* and there were many others. The works of John the Exarch have recorded for us the enthusiastic words of admiration which the magnificence of Preslav roused in every visitor. According to his report, even outside the town gates there stood large buildings decorated with stone, wood and paint. When a pilgrim entered the inner city and saw the magnificent palaces and churches, and interiors richly adorned with marble, copper, silver and gold "he went out of his mind in amazement".

Today only insignificant ruins have survived of all this glory, which generations of archeologists have been digging out of the ground. Thanks to their efforts it has been possible to reconstruct the fortifications, which in their outer line of an irregular pentagon encompasses an area of 3.5 square kilometres (1.3 square miles) while the inner walls protected the palace complex which covers 0.25 square kilometres (15 acres). Preslav was smaller than Pliska, with which it has a number of features in common, but differed in other respects. It was not built on a plain like Pliska, but, in the manner of Byzantine cities, on terraces above the river Ticha on the slopes of the Zăbuy Mountain. Hills protected it on three sides; only to the north-east it opened on a broad valley, surrounded by mountains in the distance, with the rocky massif of Madara the most outstanding point.

The fortifications were built using the same techniques — *opus implectum* and *opus quadratum* — as at Pliska. Here, too, in the inner town stood the two-storey building of the palace (35 × 22.5 metres or 38 × 25 yards in size), with walls of ashlar, which formed the inner and external sides of the walls and were filled in with rubble and mortar. Water pipes were let into the walls. The one standing column with an ornamental capital gives an idea of the magnificence that once stood there. Slightly higher to the west on a terrace rose the "Small Palace", a basilican type of building with an apse on the southern side; it had been altered several times, and its earliest form perhaps dated from the period of Omortag. Among other buildings in the inner town there was a basilica to the south of the palace and an enormous building, 107 metres (350 feet) long, along the southern fortifications. This was divided into eighteen equal sections, each with a separate entrance and may have served as a centre of trade.

In the outer town, especially in the northern section, were the workshops of craftsmen who worked precious metals, glass, iron and clay, all to a very high level. Preslav also had numerous churches and monasteries, scattered about the town and beyond the walls along the banks of the river Ticha. A true jewel of Preslav architecture was Symeon's "Golden Church", a rotunda with twelve semicircular niches and twelve marble columns (symbols of the twelve Apostles) which supported the cupola. On the western side there was a tripartite narthex with two towers, to which later an atrium was attached, and a pillared court with a well. The entire layout followed a late Roman style. Of the other churches in the outer town some were basilicas, some domed. The basilica with nave and aisles in the north-eastern part of the town (Cheresheto) was probably built entirely of wood.

Among the Preslav monasteries, Patleyna, lying 2 kilometres (about 1.2 miles) south of the town, deserves special mention. It became famous for its workshops which produced painted pottery, used to decorate the walls of the local church of St Panteleimon (of which the name Patleyna is a corruption). An icon of St Theodore, a rare example of the artistic style of the Preslav School, has survived in relatively good condition. In the monasteries there survived a number of inscribed monuments, documenting the original form of both spoken and written Slavonic. Preslav also has Greek inscriptions, which were put on luxury objects, such as on the bottom of a silver cup belonging to Governor Sivin in the ninth to tenth century, which is a magnificent example of Old Bulgarian metalwork influenced by Byzantium.

Preslav continued to exist for centuries. At the time of the Byzantine domination in the eleventh and twelfth centuries a military garrison was stationed here; after liberation in the thirteenth century the town became the residence of Peter, brother of Tsar Asen. But it held a secondary position, since the centre of the Empire had been moved further west — to Veliko Tărnovo.

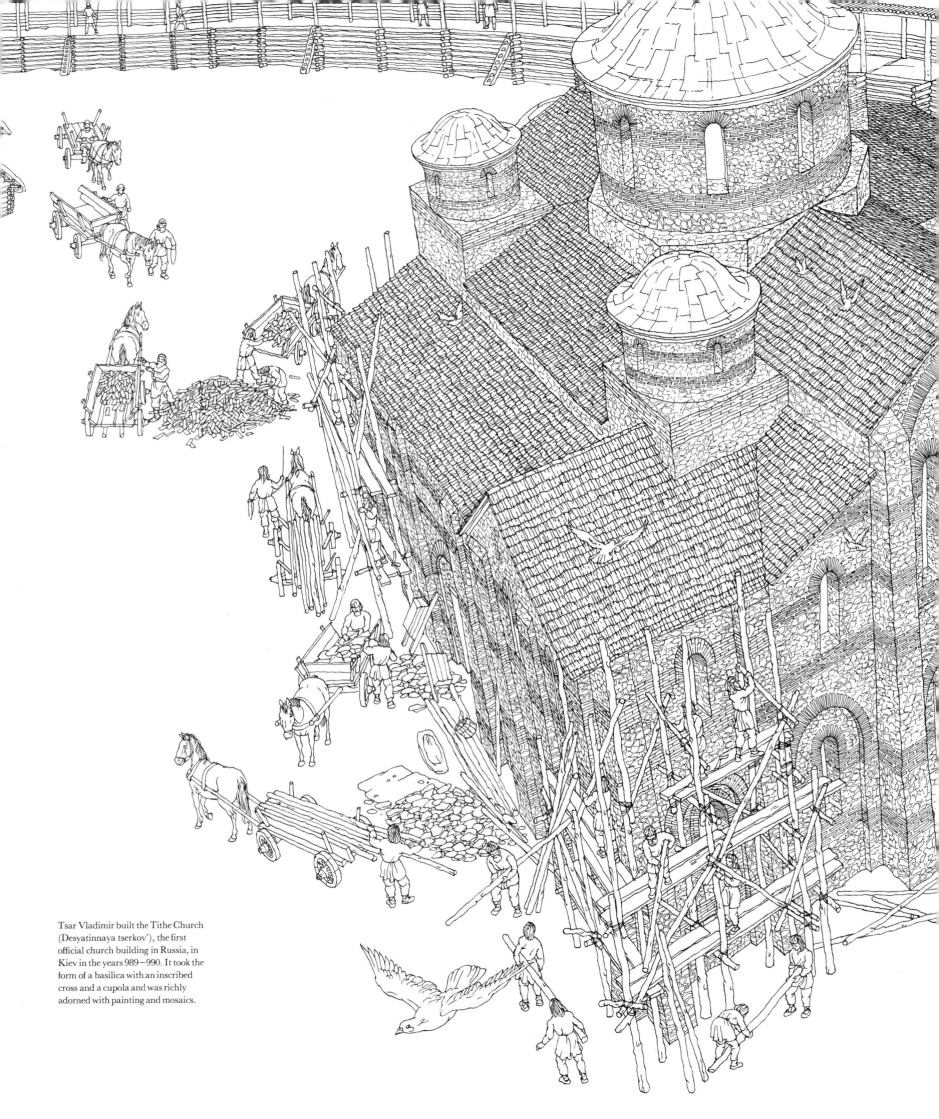

Tsar Vladimir built the Tithe Church (Desyatinnaya tserkov'), the first official church building in Russia, in Kiev in the years 989–990. It took the form of a basilica with an inscribed cross and a cupola and was richly adorned with painting and mosaics.

THE EARLY HISTORY OF KIEVAN RUSSIA

The broad stretches of the Russian lands are drained by innumerable rivers that merge into several mighty watercourses which ultimately flow into three seas: the Caspian, the Black Sea and the Sea of Azov. Most of the watercourses fall into these and, since time immemorial, they were the links between the tribes in the far North and the major cultures of the south. The Slavonic people loved these life-giving rivers and to this day show their respect in songs and herbs bearing the gentle names of "Mother Volga", "Father Dnieper", whose fertile banks have always been a source of food. And over long centuries the Slavs set out along them from their original home between the Dnieper and Dniester to the sparsely inhabited regions of Eastern Europe, while merchants

←

The present appearance of the Kiev St Sophia's Cathedral is only remotely reminiscent of the magnificent cathedral built by Yaroslav the Wise in the first half of the eleventh century.

The original appearance of the Kiev St Sophia's is shown only on a model. It resembled the Cathedral of Hagia Sophia in Constantinople and became the pattern for all further Russian cathedrals.

came travelling on their waters from distant lands. One of the most important of the rivers was, undoubtedly, the Dnieper, running through the very centre of the Slavs' original homeland. To the ancient Greeks, who set up their trading stations and colonies along the Black Sea coast, the river was known as the Borysthenes. In the Byzantine period the Dnieper was a major trade route. Particularly in the ninth century, when the enterprising Scandinavian Varangians began their long-distance trade, most of the "routes from the Varangians to the Greeks" led down the Dnieper. Trade links spread along all its tributaries to the west and east. Soon suitable places on the edge of the steppe and the forest lands began to develop at points where the trade routes from Ukraine and Byelorussia crossed those to the Black Sea coast. In this manner the first state of the Eastern

Slavs arose and Kiev became its political and cultural centre. We call this state, which envolved in the ninth century, Kievan Russia.

The development of the state was determined by internal economic and social conditions and by external causes in the form of constant pressure from the nomads in the steppes, especially the Avars, Bulgars, Khazars, later the Magyars and Pechenegs, and others. For the Slav tribes, scattered into minor tribal princedoms, there arose the need for a more permanent unification, which would enable them to counter these internal and external pressures. Such was the situation when, in the ninth century, groups of Scandinavians arrived, armed military and merchant companies who followed the Volga and Dnieper in their search for a way to the rich cultures of the Near East. The customary routes between Western Europe and those areas across the

Mediterranean Sea had been cut by Arab pirates. A mighty company led by Askold and Dir thus arrived in the Kiev region some time after the middle of the ninth century and formed an alliance with the local tribe of the Polyane, and they then became central to developing the organization of the state. What role the Norsemen played in this process has long been debated by historians and archeologists. What is most likely is that the Scandinavians simply took an active part in a process which was already in progress among the Slav communities and helped bring it to fruition. In no case was it a question of forceful domination, but a voluntary alliance, as between the Bulgars and the Balkan Slavs. Conjecture as to the origin of the name Russia, which soon came to be applied to the entire group of people and the whole country, has not yet been settled. It may have come from the Finnish *Ruotsi* for which a Swedish

In the eleventh century a monastery — the Pechora — was built above the hermits' caves on the rocky banks of the Dniester south of Kiev. It came to play an important role in the cultural and political life of Kievan Russia.

The workshops of Kievan craftsmen produced luxurious works of art, e. g. these silver bracelets with hammered patterns.

forerunner is being sought, or perhaps it was a local tradition in relation to the river Ros', a tributary of the middle Dnieper, which seems to be suggested by certain Oriental sources. The Slavs themselves called the Scandinavians, most of whom came from Sweden, "Varyagi" (in Byzantine sources Varangoi), which is derived from *varing* or *vaering* and corresponds to the Slavonic term *druzhina*, "company", that is a group of armed men bound by mutual pledges and linked in a common undertaking, military or commercial.

The alliance of the Varangians with the Slavs in the Dnieper region, the important north-south route to the Black Sea, soon became an unexpected threat to Byzantium. In the year 860 the Russians unexpectedly appeared in ships outside the gates of Constantinople and during the absence of Michael III, who was fighting the Arabs, very nearly took possession of the city. The Byzantines saw themselves forced to take account of this new political and military rival and concluded a treaty of friendship with the Khazars (here the Thessalonican brothers Constantine and Methodius played an important role) to keep them in check. Nonetheless, after this event, Kievan Russia became exposed to the strong influence of Byzantine culture; missionaries were sent, and in 864 a bishopric was established at Kiev. This development was forcefully interrupted by Prince Oleg of Novgorod, who some time around 880 conquered Kiev and suppressed the beginnings of Christianity.

The link between Novgorod and Kiev (Upper and Lower Russia) led to the origin of the Old Russian state proper, which by stages unified all Eastern Slav tribes. Its foundation is associated with the name of Oleg, who subdued the Drevlyane, Severyane and Radimichi, and eliminated the influence of the Khazars. He made closer contacts with the Byzantines, and in 911 (after a second unsuccessful attempt to conquer Constantinople in 907) concluded a trade agreement. Oleg's successor Igor vainly tried to break down the fortifications of Constantinople in 944. He had no choice but to continue to live in peace with his southern neighbour, whose influence strengthened particularly after Igor's death in 945, when the regency for the minor Svyatoslav was taken over by his mother, the energetic and prudent Princess Olga. Christianity began anew to penetrate to Russia; in Kiev the Cathedral of St Elias was built and Olga herself was baptised in Constantinople in 957. But when her son Svyatoslav ascended the throne (964—972) another anti-Christian reaction set in. Svyatoslav was an able warrior, who substantially enlarged his country particularly in an easterly direction. He subdued the Vyatichi, the last Slav tribe that had remained beyond the reach of the Kiev princes. He destroyed the empire of the Khazars, defeated the Bulgars in the Volga region and moved the frontier of his state as far as the Volga, the Caucasus and the shores of the Caspian Sea. His dream of founding a large Slav Empire, encompassing the Slavs in the Balkans, failed, however, despite an expedition which he led against the Bulgars in the Danube region. He was prevented by both Byzantium, which realized the dangerous consequences of his intentions, and the invasion of the Pechenegs, during which he met his death.

His son and successor Vladimir (980—1015) gave Kievan Russia its final form. Once again, the rebellious Radimichi and Vyatichi were subdued and Vladimir extended the frontier of his country towards the west as far as Przemyśl and Grody Czerwieńskie in south-eastern Poland. During his reign Christianity was finally adopted in the Byzantine form, the ostentation of which impressed the mentality of the Scandinavian and Slavonic Russians. But under the influence of Bulgarian Ohrid the Slavonic liturgy was adopted and Slavonic became the language of worship. This helped the rapid spread of Christianity, the closer unification of the Eastern Slav tribes and the adoption of Slavonic ways by the Varangians. The results were similar to those in Bulgaria. Vladimir's work was brought to fruition by his son Yaroslav, who came to power after long years of struggle (1015—36) between Vladimir's sons. During his rule (1037—54) Kievan Russia flourished politically and culturally; the organization of state became firmly established and its borders were extended to the north and north-east. Literature, architecture, arts, and crafts developed and by establishing a metropolitan centre in Kiev the Russian Church became independent. These achievements were followed by a gradual decline. The extensive empire could not be kept together in permanent unity. After the second half of the eleventh century, independent princedoms gradually arose, most of which acknowledged the sovereignty of Kiev only nominally — except for several strong personalities, such as Vladimir II Monomakh (1113—25). This development was hastened by the invasion of the Polovtsi into the Ukrainian steppes, which caused shifts in population and the centre of the state was moved to the more northerly parts of Eastern Europe, which meant Kiev's decline. Its fate was sealed by the invasion of the Mongols in the first half of the thirteenth century.

Archeological excavations have greatly contributed to a better understanding of Kievan Russia and its centres, starting with Kiev itself. It is possible to observe archeologically how different cultural groups on the middle Dnieper, representing the local tribes, merged to produce the unified culture of the emerging state, and how the prerequisites for the rise of Kiev were formed long before the tribes actually unifed. In this regard legends proved to be valuable; such as the legend of the oldest princes of the Polyane, recorded in the eighth century in the Armenian chronicle *History of Taraun*, attributed in part to Zenob of Glak (a legend more famously recounted in the Russian *Primary Chronicle* mentioned below). This tells of three brothers named Kiy, Shchek and Khoriv. The first is said to have given the name of Kiev. This legend is reflected in the

archeologically proven existence of three great hill-forts on the territory of Kiev in the eighth to tenth centuries: on Andreyev or Kiev Hill (which later acquired decisive importance), on Kiselevka Hill and finally to the north-west of Andreyev Hill. These hill-forts bear proof of the local social and political

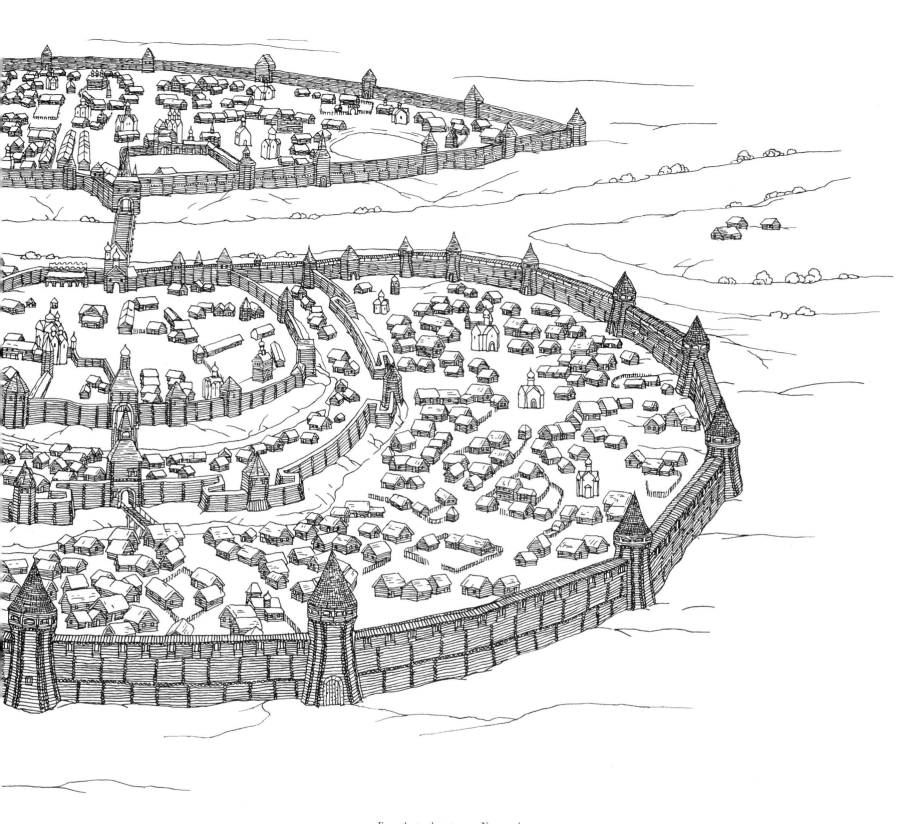

development, which was given a major boost by the arrival of the Scandinavians Askold and Dir, whose successors founded the first Russian dynasty.

Until the ascent to the throne of Vladimir the Great, Kiev Castle on Andreyev Hill was relatively small in size (2 hectares or 5 acres). Vladimir built a mighty and

From the tenth century on Novgorod became the true metropolis of the Russian North. In the Scandinavian sagas it was called Holmgardr, and it served as a centre of long-distance trade and political and cultural life, and had an unusual city administration. The river Volkhov divided the city into two halves: the western called the Sophia Side and the eastern known as the Market Side.

spacious castle with fortifications at the end of the tenth century, where his retinue of noblemen and boyars lived and, after the adoption of Christianity, the higher clergy lived too. Some time in the year 989 or 990 the Tithe Church (Desyatinnaya tserkov') was built in his residence, the first official church building in Russia, which,

144

at that time, served only the family of the prince. It was a basilica with an inscribed cross and cupola, erected by Greeks, and richly adorned with paintings and mosaics. The wealth of Kiev was ensured by merchants and craftsmen, who settled in the fast growing settlement below the castle called Podol, which lay to the north-east of Andreyev Hill and Kiselevka on the right bank of the Dnieper. This gave Kiev the typical polarity of the Hill as the residence of the prince and Podol as its economic hinterland.

Kiev grew particularly under Yaroslav the Wise, when it acquired the form so much admired by foreign visitors from the East and the West. The actual town on Andreyev Hill — with the prince's palace, the seat of the metropolitan clergy, churches, monasteries, the courts of the boyars — was fortified with ramparts twenty metres (sixty-five feet) wide and 5.5 kilometres (about 3.5 miles) in length. Yaroslav built it on the pattern of Constantinople, and so he had a Golden Gate with the Church of the Annunciation built, the copy of the Constantinople gate, and especially the magnificent Cathedral of St Sophia as a pendant to Constantine's Cathedral of the Holy Wisdom *(Hagia Sophia)*. It had the typical Byzantine ground plan of a cross inscribed into a square, divided into five naves and covered with thirteen cupolas. Its magnificence was heightened by a lower gallery that surrounded the building on three sides. The Byzantine architecture was applied in its original conception, but it was the work of local artists, as were the rich interior decorations where by the side of the customary Bible scenes secular motifs appeared (hunting scenes, races, clowns, etc.). The Kiev St Sophia became the "Mother of Russian Cathedrals", serving as a model in the construction of other important religious buildings — at Novgorod and Polotsk.

Outside the town fortifications numerous churches and monasteries were built. The most famous of these was the Pechora Monastery some 3 kilometres (about 2 miles) south of Kiev, originally a cave for pilgrims on the rocky banks of the Dnieper. From the middle of the eleventh century it became a complex of monastery buildings and churches, built above the caves. This monastery became an important centre of cultural and political life in Kievan Russia. It had an independent status and kept close contacts with the Byzantine sphere of culture, particulary with Athos. Literature flourished, particularly historical writing. From this setting came the Russian *Primary Chronicle (Povest' vremennykh let)* often attributed to the editorship of Nestor. Among the churches the most outstanding decorations were found in the Uspensky sobor (from the years 1073—88). Its destruction by the Nazis during the Second World War meant a great loss for Russian culture. Thanks to archeological research it was, however, possible to reconstruct the original appearance of the monastery.

Most of the people of Kiev in the eleventh century lived below the castle at Podol, where poor semi-subter-

←
The Novgorod Kremlin is dominated by the Cathedral of St Sophia, which was built along the lines of the one in Kiev by Bishop Luka Zhidyata and Prince Vladimir Yaroslavovich in the eleventh century. Close to the cathedral stood the house of the bishop and later of the archbishop, the most powerful figure in the city from the twelfth century on.

ranean dwellings of the old type contrasted sharply with the magnificence of the palaces and churches. Here there was a thriving market and the living quarters of foreign merchants, who brought goods from distant lands. In the twelfth century this part of Kiev was likewise fortified, though less strongly than the seat of the princes on Andreyev Hill. All contemporary local, Western, Arab and Byzantine writers speak of the ostentation and dense population of Kiev. A fatal fire in 1124, internal strife, the growth of rival centres and raids by nomads led to its decline in the twelfth century and the centre of Russia moved further north.

The greatest danger to Kiev always threatened from its southern border, from where hordes of looting nomads kept coming. Under Vladimir, therefore, the approach to Kiev was protected by several lines of fortifications, which lay on the left tributaries of the Dnieper. The first line was along the river Sula, the second on the Trubezh and the third on the edge of the forests surrounding Kiev. The northern gate to Kiev was the town of Lyubech, often cited in records and investigated by archeologists in the years 1957—60. Its castle was divided into a palace section (the *kremlin*) and an area for the guards and for supplies *(detinets)*. It was separated from the town by a moat. Access was over a draw-bridge, through a gate, and then along a narrow wooden paved corridor to the main gate with two towers. Just behind it there stood the highest, a five-storey tower, something like the donjon in the West, which was undoubtedly the seat of the commander of the castle and the ultimate refuge. Beyond this tower the way led to the palace itself, a four-storey building with three towers. The family of the prince lived in richly adorned rooms on the second door. Then there was a small wooden church, behind which an underground passage was discovered that led out of the castle. The large number of store-rooms and tanks for drinking water show that the inhabitants might have withstood a siege for at least one whole year.

Lyubech was the residence of the Chernigov princes, who often competed for power with those in Kiev. According to Byzantine records Chernigov was the most important town in Kievan Russia after Kiev itself. With its location on the right bank of the Desna, on the edge of the forest-steppe region, it became the key to ruling the entire left bank of the Dnieper and the route to the sea coast. Before the unification of Russia it was the tribal centre of the Severyane; in the eleventh century it became the residential town of the extensive Chernigov princedom, with varying degrees of dependence on Kiev. Under Mstislav Vladimirovich, Prince of Tmutarakan', and Chernigov, it assumed for a time the role of capital city of Russia (1026—36). Mstislav built the Spaso-Preobrazhensky sobor — a basilica with nave and side aisles and five cupolas, the oldest surviving cathedral in Russia.

In cultural life, too, Chernigov was second in importance only to Kiev. Its wealth is attested to in finds in barrow graves scattered along the edge of the town. The warriors were often buried with their horses, in full outfit and armour, in log chambers. The most famous are two immense *kurgans* (barrows), which have survived in the outer ward and are known as the Black Barrow and the Barrow of the Black Princess. The former, which was fully excavated, was the grave of a Chernigov prince with his wife and young son; it contained a large number of weapons, and objects showing the exceptional social status of the interred persons. In the twelfth century the fame of Chernigov faded — and in this respect it shared the fate of Kiev.

The most important of the towns in Upper Russia was Novgorod the Great — the true metropolis of the North. Scandinavian sagas referred to it as Holmgardr, Byzantine records as Nemogardas. It grew up on an important crossroad of watercourses along the river Volkhov near Lake Il'men', out of which ships moved down the Volkhov to Lake Ladoga and from there along the Neva to the Gulf of Finland, or up the Msta with the aid of tow lines to the Volga. Further, along the Lovat' and with the use of tow lines to the Western Dvina and the Baltic Sea. Or along the Dnieper to the Black Sea — this was the well-known "route from the Varangians to the Greeks" mentioned before.

The town of Novgorod was founded in a location which was predestined for long-distant trade. This constituted the economic basis of its existence and influenced its remarkable political development and its quite exceptional status among the early medieval Russian towns. For a long time it existed as a city republic with its special, one might say, democratic set-up, and, to a certain extent, it remained independent of the Russian principalities. The territory that belonged to it included the broad forest regions of northern Russia, from where the Novgorod merchants derived their main export articles (furs and wax).

According to Nestor's *Primary Chronicle* Novgorod was built by the Slovene, a Slav tribe that lived between the Valday Hills, the Lake Peipus and Lake Ladoga. Together with the Krivichi they systematically penetrated the sparsely settled regions of the Finnic and Baltic tribes. A certain milestone in development was the arrival of the Scandinavian Varangians, whom Nestor describes as following an invitation for Rurik to take over the rule. This is said to have happened in 862, shortly before Rurik founded Ladoga (Aldeigjuborg). Another legend, however, speaks of fights between the Slovene and Varangians, during which Rurik killed Vadim the Brave and many other men of Novgorod. All these reports are, of course, legendary, just like the figure of the first mayor (or lord mayor) of Novgorod, Gostomysl. If the facts about Rurik reflect a real event, then the castle that Rurik built must have been located elsewhere than in the town where excavations have so far discovered no settlements from the period before the tenth century. It might have been at a place called "Rurik's Hill-Fort", some 5 kilometres (3 miles) from

Novgorod, where ninth- and tenth-century pottery has been found together with imports from Byzantium. Whatever the case may be, at the time of the Kievan state, Novgorod was associated with the Rurik dynasty. Vladimir the Great ruled here before he conquered Kiev and became ruler of the whole of Russia in 980. During his reign the prince in charge of Novgorod was his son Yaroslav. And it was the people of Novgorod who, after Vladimir's death, helped Yaroslav to the throne of Kiev for the first time in 1019. And so it went on with the one difference that the princely power gradually weakened as the separatist trends of Novgorod strengthened and as it strove to attain an independent autonomous position. This was achieved by an uprising in 1136. The princes were then more or less tolerated and installed or expelled according to the prevailing political mood. Only some of them were true rulers of the town, for example Alexander Nevsky, the heroic defender of Novgorod against the expansion of the Swedes and the Order of Teutonic Knights in the thirteenth century.

The river Volkhov divided the town into two parts: the western, called the Sophia Side, and the eastern known as the Market Side. They were joined by a wooden bridge. The centre of the western part was the Kremlin, fortified in the earliest period by a palisade and surrounded by a moat filled with water, as was the whole town. It was dominated by the Cathedral of St Sophia, originally a wooden structure, which is said to have been erected, under Vladimir, by the first bishop of Novgorod, Akim. Before the fire in the year 1049 building began on a new stone St Sophia slightly further south, erected by Bishop Luka Zhidyata and Prince Vladimir Yaroslavovich. It was undoubtedly designed along the lines of the St Sophia in Kiev, from which it differed, however, in that it had five naves in the shape of a cross and five cupolas. Close to the cathedral there was the House of St Sophia, the residence of the Bishop and from 1165 of the Archbishop, the most powerful figure in the Novgorod city republic.

Surrounding the Kremlin lay three quarters or districts (*pyatiny*, meaning "fifth") of the town: the Potters', where in the twelfth century lived the merchant Sadko, clearly the pattern for the legendary figure Sadko of Russian legends and the well-known opera by Nikolay Rimsky-Korsakov; the Suburban Quarter, where the boyars and craftsmen, especially blacksmiths and silversmiths, lived; and the Nerev Quarter, where excavations are still continuing.

The centre of the Market Side on the right bank of the Volkhov was Yaroslav Court, originally the residence of the princes, but from the first half of the twelfth century the town hall. The square in front served for assemblies of the *veche*, the city council. In relation to the Archbishop's Kremlin this was the opposite pole of the town, whose wealth came via the nearby harbour, where ships anchored with cargoes of material, precious metals, food, spices and other valuable goods and from where they set off on long voyages carrying priceless furs and wax. The Market Side was divided into two parts. The carpenters', where lived the master carpenters who were renowned throughout Russia for their skill; together with the blacksmiths from the Sophia Side they belonged to the most powerful guilds in Novgorod. The merchants and tradesmen lived in the Slavene Quarter. Excavations here have shown small dwellings of shoemakers and tanners.

The excavations of Novgorod were no easy undertaking, since the town had bustled with life for many centuries, wooden houses and streets were renovated in each generation and thus gradually the level of the ground rose by 8.5 metres (about 9 yards). Thanks to seeping ground water organic matter such as wood, textiles and furs have survived. By applying dendrochronology to well-preserved wood it is possible to date events to the exact year. For example, wooden paving in the Nerev Quarter, renewed a total of twenty-eight times, existed from 953 to the year 1462.

The streets were laid out almost at right angles and according to the cardinal points, which shows that building construction was regulated and related to the administration of the town. The administrators were in charge of drainage and sewerage, of which wooden pipes and barrels have survived. The wooden houses, all built in the technology of log cabins, had one to three rooms and often a first floor, which served as living quarters while the ground floor was normally used for administrative or production purposes. The rich merchants and boyars lived in homesteads. Smaller houses were grouped around larger buildings to form one unit, inhabited by several families. The total number of the population has been estimated, from the size of the town and density of buildings, at 20,000 in the eleventh century and 50,000 in the thirteenth century — in other words, it was an agglomeration of dwelling houses that had no like in contemporary Europe.

The favourable soil conditions and mighty culture strata brought the archeologists rich finds of numerous objects of daily use — craftsmen's tools, firesteels, ornamental combs, jewels, remains of clothing and footwear — from which various production techniques and certain features of fashion can be deduced. Proof of trade were finds of coins, seals, punches, ships and sledges. The burghers shortened their leisure-time by playing chess, draughts or musical instruments such as *gusli* (zither-like psalteries). Business life was impossible without accounting, written contracts and correspondence. They used sharp instruments to write on strips of birch bark, which kept well in the moist soil of Novgorod. These are the famous *gramoty,* several hundred of which have been found in Novgorod and more continue to be unearthed. They give an intimate view of commercial, trade, legal, family and personal affairs. It is a priceless source that tells us in detail about the daily life of the town in the eleventh to sixteenth centuries. They, furthermore, give a picture of the development of the language, for they are written in the

The Korsun' Door of the Cathedral of St Sophia in Novgorod is a masterpiece in the Romanesque style. It is decorated with reliefs in bronze depicting scenes from the Gospels and portraits of the twelfth-century craftsmen who made it.

spoken language — by contrast to contemporary literature, where Church Slavonic was used.

Literature and art flourished in Novgorod in the eleventh century, as shown by the *Ostromir Gospel* with valuable miniatures, which was made in the years 1056—7, commissioned by Mayor Ostromir. In the eleventh century *Teaching the Brethren* by Bishop Luka Zhidyata appeared, containing prayers, samples of liturgical music, etc., and even his own literary writings. The *Novgorod Chronicles,* of a later date, are immensely valuable for the study of the history of the town.

The literary and artistic life was concentrated mainly in the monasteries, which were also of economic and military importance, for they formed a protective zone around Novgorod controlling access to the town. Pilgrims and monks from the Novgorod monasteries, seeking the loneliness of the deep forests, were often among the first pioneers to penetrate the virgin regions of northern Russia and set the process of colonization in motion.

Closely linked with the history of Novgorod is the fate of two further towns that played an important role in international trade and protected the threatened northern and western frontiers of the Novgorod territory. One was Staraya Ladoga on the river Volkhov, some twelve kilometres (eight miles) south of Lake Ladoga, and the other Pskov, lying to the south of Lake Peipus (Chud), on the confluence of the Velikaya and Pskova rivers. These two areas were settled in the eighth to ninth century by the Krivichi, but when the towns grew in the tenth century, they soon became dependent on Novgorod as "associated towns" — first Pskov and then Ladoga in the second half of the eleventh century.

In Ladoga, far to the north and known to the Scandinavians as Aldeigjuborg, a large group of Varangians settled. According to legend, the town was founded by Rurik himself with his retinue. There exist runic inscriptions, patriarchal houses of the Scandinavian type and *kurgans* with burials on ships according to Viking customs. Where the little river Ladozhka flows into the Volkhov, there was a busy harbour, which served for transhipment from sea-going to river boats. Later the big houses disappeared and their place was taken by smaller log cabins of tradesmen and craftsmen, as in Novgorod.

Pskov was the main destination of the German Hanseatic merchants, who called it Pleskow. They reached it along the Western Dvina, on the mouth of which they built a trading station called Portus Sanigal-lorum. Later Pskov became the target of the military expansion of the Order of Teutonic Knights, who were successfully defeated by the Novgorod prince Alexander Nevsky in 1242 in the memorable battle on frozen Lake Peipus to the north of the town. As an "associate" of Novgorod Pskov had a certain degree of autonomy and a similar organization to that of the main town, where Pskov was represented on the administrative council. It was an important trade and cultural centre and gained its greatest fame from the work of its architects and artists.

Novgorod, with its "associates" and with an extensive colonized territory, developed successfully throughout the Middle Ages. It did not suffer the ravages of the Tatar invasions, whose Golden Horde, with its capital town of Sarai on the Volga, was interested in trade contacts with Europe, and Novgorod served them as an intermediary. The decline of the town was inevitable when a new centre of power arose in Russia in Moscow, for the centralist tendencies of the Moscow Tsars found that the exceptional position of Novgorod stood in their way. In 1478 the town privileges were greatly reduced by Ivan III; a hundred years later this proud town was completely humiliated by Ivan the Terrible. From that time on it led a miserable existence until its role as a "window on Europe" was taken over in 1703 by a new town, founded by Peter the Great, St Petersburg, today's Leningrad.

The Novgorod *gramoty*, letters and documents written by stylus on strips of birch bark, is an invaluable source for the study of the daily life of the town in the eleventh and twelfth centuries.

150

PEASANTS, CRAFTSMEN, MERCHANTS AND WARRIORS

The historical development of the ancient Slavs, which we have been trying to outline, was based on their economic life, agricultural and crafts production and the barter that it involved. Historic sources provide only sparse information in regard to the earliest period. Here archeology comes to our aid with its finds of work tools, production tools and the resulting products, workshops and other premises, and evidence of trade. This is true even for such an integral part of life as military involvement, whose level determined possibilities of expansion and the settlement of new territories, internal social development and even the first political organization. We shall now try to take a look at these aspects in the life of the Slavs in the early Middle Ages.

PEASANTS

Finds of carbonized remains of plants in the Slav villages from the sixth and seventh centuries (e.g. at Březno near Louny in Bohemia) show that their inhabitants cultivated cereals: wheat, rye, barley, oats and millet. But they also grew pulses such as peas and lentils as well as plants like hemp whose fibre was used in craft work. As far as fruit trees are concerned there have been finds only of plum tree wood, and there are no traces of vegetable growing.

The cultivation of a large number of different crops suggests a relatively advanced agriculture, in which crops requiring fertile soil alternated with less demanding types. This corresponds to the manner of working the soil in which part of the fields were left to lie fallow for more than a year.

What was especially important was the discovery that the Slav settlers brought along with them to their new homes — a species of wheat which gave higher yields. From the sixth century on this replaced the more primitive wild einkorn and wild emmer, which were widespread in Central Europe before their arrival. This shows that the economic level of the earliest Slavs was by no means low; on the contrary, it shows that they were good farmers who raised agricultural production in the newly occupied lands to a higher level.

←
The basic importance of agricultural production in the life of the Slavs is documented, among other things, by the Czech legend of Přemysl the Ploughman, the founder of the first local dynasty. The mural paintings in the rotunda at Znojmo depict the scene when Přemysl was summoned to the court while he was ploughing (twelfth century).

The finds of the better wheat and bones of oxen are proofs that the land was tilled and the ox used as a draught animal. The soil was manured by grazing cattle on the fallow fields and with ashes from the burnt stubble. The fallow fields were also burnt off from time to time. Otherwise burning was used when new villages were laid out and new ground opened up for cultivation.

Since, after a certain time, the soil around the village became exhausted, villages were temporarily abandoned. A similar, mostly locally limited shifting of villages, or possible return to the original sites can be observed in Slav settlements of the sixth century in Poland and the Ukraine, and this phenomenon is even recorded in Byzantine reports for this period (for example, by Procopius of Caesareia). In view of the advanced level of agricultural production this form of agriculture cannot be considered nomad.

A very important aspect of the economy of the early Slavs was cattle breeding. Without large herds of cattle, which provided food and served as beasts of burden for transporting supplies and the modest amount of property, the long journeys of the Slav tribes at the time of the migration of nations would not have been possible. Cattle breeding, however, was not the main but a subsidiary way of making a living — in this the Slavs differed from the typically nomad tribes such as the Huns, Avars or the ancient Magyars.

According to finds of bones they kept mainly beef cattle *(Bos primigenius f. taurus L.)*, relatively small in size with short curved horns. Then pigs, but it is not certain to what extent they hunted wild pigs, from which the domestic animals do not greatly differ in appearance. Sheep and goats held third place together, it being difficult to distinguish the bones of one from the other. Then followed domestic or wild poultry, and the rest comprised the horse, dog, and hunted animals. In the case of domestic animals, they were hardy beasts that ran free around the village and did not require roofed stables or pens, which were a later feature.

In the early Middle Ages advances were made in farming methods not always on the same level. In the eighth and ninth centuries there was a substantial improvement in agricultural techniques and a certain intensification of production, as shown by the larger quantity of tools found and a dense network of permanent settlements that were no longer shifted. This development is in accordance with social changes, which led to the establishment of the first Slav states in the ninth century.

The overall statistics of finds of grain from the time show that an important role was played by millet, roughly equal to wheat, followed by rye, oats, barley, peas, vetches and hemp. Cultivation of flax is proved only indirectly in finds of textiles.

We can learn about the shapes of agricultural tools from several large-scale finds — probably forgotten stores of merchants or peasants in difficult times, as well as finds of individual objects in the villages. These make it clear that ards were used primarily for tillage, equipped with small iron shares, suitable only for shallow turning of the sods. Larger shares that could be used for deeper tillage were very much the exception. Some ards had coulters, which cut apart the soil in front and made it possible to open it up from underneath. They even used sole ards with long oar-shaped shares made of iron or wood. This was shown by a rare find at Dabergotz near Neuruppin in the German Democratic Republic, dated, with the aid of radio-carbon tests, to the eighth century. More rarely ploughs were used for tillage even though their existence has been proved during the eighth century. This is confirmed by finds of asymmetrical plough-shares which together with a mouldboard and coulter served to cut the furrow from underneath and turn it over. In the shallow tillage there was no great need to turn over the soil and therefore the plough was not widely used in the early Middle Ages. A change occurred only in the thirteenth century when, together with the general changes in farming methods, tillage using large and heavy ploughs began to be

Numerous archeological finds reveal to us the shapes of agricultural implements — ploughshare, coulter, sickle, scythe, etc. used in the early Middle Ages.

The soil was tilled with an ard with an attached share, suitable for shallow ploughing. A rare find was this ninth-century ard from Dabergotz near Neuruppin (GDR), to which an oar-shaped share was attached.

introduced. From that time on we have proof of the use of harrowing with iron harrows.

At harvest time the early Slavs did not use scythes but sickles with which they cut only the ears held in the hand. It was hard work but only a relatively small amount of grain was lost. Straw remained on the fields, where it was either burnt or ploughed under. From the thirteenth century on they began to use the straw to make manure, and so the corn was cut lower to the ground with longer sickles, adapted in shape for the purpose. The scythe was known in the eighth century, but it was only used for cutting grass.

The corn was threshed with flails, husking was done on wooden crushers by hand or foot, and the grain was stored in pits. These were two to three metres (six to ten feet) deep, usually pear-shaped or in the form of a pouch with a narrow neck and the walls were burnt dry and lined with straw. Once the corn had been poured in, the opening was closed tightly, covered over with clay and protected by a little roof. This method of storage, providing conditions that were airtight and at an even temperature, had the advantage of protecting the grain from pests, and automatically conserved the grain and did not impair its germinative power. For those reasons it survived in many regions until the nineteenth century. In places the home grinding of corn on millstones turned by hand, survived into the modern era in the exact way it was already known from the early Middle Ages on. Only in the eleventh and twelfth centuries with the onset of feudalism were watermills and windmills increasingly used.

The pulses they cultivated included peas, lentils and beans. Cucumbers were grown as early as in the ninth century, other kinds of vegetable only being referred to in later records.

Grain was harvested by sickle with which the ears of the crops, held by hand, were cut off the stalks. This is depicted in an illumination in the *Legend of St Wenceslas* of the *Velislav Bible* (Prague).

Vines were grown in Central Europe from the ninth century on. In the tenth century this activity was depicted in the same *Legend of St Wenceslas (Velislav Bible)*.

Even fruit was cultivated: we know of most kinds of fruit only from medieval finds or reports, but peach- and plum-stones as well as walnuts were found in ninth-century strata. At that same time the Slavs were already growing vines in some areas, e.g. in Moravia, though rather crude varieties. Improvements took place only in the late Middle Ages. Hops to make beer were only gathered to begin with, but from the thirteenth century on they were actually cultivated. The Slavs' favourite drink — mead — points to bee-keeping, but there is no archeological evidence of this.

In livestock production, throughout the early Middle Ages, attention was mainly devoted to the breeding of beef cattle, while pig breeding gradually assumed increasing importance so that in some excavations it predominates. The third place is reserved for sheep and goats, then poultry; geese were relatively rare at the beginning. Duck and pigeon were recorded only in later reports. Apart from the bones of animals kept for food, bones of horses have been found in the villages, which served chiefly for transport and as beasts of burden. After the thirteenth century they were used as draught animals; until that time only oxen had been used for this purpose. There were also bones of dogs, cats and, on isolated occasions, donkeys.

Among the first settlers cattle breeding was extensive for many centuries, which means that the cattle were grazing freely most of the year. Only in winter was fodder provided, as shown by finds of scythes which were used to cut grass. Initially they were short semi-scythes, and from the fourteenth century on they were replaced by today's long-handled scythes. Rakes and forks were likewise found only in the later Middle Ages.

Old hunting practices included falconry. This is confirmed on a silver plaque with the motif of a falconer from Staré Město in Moravia (ninth century).

At that time there appeared the horseshoe — in connection with the increasing use of the horse as a draught animal. Finds of hunting arrows and fish-hooks suggest the existence of hunting and fishing, which, however, did not play such a great role as the breeding of animals.

Among the early Slavs both crop and livestock production were extensive. That does not mean that they were not profitable — on the very contrary: extensive agricultural production was less exhausting, needed smaller quantities of seeds and did not suffer so much from bad harvests and bad weather. But its disadvantage was that it required large areas. This meant that, as the population grew, it could not continue for long.

In the thirteenth and fourteenth centuries, therefore, the existing grass and field system of enclosures was replaced — as an innovation of feudalism — by the relatively more intensive "three-field" system where two-thirds of the land was sown alternately with winter and summer crops and one third was left to lie fallow and used for pasture. In this way it was possible to use larger areas of land, which were readily at their disposal, to achieve higher production and fed a larger number of people — but at the cost of far more labour, which involved tillage with a heavy plough, more exhausting harvest work, manuring and harrowing the fields. For the country people this technical improvement meant a worsening of living conditions and feudal serfdom. But such was the fate of the whole of Europe at the time.

CRAFTS AND TRADE

The first Slav settlers made all their own things — tools, crockery, clothing, footwear and weapons — or they acquired them through barter or as loot. As soon, however, as the newly occupied lands were consolidated and agricultural production began to increase, there was a greater need for better adapted tools, and substantial changes occurred. By degrees division of labour evolved as a prerequisite of the new stage of economic and social development. People began to specialize in individual crafts and this made trade possible, led to the origin of town centres and the social stratification of the population.

The first to become specialized were the iron smelters and blacksmiths, who prepared and utilized the basic raw material for the production of working tools and weapons — iron. The technology of iron smelting spread to Europe from Asia Minor in the first millennium B.C. and was already known to the Slavs when they were in their original homeland beyond the Carpathians. At the turn of the eighth to ninth century this production began to be concentrated in iron forges, which ensured production on a larger scale. At Želechovice in Moravia twenty-four smelting ovens were discovered from that period, and similar finds have been made elsewhere. As the analysis of iron objects has shown, the Slavs had mastered the production of steel by the ninth century.

The technique of iron smelting, known to the Slavs when they were still in their original homeland, began to be concentrated in ironworks at the turn of the eighth to ninth century, where larger-scale production could be achieved.

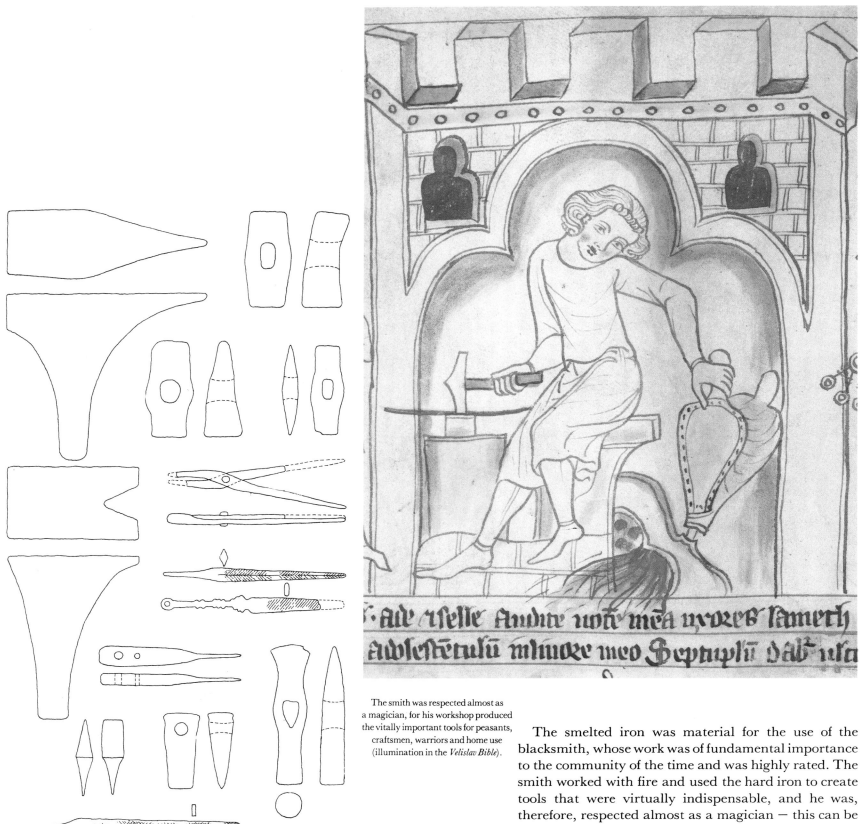

The smith was respected almost as a magician, for his workshop produced the vitally important tools for peasants, craftsmen, warriors and home use (illumination in the *Velislav Bible*).

Archeological finds of the tools of the smith show the advanced techniques and specialization of this craft.

The smelted iron was material for the use of the blacksmith, whose work was of fundamental importance to the community of the time and was highly rated. The smith worked with fire and used the hard iron to create tools that were virtually indispensable, and he was, therefore, respected almost as a magician — this can be seen in the numerous motifs in legends and fairy-stories. His forge produced mainly tools to work the land, instruments for craftsmen, articles needed in the home and in particular the essential outfit and equipment of warriors.

Metallographic analysis has revealed the techniques used by the smiths. It was found, for instance, that the smith was already able in the ninth century to attach steel edges to the iron blades of swords and daggers. They were also acquainted with the technology of Damascus blades, otherwise known only in the Orient and in the Rhineland. The location of forges inside and outside the hill-forts is indicated by finds of hearths, anvils, tongs, half-finished items and waste. In the tenth to eleventh centuries whole hamlets came into being, of which the inhabitants were specialized in blacksmiths' work and paid their tithes to the prince in the form of products, i. e. they were service villages. Similar villages existed also for other crafts.

By the side of the iron smelters and blacksmiths there soon appeared the potter. His craft is the oldest extant, for the production of pots was known from the Neolithic Age on. For a long time it was practised in each family and was considered the work of women. Pottery as a craft eventually appeared in the more advanced cultures of antiquity. But among the barbarian nations of Europe the potter only appeared with the transitory feudalism. This was the case among the Slavs. Large-scale production began only in the ninth and tenth centuries; it was carried out by specialized craftsmen and depended on technical improvements. From the free shaping of a pot by hand they went on to turning it on a wheel moved by hand and finally to turning pots on a rapidly turning wheel set in motion by foot. The finished products were then baked on grates in clay kilns, whole batteries of which were located in the vicinity of the main centres. The work of the potter was also reckoned to contained a bit of magic — hence the various symbols on the bottom of the pots (cross, cross in a circle, swastikas, wheels, pentagrams, hands, etc.), which, after the transition to craft production, became potters' marks. The potter produced not only pots, dishes, and bottles, but also whorls, little figures, toys, and cult objects, among them painted eggs (*pisanki*) which spread from Kievan Russia in the ninth century.

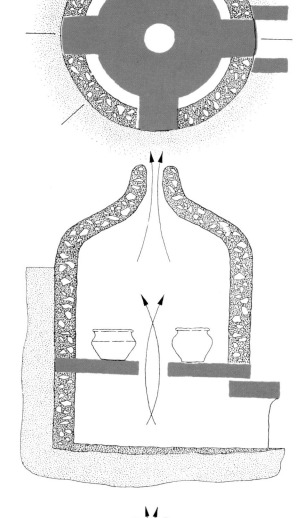

In the early Middle Ages the Slav potters mainly used a slowly rotating wheel, on which hand-made pottery was only turned in its final stages. The fast rotating wheel, set in motion by foot, which made it possible for the entire vessel to be turned, did not come in until later. Pots were baked on grids in kilns, the construction of which (ground plan and side face) is depicted here (right).

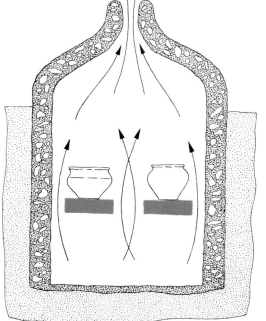

For a long time wood was worked only in the home, and various tools, spoons, plates, little statues, toys and handles were cut from it; beams, posts and boards for building houses were hewn; fortifications, bridges and wheels were made of it and wood was used to fashion wagons, sledges, ships, boats, barrels, buckets, chests, and the like. Byzantine chroniclers report wagons as having been used by the Slavs from the sixth century. Without these their long-distance migration would have been unthinkable. We do not know what these wagons looked like, for all that has been found are wheels excavated in Mecklenburg. Wood, a material that is perishable, survived only in highly favourable soil conditions, such as exist in the northern parts of the German Democratic Republic, in Poland and Russia, where a large number of wooden objects from the ninth to twelfth century have been unearthed. Specialization in making things with wood took place only under feudalism, when there appeared joiners, carpenters, coopers, wheelwrights, and turners.

Up to the tenth century cloth was woven mainly in the home. Spindles with whorls were used by women at all levels of society. They used them to spin flax and sheep wool. The wooden spindles have not survived, but whorls made of clay or stone can be found in Slav settlements in large numbers. From the spun fibres they wove various kinds of fabrics, some rougher, others smoother, and in various colour combinations. Their quality was discussed in the tenth century by a Jewish merchant from Spain Ibrāhīm ibn Ya'qūb, who noticed that in Prague things were paid for in kerchiefs. (In fact the Czech word for "pay" — platit — is related to the word for "linen cloth" — plátno.)

The narrow strip of material was woven with doffer combs or plates, broader material on a weaver's loom. Originally it was a vertically placed frame with clay weights, which, in the ninth and tenth centuries, was replaced by a horizontal loom which probably spread to Central Europe from Byzantium via the Balkans. With the improved loom there arose the independent craft of

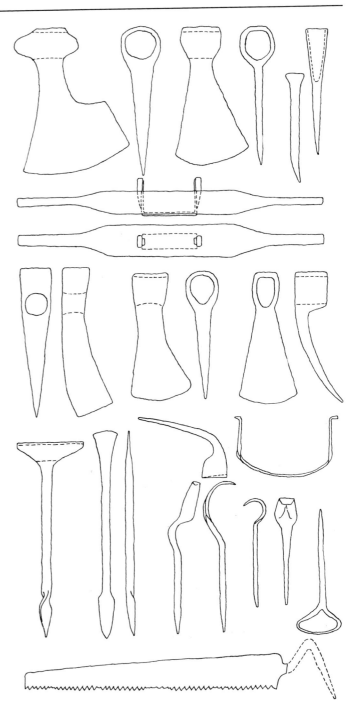

Wood was worked by means of axes, chisels, saws, files, drills, knives and planes.

A number of work tools were made of wood which survived only on exceptional occasions, e.g at the hill-fort of Behren-Lübchin in Mecklenburg (eleventh to twelfth century).

the weaver. But clothes continued to be sewn by women, even among the nobility, as shown by the find of a golden needle in the tomb of a Slav princess at Alt Lübeck.

Tanned animal skins were made into boots, fur coats, caps, and gloves and they were also used for shields, saddles, quivers and sheaths. The work of tanning has been proved on Slav sites by finds of pits with marks of lime and remnants of skins. Tanning as a craft came into being under feudalism, as did the production of footwear, which can be shown by finds of carefully shaped, sewn footwear decorated with hem-stitching at Polish Wolin, Opole, Gdańsk, and elsewhere. Ibrāhīm ibn Ya'qūb speaks of the production of saddles and shields in Prague. The products have not survived but the form of the shields is known from pictures on stone walls at Libušín, dating from the turn of the tenth to the eleventh century, from the *Vyšehrad Codex* (end of the eleventh century) and mural paintings at Znojmo in southern Moravia.

Work involving horn and bone was also of a high standard; it was used to fashion combs, handles, ornaments, dice, pipes, needles, awls and "skates". Many of these objects were richly adorned with engraved patterns. An example is a comb from the residence of the Czech princes at Budeč, the product of the local tenth-century workshop.

The craft of the stonemason likewise did not develop until the feudal period, when it arose in connection with the building of cathedrals and palaces. Prior to that, stones had been hewn only as millstones, whorls, grindstones, moulds for casting metal objects and as building material for fortifications. They also worked semi-precious stones, from which they polished beads and ornaments to be set in metal. Glass was originally imported from the Orient, Byzantium or the Rhineland, but from the ninth century on the Slavs were capable of making it themselves.

Combs were produced from horn and bones, and sometimes decorated with incised patterns (Budeč, Bohemia, tenth century).

The spindle and the whorls were the attributes of women at all levels of society. They were used to spin flax and wool (illumination in the *Velislav Bible*).

The uncrowned king of craftsmen — even if his status was usually that of slave or serf — was, undoubtedly, the goldsmith and jeweller, whose products belong to the sphere of the arts and crafts and are a sensitive barometer of the cultural level of their time and setting. In the Slav countries this craft flourished in the ninth and tenth centuries; the beginnings, however, date back to the seventh and eighth centuries. They worked both less precious metals — copper and pewter, from which they cast bronze — and silver and gold, by casting them into stone or wax moulds and by hammering, plating, engraving, punching, granulating, filigreing and latticing with enamel. This gave rise to the multi-coloured, highly original magnificence of the jewels of the Great

159

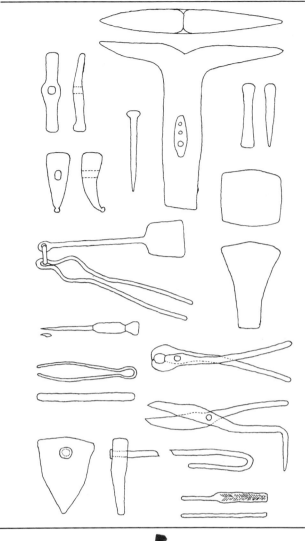

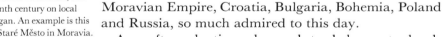

In the beginning glass was imported to the Slav countries from the Orient, Byzantium and the Rhineland, but from the ninth century on local production began. An example is this necklace from Staré Město in Moravia.

The art of the Slav jewellers flourished first in the ninth and tenth centuries. This is confirmed not only by the items themselves, but also by finds of specialized tools.

That trade flourished is borne out by finds of scales and weights at hill-forts in Mecklenburg from the eleventh to twelfth century (Neu Niekőhr, Behren-Lübchin, Teterow, Alt Bartelsdorf).

Moravian Empire, Croatia, Bulgaria, Bohemia, Poland and Russia, so much admired to this day.

As craft production advanced, trade began to develop. It started at the time of Samo, but until the early ninth century trade relations between the Slav lands and the surrounding world were only sporadic. In the ninth century a change occurred. It was related to the growth of production, and the establishment of Slav states and trade centres in Northern and Eastern Europe, which mediated long-distance trade with Byzantium and the Orient.

Some of these long-distance routes were known already in the Roman period, for example those along the Danube and the Amber Route, leading from the Baltic through Moravia to the Mediterranean region. Others assumed importance in the ninth and tenth centuries, for example the north-south route that linked Scandinavia via Kiev with Byzantium; the Volga Route, which provided contact with the world of Islam; and, the West-East Route, which led from Kiev via Cracow to Prague and further to the West. In the tenth century Prague was a junction of European routes.

Before the introduction of coinage, talents (of iron or

Life in the Slav settlements depended mainly on agriculture and cattle breeding. Hunting and fishing were only of subsidiary importance. The women busied themselves with grinding corn, cooking, spinning and weaving. The first craftsmen were the smiths and potters, soon followed by bone and wood carvers, carpenters, etc. Travelling traders prospered from the exchange of commodities.

silver) served as currency, as did weighed silver, fabric, furs, salt, and the like. But before long foreign coins came into circulation, mainly Arab, Byzantine, and later Western European. In Bohemia the first local coins were minted under Boleslav I (929—967), in Poland under Mieszko I (960—992), in Russia under Vladimir the Great (980—1015). Their circulation meant a strengthening of the home market and made it possible for great wealth to be accumulated, which is illustrated by finds of treasures close to the main towns and routes. Thus, from the tenth century on, a merchant class emerged in the Slav countries to become an important element in society which helped determine economic and cultural development. Specialization of production and in the distribution of products, in the ninth and tenth centuries, connected with the growth of the towns, gave this development a basic impetus, the results of which are felt to this day.

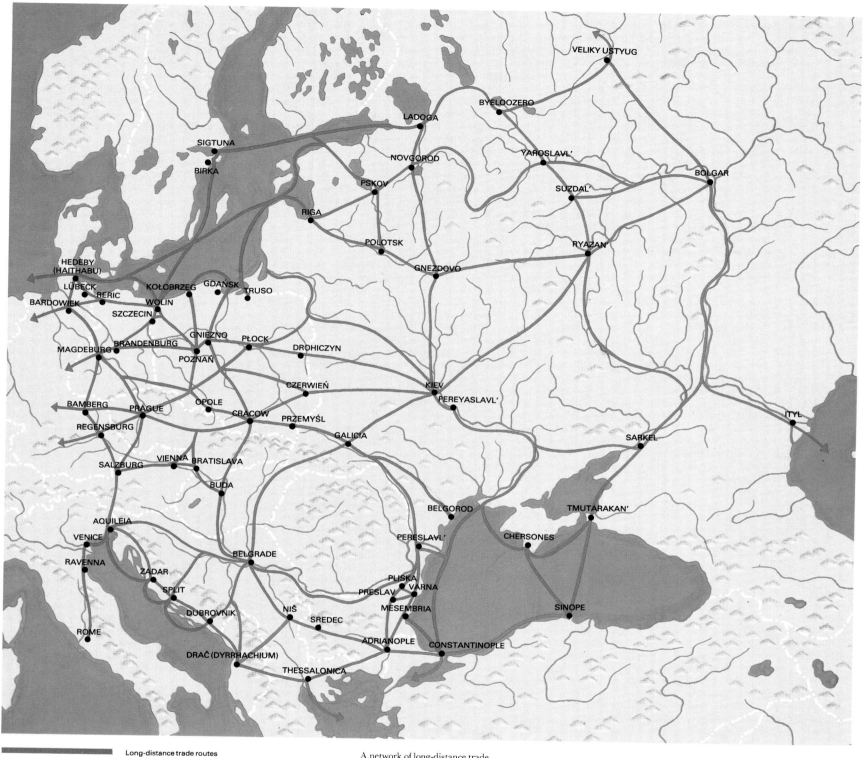

VELIKY USTYUG

BYELOOZERO

LADOGA

SIGTUNA

BIRKA

NOVGOROD

YAROSLAVL'

BOLGAR

PSKOV

SUZDAL'

RIGA

POLOTSK

RYAZAN'

HEDEBY
(HAITHABU)

GNEZDOVO

LÜBECK

KOŁOBRZEG

GDAŃSK

TRUSO

BARDOWIEK

RERIC

WOLIN

SZCZECIN

GNIEZNO

PŁOCK

DROHICZYN

MAGDEBURG

BRANDENBURG

POZNAŃ

KIEV

PEREYASLAVL'

BAMBERG

OPOLE

CZERWIEŃ

PRAGUE

REGENSBURG

CRACOW

PRZEMYŚL

ITYL

GALICIA

SARKEL

SALZBURG

VIENNA

BRATISLAVA

BUDA

AQUILEIA

TMUTARAKAN'

VENICE

BELGOROD

CHERSONES

RAVENNA

ZADAR

PERESLAVL'

SPLIT

BELGRADE

PLISKA

VARNA

DUBROVNIK

NIŠ

PRESLAV

ROME

SREDEC

MESEMBRIA

SINOPE

DRAČ (DYRRHACHIUM)

ADRIANOPLE

CONSTANTINOPLE

THESSALONICA

Long-distance trade routes

A network of long-distance trade
routes, confirmed in records and by
excavations, linked early medieval
Europe economically as well as
culturally. Influences moved along
these routes in an east-west as well as
north-south direction.

WARRIORS

In the period of Romanticism, under the influence of the German philosopher and historian J. G. Herder, the idea was widely accepted of the "dove-like" character of the Slavs as peaceful peasants in contrast to the belligerent Germans. More profound historical and archeological studies, however, have invalidated this idea. Without skill in warfare the extensive Slav expansion in the sixth to eighth centuries would never have taken place, even if it was aided by propitious external conditions. The two great powers of the early Middle Ages — the Byzantine and the Frankish Empires — waged heavy battles against the Slav tribes and states along their borders with varying success over the centuries. The same is true of the constant conflicts between the Eastern Slavs and the nomads from the steppes. The Slav warrior did not basically differ from

the German soldier in fitness and skill at fighting. This was expressed clearly by an unbiassed observer in the tenth century, Ibrāhīm ibn Ya'qūb: "Generally speaking, the Slavs are quick to attack and hot-tempered. If there were not so much disunity among them, caused by their being split up into a number of tribes, no other nation could stand up to them."

We can learn how the Slav warriors were equipped from finds made by archeologists and from later iconographical depiction. Their main weapon was the bow with arrows that had leaf-shaped iron arrowheads with hooks, or were three-edged or rhomboid in shape adopted from the nomads. Then there was the axe, either light-weight or heavy, with a broad blade, called the "beard-axe". It often had inlaid ornamentation as did the lance, which frequently had pinions. Swords of the early medieval type became highly popular from the ninth century on, despite the prohibition of imports from

Some time at the turn of the tenth to the eleventh century a guard at hill-fort Libušín (central Bohemia) whiled away an idle period by carving horses and riders on the walls of the fortifications. In his naive manner he depicted a rider with a large shield and long spear, and a fringed banner at its end.

166

the West, mainly from the workshops in the Rhineland. Soon such swords were being produced by local smiths and, like the foreign models, they had decorated hilts. The warriors carried their swords in wooden or leather sheaths sometimes adorned with wrought-metal ornaments. The shields, of inferior quality (as the observant Ibrāhīm noticed), were made of wood and leather. In the earlier period they were circular in shape, but from the eleventh century on the predominant type was the Norman shield of oval shape running to a point.

Cavalry formed an important part of the Slav army, even if not as decisive as in the case of the Avars, the Bulgars, Magyars and other nomads. The Slav horsemen differed from these, among others, by wearing spurs. In the sixth to eighth centuries these spurs had hooks at the heel, later loops and, from the ninth century on, there were little side tabs at both ends. They were often highly elaborate with relief decorations and

The magnificent stirrup adorned with gilt bronze layers and inlaid with silver probably belonged to a member of the prince's retinue (Zbečno, Bohemia). It came from a Scandinavian workshop and shows that Bohemia had contacts with that area in the tenth century.

gilding. This was equally true of the rest of the horseman's outfit, in which the straps often had ornamental metal-work. The Slavs probably adopted this custom from the nomads from whom they had learnt to use stirrups. The outfit further comprised cudgels, spiked clubs, scimitars, daggers, and slings. They even wore helmets to begin with of foreign make but soon produced in local workshops. Most of the helmets were conical in shape and in the eastern regions had elongated tops. A beautiful ninth-century example is the St Wenceslas helmet, kept in the Treasure of St Vitus's Cathedral at Prague Castle.

Numerous buildings that served the purposes of warfare provide evidence of the Slavs' skill at fighting and defence: fortifications of hill-forts, castles and even the first towns. Each one was set up at a strategically important location: crossroads of important routes, the confluence of rivers, near fords, on mountain passes or in

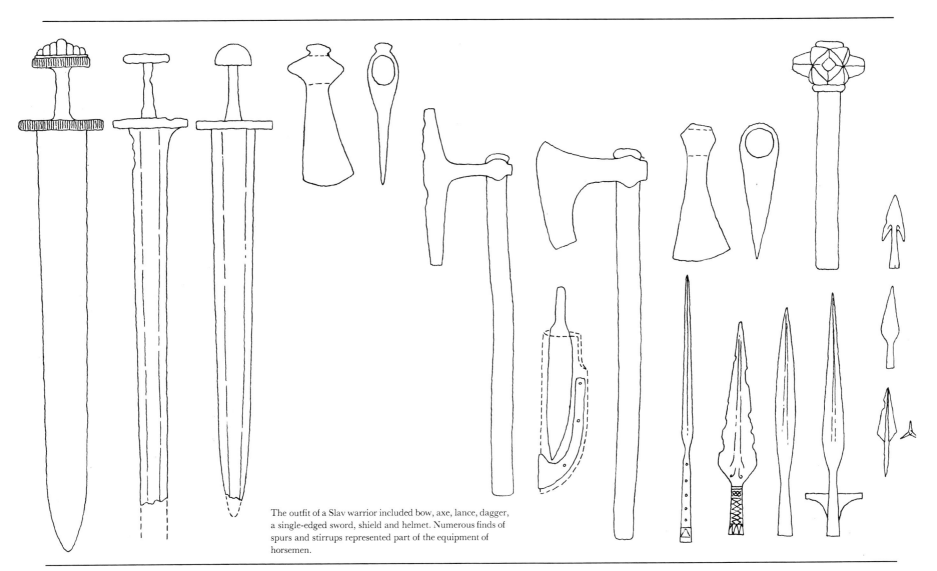

The outfit of a Slav warrior included bow, axe, lance, dagger, a single-edged sword, shield and helmet. Numerous finds of spurs and stirrups represented part of the equipment of horsemen.

places protected by nature, where inaccessibility was further strengthened by ingeniously located ramparts. In the majority of Slav countries the ramparts were constructed of wood. There was a great variety of different types from simple palisades to complex structures with chambers and soundly secured gratings. The Bulgar regions differed in this respect since even at a very early stage they built stone ramparts in the style of antiquity. In Bohemia and Moravia ramparts were built in the ninth century that were a revival of earlier Celtic fortifications. They had frontal dry-stone walls and broad galleries of wooden construction filled up with clay. This type survived until the twelfth century when stone walls began to be built with mortar. Siege

instruments to take castles by storm are mentioned in written sources. The Slavs must have copied these from those of Byzantium, and though their own tools did not attain the perfection of the originals, they were highly effective, for they even enabled the Slavs to penetrate the strong ramparts of Greek towns such as Thessalonica.

The abilities of the Slav warriors proved themselves even at sea, especially on the Baltic and Adriatic Seas. On the Baltic they built ships similar to those of the Vikings and often became as accomplished as those feared sailors, even in their skill at warfare, not only in defence of their own shores but also in attacks on the Scandinavian coast.

In the early Middle Ages to wear armour was a privilege of princes and leading warriors. This magnificent example of a wire shirt and a coat of mail with a collar, is allegedly the property of St Wenceslas (St Vitus's Treasure at Prague Castle).

The helmets of Slav warriors were mainly conical in shape. A precious example is the St Wenceslas Helmet in the Cathedral Treasure of St Vitus's in Prague. It came to Bohemia as an import of Western origin in the ninth century.

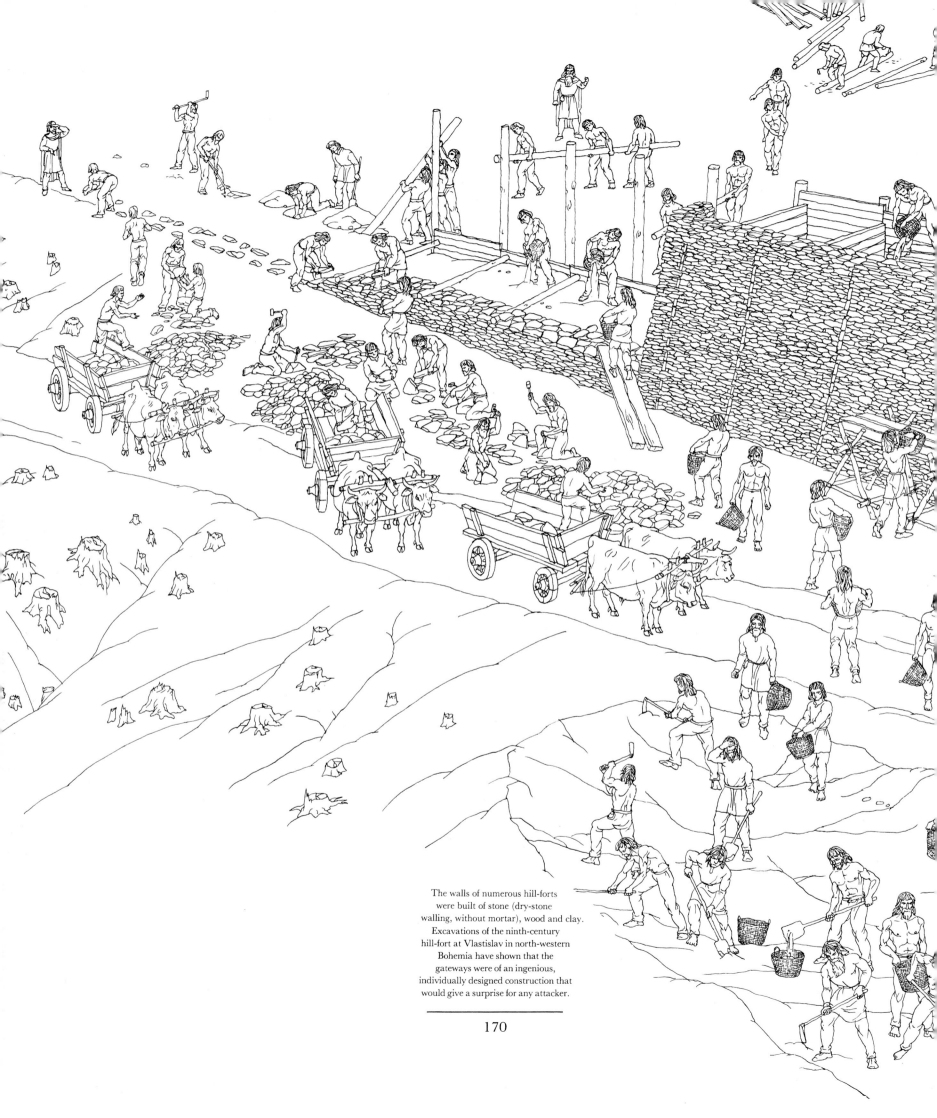

The walls of numerous hill-forts were built of stone (dry-stone walling, without mortar), wood and clay. Excavations of the ninth-century hill-fort at Vlastislav in north-western Bohemia have shown that the gateways were of an ingenious, individually designed construction that would give a surprise for any attacker.

The first historically known Czech Prince was
Bořivoj, who together with his wife Ludmila
adopted the Slavonic form of Christianity from
Moravia and around A.D. 870 built St Clement's
Church at Levý Hradec — the oldest church
building in Bohemia.

THE BOHEMIAN STATE
OF THE PŘEMYSLIDS – THE HEIR TO THE
GREAT MORAVIAN EMPIRE

Until the ninth century Bohemia lay beyond the mainstream of historical development, hidden behind its veil of border mountains and forests, still sunk deep in the mythical period of its development on which legends cast but a dull light. The territory was divided into natural regions inhabited by groups of tribes. Of greatest importance were the Czechs proper, who ruled in the strategic centre of the land on the lower reaches of the river Vltava and by stages built their main castles there: Budeč, Levý Hradec, Libušín, Tetín and Prague. The first records of the existence of the Czechs are to be found in the *Moissac Chronicle,* which describes a mighty Frankish expedition to Bohemia in the year 805 and calls the local Slavs "Cichu-Windones". (But there are still doubts as to the correct reading of this largely illegible manuscript from southern France.) Later records do not

reveal a great deal more. They report simply the presence of Bohemians and Moravians at the Imperial Council at Frankfurt in the year 822 and the baptism of fourteen Bohemian princes at Regensburg in 845. But the number of the princes shows that the political organization of the Bohemians was still split up into groups. Apart from the Czechs, the only tribes who played an important role were the Lučané from north-western Bohemia on the river Ohře, the Zličané in the fertile regions of the central Elbe valley, the Western and Eastern Charváti in north-eastern Bohemia (Czech Croats), and the Doudlebi in the south of the country. In addition there were a number of smaller tribes: in the north the Pšované, Litoměřici, Lemuzi, Děčané, and in the western part the Sedličané and the Chbané.

The legends recorded by chronicler Cosmas in the early twelfth century refer only to the tribe of the Czechs. They relate the story of an ancient ruler, Krok, and his three daughters. The youngest, Libuše, endowed with

The hill-fort of Libušín was founded, so legend has it, by Libuše, the mother of the Přemyslid dynasty. Excavations have confirmed an old settlement from the sixth to seventh century, but the fortifications did not come into being until the ninth century when Libušín played the role of a border fort on the frontier of two tribal territories.

The unknown princess of the Lemuzi tribe, buried at Želénky near Duchcov in Bohemia, owned gold and silver jewels of a Great Moravian origin: ear-rings, buttons, an ancient cameo set in a gold case hanging on a gold chain, and a unique silver plaque with a deer and falcon depicted in relief.

the gift of prophecy, assumed the crown after her father's death. But the men were not satisfied with this woman ruler and forced Libuše to marry Přemysl, who thus became the founder of the ruling dynasty. Cosmas lists its members up to the historical period but does not say anything about them except for Neklan, under whom there was a big battle between the Czechs and the Lučané led by the ambitious Prince Vlastislav. This tribal conflict, which must have occurred some time after the middle of the ninth century, imprinted itself upon the memory of the people as an event with a fundamental bearing on the later development of Bohemia. It was one of the main stages in the process of

unification. In the year 872 Western sources still speak of five Bohemian princes (Světislav, Vitislav, Heřman, Spytimír and Mojslav, and later Bořivoj was added to these). They were defeated by Archbishop Luitbert during a large expedition against Moravia under Carloman, but at that time the political core was beginning to form in the centre of the country and gradually all the other parts of Bohemia became attached to it.

The first historical ruler appeared next on the scene. He was Bořivoj, who, so the old Slavonic legends relate, adopted Christianity from Moravia, perhaps from personal contact with Methodius, some time in the years

Old Kouřim was the residence of the princes of the Zličané tribe in the ninth and tenth centuries, whose territory lay to the east of the tribe of the Czechs. The wealth of the princes of Kouřim, rivals of the Czech Přemyslids, is proved by the magnificence of the jewels found in the local cemetery, including insignia of the prince's power (the spike of the flag-pole and a silver-plated stick).

869 to 870. But not even Bořivoj's rule extended over the whole of the country. He probably commanded only its central and north-western parts. His baptism and that of his wife Ludmila brought about a pagan reaction, the rebellion of Strojmír or Spytimír, in which political aspects — that is, opposition to a certain dependence on Moravia — must have played a part. This gradually increased, especially under Svatopluk, and from 890 on it was acknowledged even by the Frankish Empire. This was, however, merely a short episode, for after the death of Svatopluk in 894 the Bohemian princes came to an agreement with Arnulf at the congress of Regensburg in 895 and renounced all dependence on Moravia. The subsequent political and cultural development of Bohemia assumed a definite orientation towards the West.

The degree of unification at the end of the ninth century can be judged from the fact that only two princes from Bohemia were present at the ceremony in Regensburg: Spytihněv, Bořivoj's successor, and an otherwise unknown Vitislav, probably the ruler of some tribes in eastern Bohemia who retained a certain degree of independence even in the tenth century, although nominally they acknowledged the sovereignty of the Czech Přemyslids. After the fall of the Great Moravian Empire in the early tenth century, the centre of events shifted to Bohemia, and the power of the Přemyslids reached far to the east into the areas of the vanished Moravian state. The cultural and political prestige of Bohemia grew in the eyes of Christian Europe when the first two Bohemian saints came from that dynasty: St Ludmila, the wife of Bořivoj, murdered at the instigation of her daughter-in-law, and her grandson St Wenceslas, the patron saint of Bohemia, who was assassinated in the year 929 (or 935) by his ambitious younger brother Boleslav. St Wenceslas, a remarkable and, for his time, a highly educated man, was already revered in the tenth century in a number of Old Slavonic and Latin legends, and soon both the West and the East paid homage to him. Furthermore, he became the symbol of Czech statehood. The crown of the Kings of Bohemia is, to this day, called the St Wenceslas Crown.

An important contribution to the development of the state of Bohemia was the foundation of the Prague bishopric in 973, under Boleslav II. Outwardly Bohemia was part of the Holy Roman Empire, but its internal political life was independent. This was underlined by the new ecclesiastical organization whereby its former dependence on Regensburg ceased. The first Bishop of Prague was Thietmar of Saxony, but he was followed by Adalbert (St Vojtěch), who was to become another Bohemian saint and gained merit from his Christianization of the Magyars and Poles.

Early feudal Bohemia rose in importance in the tenth century, but political duality continued until the end of the century since, apart from the ruling Přemyslids, eastern and southern Bohemia came under the sphere of influence of the Slavník family. One of their descendants was Adalbert. The Slavníks maintained their own political and cultural contacts with, for instance, Saxony

Jewels of that cemetery.

and Poland, and they even minted their own coins. Their power was finally broken by the treacherous assassination of the entire family at their castle at Libice in 995. This bloody act removed the last rivals of the Přemyslids and completed the process of unification. At the turn of the tenth to eleventh century there was a temporary decline during which, for a time, Bohemia was ruled by Prince Bolesław Chrobry (the Brave) of Poland. But under Prince Oldřich (1012—34) and especially under Břetislav I (1034—55) the state of Bohemia, with Moravia now firmly a part of it, reached its basic form, which it kept throughout its further century-long development.

Archeologists have drawn a full picture of the early historical development of Bohemia. They excavated the main centres of the Přemyslids and their tribal rivals as well as localities not mentioned in written records. They have provided valuable facts about periods of which all previous knowledge came from oral tradition.

This includes a hill-fort that the chronicler Cosmas linked in his Legends with Libuše, who gave rise to the Přemyslid dynasty. This hill-fort really exists. It is called Libušín and is located on a spur of land west of a village of the same name. More thorough excavations have been carried out here than anywhere else in Bohemia. True enough, its fortifications were raised only in the historical period, probably in the last third of the ninth century, when Libušín served as a border fort along the tribal borders with the Lučané. But there have been finds of pottery of the Prague type, which shifts the

beginning of settlement on the spur back to the sixth or seventh century, the very time to which the legend of Libuše refers. The place must then have served as a cult site. This is suggested both by its location on the top of a hill and the presence of a spring, which played such an important role in the cult of the early Slavs. Among the finds was a clay disc with the symbol of the sun — a cross inscribed in a circle. So it would seem that the legend of Libuše was inspired by some local tradition which survived in the minds of the people into historical times.

A similar case can be cited in regard to the legend of the war between the Czechs and the Lučané, which can also be pinpointed to an archeological site: hill-fort Vlastislav in the Central Bohemian Massif. Cosmas tells us that it was built by Vlastislav, the ruler of the Lučané, and he kept the local allies of the Czechs at bay from there. This strategic position is fully upheld both by the location of the hill-fort as such and the results of excavations, which brought proof of its function as a border fort at the time of tribal conflicts.

The northern neighbours of the Lučané were the Lemuzi. Legend relates that the founder of the Bohemian dynasty, Přemysl, came from their territory in the valley of the little river Bílina below the Ore Mountains. They were naturally allies of the Czechs in their struggle against the Lučané. The tribal centre of the Lemuzi was discovered at a hill-fort between Duchcov and Teplice, called Zabrušany. In the vicinity of this hill-fort — at Želénky near Duchcov — a burial mound of an unknown

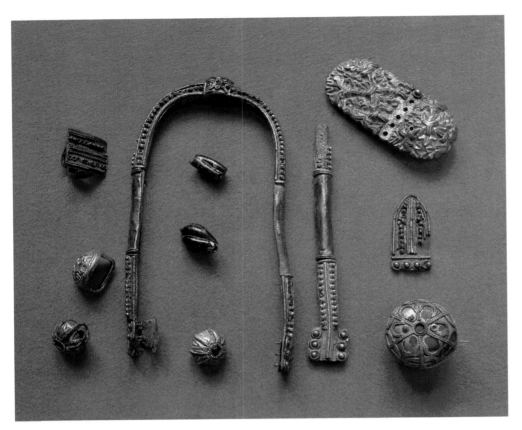

in the legends about St Wenceslas and St Ludmila, written by a monk named Christian probably at the end of the tenth century, when he talks about St Wenceslas's miraculous victory over the rebellious Prince of Kouřim. Long years of excavations at this hill-fort have brought to light triple fortifications with gates, a shrine with a little lake and a hall 89 metres (200 feet) long, which was the public chamber of the prince's palace. It must have served for assemblies, banquets and other festivities. This unique find in Bohemia has numerous contemporary analogies in Scandinavia and in Russia. Other valuable finds were made when a burial ground was discovered in which members of the prince's family had been interred.

The tomb of a prince was also found not far away, at Kolín, and in it jewels of the Great Moravian type as well as Carolingian imports including a chalice, spurs, stirrup mounts and glass vessels. This shows that the area must have had contacts with the West.

The original tribal centre of the Czechs was probably the hill-fort of Budeč near the village of Zákolany, 25 km (17 miles) north of Prague. It is mentioned in the earliest Czech legends, written in Old Slavonic and in Latin and dating from the tenth century. The second historical

Contacts with the Western Carolingian sphere are proved by the items found in a prince's double grave (man and woman) at Kolín, also on the territory of the Zličané: a goblet (only the upper half and part of the foot are original), spurs, belt mounts, and glass vessels. Beside these objects there were also jewels of the Great Moravian type.

Lemuzi princess was excavated. It contained gold jewels which were worked in a style very similar to that of the Great Moravian Empire. Perhaps the princess who ruled over the Lemuzi and had her seat at the hill-fort of Zabrušany came from Moravia.

The centre of the second important rivals of the tribe, the Zličané, was the hill-fort at Kouřim. It lies on a spreading hill that forms part of the northern foothills of the Czech-Moravian Uplands. Kouřim is mentioned

prince, Spytihněv, built a St Peter's Rotunda there some time after 895, which is the oldest stone structure still standing in Central Europe that has survived almost in its entirety. His successor Vratislav sent his under-age son Wenceslas there to study Latin under priest Ucenus (or Wenno) so that the first known school on Bohemian soil must have stood there. For a short time Princess Drahomíra lived at Budeč after a disagreement with her son Wenceslas.

Excavations, which have been in progress since 1972, have revealed that the inner part of the hill-fort was fortified some time around the year 800. Later the ramparts were twice enlarged and renewed, for the hill-fort was permanently settled from the ninth to the thirteenth century. The actual palace of the princes was separated from the inhabited area of the hill-fort by a palisade. Inside it stood the rotunda with an eastern and a northern apse — the latter probably serving as a burial chapel. Today a Romanesque tower stands on the foundations of this northern apse. Tombs with jewels of the Great Moravian type prove that burials took place inside and around the rotunda in the first half of the tenth century. The princes' palace has not survived, for its area was disturbed when a modern cemetery was laid out. But the seat of the prince's warden has been discovered. He assumed rule over the hill-fort when the Přemyslids went to settle permanently at Prague Castle. This residence was a complex of wooden and stone buildings surrounded by a palisade and linked by a paved road both to the settlement below and to the Church of Our Lady, which was built towards the end of the tenth century. Its foundations on a rectangular ground plan with an apse were discovered by the archeologists not far from the residence.

To the east of Budeč on the high left bank of the river Vltava rises another Přemyslid castle, Levý Hradec. Its beginnings likewise go far back into the mythical period, but it was established slightly later than Budeč. After being baptised by Methodius, Bořivoj built the first church in Bohemia there. In the year 982 the second bishop of Prague Adalbert was elected in this church. Excavations in 1947—54 have shown that a prince's fortified residence with an outer ward existed there between the early ninth and the first half of the eleventh century. The fortress was abandoned probably during the expedition led by Henry III against Břetislav I. The prince lived inside the hill-fort with his retinue, who had at their disposal log cabins with timber floors, each divided into two rooms with an entrance hall. In the outer bailey, separated from the castle by a ravine, stood simpler dwellings of peasants and craftsmen, built of posts and stakes interwoven with twigs. Only the homestead of a free peasant, which had several chambers and outbuildings, was above average. The prince's palace has not been discovered, but it is quite possible that it stood where traces of a burnt-down building have been found below the foundations of medieval homes. The remains of Bořivoj's Church of St Clement were uncovered inside the present Baroque church with its Gothic presbytery. It was a rotunda with a semicircular apse of the type brought to Bohemia when Christianity was introduced from Moravia. That influence is also suggested by jewelry with which the inhabitants of Levý Hradec were buried at Žalov near the hill-fort.

Originally the Přemyslids had several centres in central Bohemia where they resided in turn and which sustained their power. In the end they recognized the

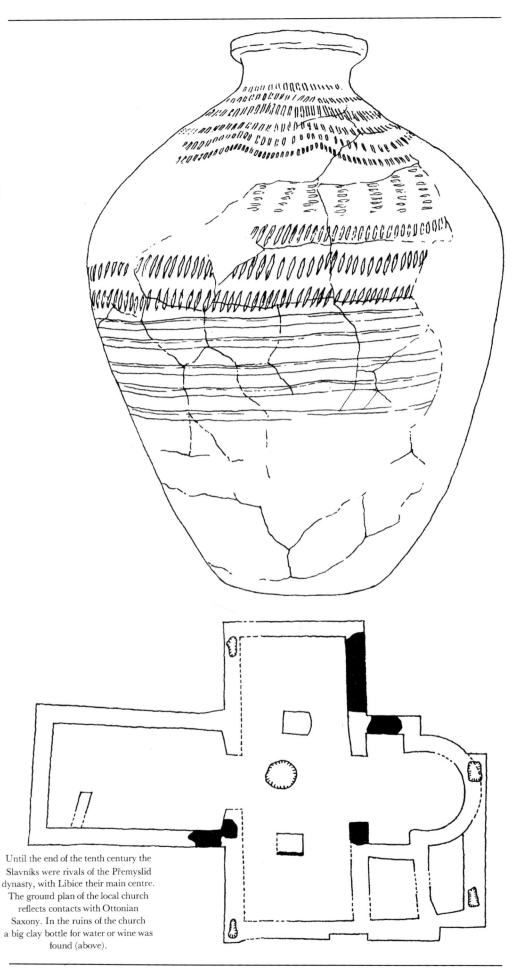

Until the end of the tenth century the Slavníks were rivals of the Přemyslid dynasty, with Libice their main centre. The ground plan of the local church reflects contacts with Ottonian Saxony. In the ruins of the church a big clay bottle for water or wine was found (above).

179

The original tribal centre of the Czechs was probably the hill-fort of Budeč, north of Prague. It still
played an important role at the end of the ninth century and in the first third of the tenth, when written
records mention it in connection with the first historical princes — Spytihněv, Vratislav, Wenceslas and
Princess Drahomíra.

The most important building at Budeč is St Peter's Rotunda which was built by Prince Spytihněv around the year 900. While only the foundations of the other Czech churches of the ninth to tenth century have survived this building in its original core still stands right up to the vaulting (the tower was added in the twelfth century). Legend relates that St Wenceslas learnt Latin here as a young boy.

Excavations at Budeč led to the discovery of a fortified homestead with the remains of stone and timber buildings and a paved lane — the residence of the warden of the hill-fort who ruled here on behalf of the prince from the end of the tenth to the twelfth century.

quite exceptionally suitable position of one of these and made it their permanent residence while the others declined in importance and gradually fell into decay. That centre was Prague Castle. It lay almost exactly in the heart of the country and long-distance routes converged on it from all directions. Here the threads of the country's destiny became interwoven. According to the legends recorded by chronicler Cosmas, Prague was founded by Libuše herself. He adds that the Czech name for Prague, Praha, derives from *práh* (threshold) which a man was just building in his house on the site of the future castle when Libuše's men found him. It was regarded as symbolic of the fate and historic role of the city, which has always been the entrance gate for cultures from the east, west, north and south of Europe. Philologists, however, are inclined to see in the name of the city a term for a place that was "arid" or "bare" (Czech: *vyprahlý*). But this is not very certain either.

The greatest hopes of uncovering the very beginnings of Prague, and in particular of Prague Castle, which is its core, rest with the archeologists. For five decades now they have been searching for traces, wherever this was possible in view of the density of housing construction in the modern city. The narrow, elongated spur above a bend in the river Vltava presented an ideal location for a fortified residence. At one point there rises a knoll

Another important hill-fort in Bohemia in the ninth and tenth centuries was Levý Hradec on the left
bank of the river Vltava. It is linked with Prince Bořivoj and the first church building in Bohemia arose
here. For that reason the hill-fort is considered a predecessor to Prague.

→
Prague Castle came to the fore of Czech history only at the end of the 9th century. Around it there grew up one of the oldest and most beautiful cities of Central Europe, upon which centuries of history have left their indelible imprint.

called Žiži, where, to judge by the name, sacrificial fires must have burnt on an ancient cult site. It was there that the ancestors of the Czechs buried their dead long before they adopted Christianity. They raised a barrow on one such grave to cover the bones of a warrior in full outfit. He was interred with his sword, an axe, a knife and a dagger and in addition there was a fire-steel to light a fire and a little wooden water bucket with wrought-iron trimmings. Later, when Prince Bořivoj adopted Christianity from Moravia, he intentionally built the first Prague church, consecrated to the Virgin Mary, on the pagan cult site.

We possess no historical records of the time when Prague Castle was founded and can only refer to legends. Excavations suggest that it might have occurred roughly in the last few decades of the ninth century, but it may have happened much earlier. What is sure is that Prague Castle was already standing by the end of the ninth century. It was surrounded by fortifications with a wall of marl in front, supported by earthworks strengthened with wooden grating, which held the entire structure in place. The fortified area was divided into three parts, separated by earthworks with palisades and a moat. The prince's residence stood in the middle

On his long travels through the countries of the Western Slavs Ibrāhīm ibn Yaʻqūb, the Jewish merchant from Moorish Spain, reached Prague in the year 967. He set down his interesting observations of certain aspects of life, particularly economic life, and he even noticed that in contrast to the more northerly Slav regions Prague Castle had stone fortifications and buildings (referring clearly to the churches).

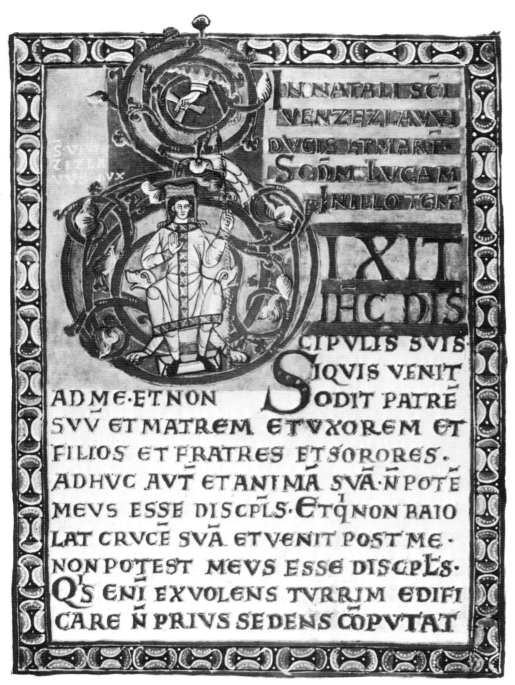

In the illuminated manuscript:

IN·NATALI·SCI
VENZEZLAVVI
DVCIS·ITMARI
SCDM·LVCAM
INILLO·TGNP

DIXIT

IHC·DIS

CIPVLIS·SVIS·
SIQVIS·VENIT

ADME·ET·NON   ODIT·PATRE̅
SVV̅·ET·MATREM·ET·VXOREM·ET
FILIOS·ET·FRATRES·ET·SORORES·
ADHVC·AVT·ET·ANI̅MA̅·SVA̅·N̅·POTE̅
MEVS·ESSE·DISCP̅L̅S·ET̅q̅·NON·BAIO
LAT·CRVCE̅·SVA̅·ET·VENIT·POST·ME·
NON·POTEST·MEVS·ESSE·DISCP̅L̅S·
Q̅S·ENI·EXVOLENS·TVRRIM·EDIFI
CARE·N̅·PRIVS·SEDENS·CO̅PVTAT

At the end of the eleventh century, during the reign of Vratislav II, the second castle in Prague – Vyšehrad – assumed the role of prince's residence for a short time. The famous *Vyšehrad Codex* dates from that period, and its illuminations are the work of the first Czech school of painting.

→

Only the St Martin's Rotunda at Vyšehrad survives from the period of Vratislav II. The remains of other buildings, the oldest dating from the end of the tenth century, have been uncovered during excavations.

one, while the other two parts formed the outer wards.

The prince's residence occupied roughly the same place as the royal palace today. In view of numerous reconstructions it has not been possible to discover its original form. We can only judge from the excavations that it must have been a log building on stone foundations, with clay tiles adorning the floors. If we are to believe the tenth-century St Wenceslas legend, it had at least two storeys. The prince himself lived humbly in those earliest times and this was even more true of the other inhabitants of the castle. Their simple log dwellings have been discovered in several places. These were the homes not only of the prince's servants and

craftsmen but also of members of his retinue, the defenders of the castle, and of the priests, whose houses were sited in the vicinity of the churches.

Apart from dwelling houses and the necessary out-buildings, there were three churches on the castle premises in the tenth century. None has survived in its original form, and the archeologists have unearthed nothing but the foundations. The oldest was the Church of Our Lady, which, as the legendist Christian relates, was founded by Prince Bořivoj after he suppressed the pagan uprising led by Strojmír. This church was pulled down in the fourteenth century and its location was forgotten. It was not re-discovered until the years 1950—1 during excavations in the western outer bailey. The foundations reveal two building periods: the older church has a rectangular nave and an apse with three curved edges. A large stone tomb inside must have belonged to the founder, but it was empty. After this oldest church had been demolished, the inhabitants built a new and larger one in a different technique and with a fully curved apse. Here a tomb with the skeletons of a man and a woman was found. The man wore a belt of hammered silver plate, the woman had grape-shaped silver earrings and a ring with a loop worn in the hair — jewelry that was in fashion in the first half of the tenth century. There is every reason to suppose that the tomb belonged to Prince Spytihněv and his wife. Spytihněv probably renovated the older building erected by his father, Bořivoj, which had been demolished for unknown reasons. As a result, certain Latin legends speak of Spytihněv, who followed the Latin rites, as the founder of the church, while they say nothing about Bořivoj, who, in fact, adopted the Slavonic form of Christianity.

The second important building in the grounds of Prague Castle was the Church of St George, founded by Prince Vratislav inside the inner fort around the year 920. This church was never completely finished and only slight traces survive. A new church arose when Boleslav II built the first central Bohemian convent of Benedictine nuns for his sister Mlada, who became the first abbess. Boleslav's tomb was discovered in a place of honour in front of the altar. Other members of the prince's family were buried by his side, including his grandfather and predecessor, Prince Vratislav. The convent buildings were altered many times and only parts of the walls date back to the period of Abbess Mlada.

The third and the most important church on Castle Hill was consecrated to St Vitus. It was founded by Prince Wenceslas. It was built north of the palace between Žiži Hill and the stone throne on which, according to an ancient custom, the Bohemian princes were enthroned. The foundations of this church were discovered when the present-day cathedral building was finally completed in 1911. During later excavations it was reconstructed as a rotunda with four apses on the basis of the surviving fragments, even though two of

191

them remain conjecture. When Wenceslas was assassinated by his brother Boleslav and soon came to be regarded as a saint and the patron of Bohemia, his remains were laid to rest here. In the eleventh century it was rebuilt as a Romanesque basilica and in the fourteenth century it was rebuilt again and became a Gothic cathedral, the main sanctuary of the nation. All the kings of Bohemia were crowned in the cathedral and the royal crown is deposited above the tomb of Wenceslas as the main national symbol.

The last survivor of the Eastern orientation of Czech Christianity was the Sázava Monastery, where Slavonic literature still flourished in the eleventh century. The expulsion of the Slavonic monks in 1096 put an end to that tradition and meant a definite leaning towards the Latin rites and the Western cultural orientation of Bohemia. Archeologists discovered the centre of a tetraconchial ground plan on the site of Sázava Monastery, for which the pattern can be found in Byzantine architecture. This helped clarify a unique chapter in the cultural history of Bohemia.

Prague Castle underwent far-reaching changes in the eleventh century thanks to the valiant Břetislav I (1034—55), who built new fortifications in an entirely untraditional manner. These were not the heavy old structures comprising clay-filled wooden galleries and a frontal wall of stone, but had a simple wall of roughly hewn marl held together with mortar. This was a novelty in the Slav region, which was adopted very gradually in other places and did not come into general use until the thirteenth century. Together with the fortifications the prince's palace itself was reconstructed in stone, but little of it remains. In the eleventh century the Bishop of Prague likewise lived in a stone building but only small parts of its foundations have survived. Another important change, in the eleventh century, was the reconstruction of Wenceslas's rotunda of St Vitus into a basilica with nave and aisles, two choirs and three towers. The work was begun by Prince Spytihněv II in 1060 and was finished by his brother and successor, Vratislav II. Excavations revealed its foundations below the cathedral. Its original appearance is given in a drawing in the fourteenth-century *Velislav Bible*.

During the reign of Vratislav, Prague Castle lost for a time its leading position to Vyšehrad as a result of a conflict between the prince and the bishop. Vyšehrad was the prince's second residence in the territory of Prague. It came into being some time towards the end of the tenth century on a bluff on the right bank of the river Vltava. The original castle of Vyšehrad was destroyed when a fort was built on its site in the seventeenth century. Its short fame is kept alive only by the St Martin's Rotunda, remains of a few buildings that have been excavated, and particularly the famous *Vyšehrad Codex*, adorned with numerous illustrations, which are the work of the first known Bohemian school of painting.

In the twelfth century the prince's residence was again transferred to Prague Castle where further building alterations were undertaken. Again new fortifications were built and the oldest tower that survives from that period is the Black Tower. The palace was rebuilt in a style derived from the Palatinates on the Rhine. A fire at this time gutted St George's Convent but it was soon rebuilt as was the Bishop's Palace and certain other houses. Every century added new buildings, churches and palaces until the typical panorama of Hradčany Castle came into being, which rises high above Prague as the symbol of the millennium of Czech history.

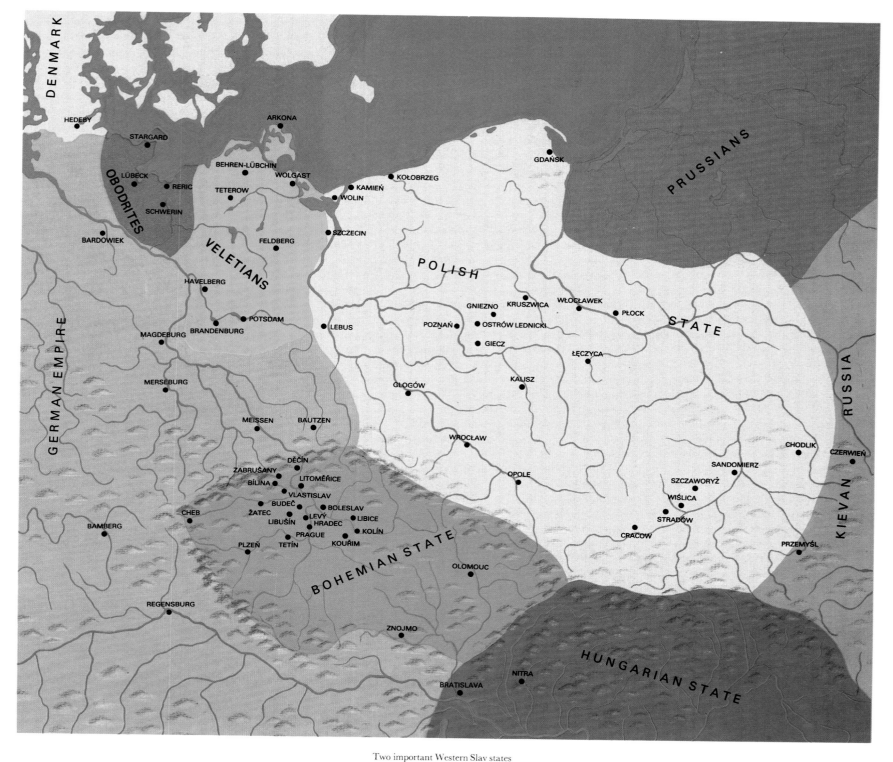

Two important Western Slav states formed in the tenth and eleventh centuries — the Czech with the Přemyslid dynasty and the Polish where the Piasts ruled. Numerous archeological sites have built up a picture of their economic and cultural life.

THE PIAST STATE IN POLAND

The beginnings of Polish history are clouded in darkness for one hundred years longer than those of the Czechs and Slovaks. Around 963 Mieszko I appears in the full light of history at the head of a strong state, able to resist even the expansion of the mighty German Empire. What is sure is that a long process of unification must have preceded this, in which the crystalizing core, in the end, was the tribe of the Polanie, who gave their name to the rest of the inhabitants, just as the Czechs did in their area. This development must have already occurred by the ninth century, but we only know tribal names from that time, often distorted beyond comprehension, and legends about the origin of the Piast dynasty, from which Mieszko emerged.

Slightly more definite reports exist from the ninth century on for the southern part known as Little Poland (Małopolska, or Polonia Minor). In the second half of the ninth century, the time when the Great Moravian

Empire flourished, the Vistulanians (or Wiślanie) established their own state along the upper reaches of the river Vistula. They were known to the Bavarian Geographer, and the Anglo-Saxon King Alfred the Great (871—901) called the country to the east of Moravia "Wisleland". It is mentioned in more detail in the *Life of Methodius*, a legend from the end of the ninth or early tenth century. Reports point to certain contacts between Moravia and the Vistulanians but largely in the form of conflicts, for the mightier state to the north of the Moravian Gate was a somewhat disagreeable neighbour for the princes of Moravia. The land of the Vistulanians was crossed by trade routes leading from Central and Western Europe to Kievan Russia. This must have been one of the causes of the economic and political development of the Vistulanians.

The history of the Vistulanians was confirmed when archeologists excavated their main centres, which included Stradów, Chodlik and Szczaworyż. But the place of greatest significance was Cracow, which became the main centre of the Vistulanians. It is related that the town was founded by the mythical Krak, who was said to have been interred in an immense burial mound found south of the town. Archeologists, however, clarified the true function of this artificially raised hill 17 metres (56 feet) high. It was only a symbolical tomb or cult centre, which, according to finds made on the site, came into being in the seventh century. The beginnings of the settlement of the Wawel, the hill that dominates the entire surroundings of Cracow, date from that very period. The Vistulanian prince mentioned in the *Life of Methodius* must have had his residence there and after a battle lost to Svatopluk his estates fell to Moravia. This is confirmed by Ibrāhīm ibn Ya'qūb, who mentions that the Bohemian Prince Boleslav also ruled over Cracow. This, in fact, is the very first mention of Cracow. Clearly Boleslav had inherited the estates from the Great Moravian Empire. By the end of the tenth century Cracow and the entire territory of the Vistulanians formed part of the Polish state. Cracow retained its significance even then. In 1000 it became the seat of a bishop. From the second half of the eleventh century it frequently served as residence of the Polish kings and played a highly important role in the cultural and political history of Poland. Factors contributing to this were its central location in a fertile agricultural area right on the trade route between Kiev and Prague, its proximity to salt mines and its highly developed crafts, particularly metalworking. Post-war excavations have shed light on the history of building in Cracow and the beginnings of stone architecture. At Wawel Castle the archeologists discovered the remain of a church of St Saviour and a rotunda consecrated to the Virgin Mary from the end of the tenth century. The church had a rectangular presbytery while the layout of the rotunda with four apses set in the form of a cross resembled the St Vitus's rotunda at Prague Castle. The remains of a basilica of the Saxon type were found in the western

wing of Wawel Castle. It had a nave and side aisles and probably dated from the period of Bolesław the Brave. Apart from church buildings excavations uncovered also the foundations of secular buildings, among them a large hall with twenty-four columns, which must have formed part of the ruler's residence.

The central part of the country, known as Greater Poland (Wielkopolska, or Polonia Maior), proved of decisive importance for the development of the Polish state. This was the land of the Polanie. Their name appears for the first time in the tenth century, prior to that the tribe must have been known by a different name, if we are to believe the facts given by the Bavarian Geographer. For in his work reliable information is

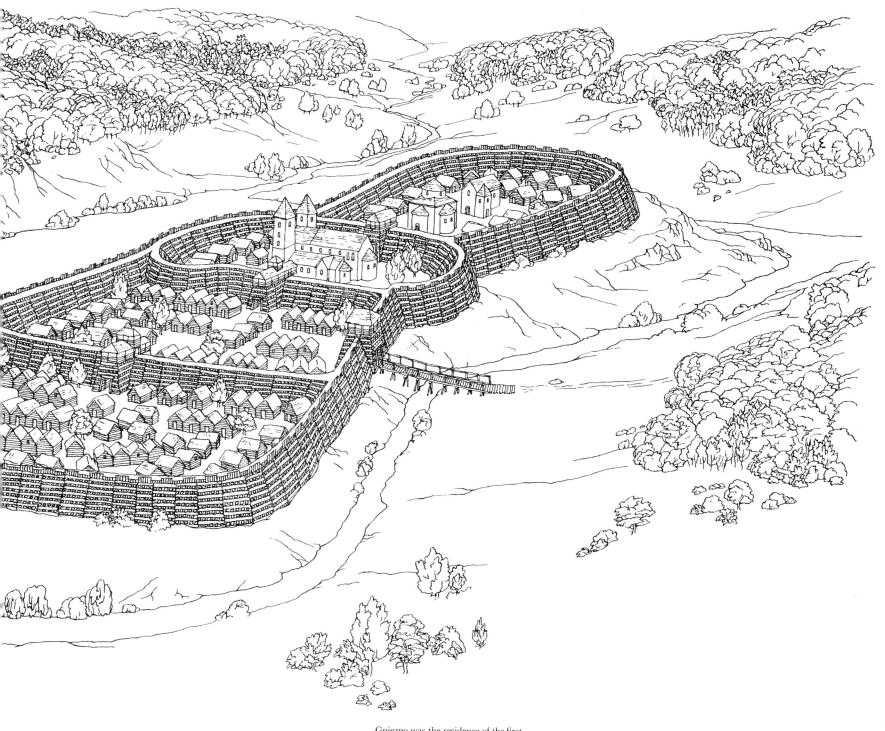

Gniezno was the residence of the first historical ruler of Poland, Mieszko I. Around the year 1000 it was a complex of four parts with the prince's residence, a St George's Church, an archbishop's cathedral and craft production in two outer baileys.

intermingled with reports that are highly questionable. He enumerates the tribes that lived on the territory of Greater Poland, among them the Glopeane and the Lendizi (Lędzianie). The Glopeane were perhaps associated with Lake Gopło in the Kujawy region; this would make them Gopłane. The Lendizi can be linked with Ląd, Lednica island, or with Lake Jelonek near Gniezno, whose northern parts were likewise called Lednica. In every case this refers to the territory of what later became known as Polanie, with whom the Lendizi can be identified. Their centre was Gniezno, while Kruszwica was the main seat of the Gopłane.

The first historical Polish Prince, Mieszko I, ruled from Gniezno according to reports by Western and Eastern sources (Thietmar of Merseburg, Ibrāhīm ibn Ya'qūb). He was a mighty ruler who commanded a retinue of 3,000 men. His original estates soon spread northwards (taking in western Pomerania with the town of Stettin) and to the south (the land of the Vistulanians, including Cracow and Silesia). Mieszko understood the political significance of Christianization introduced by missionaries from Bohemia, and he managed to have a bishopric established at Poznań in 968, which was directly responsible to Rome. He became the founder of a strong Slav state which played an important role in the history of Central Europe. This made itself known

195

already during the reign of Mieszko's outstanding successor Bolesław the Brave (992—1025), who strengthened the state by sound political and ecclesiastical organization (Gniezno was raised to archbishopric), assumed the title of King and very nearly realized his bold concept of a joint Bohemian-Polish state: this was after the death of the Czech Boleslav II in 999 and the deposition of his incapable successor Boleslav III when, for a time, Bolesław occupied Bohemia, Moravia and a part of Slovakia and proclaimed himself Prince of

Bohemia. But this plan was wrecked by the German King Henry II, who took the exiled Přemyslids Jaromír and Oldřich under his protection and helped them regain their princely throne. After the death of the otherwise capable Mieszko II (1025—34) it was, on the contrary, Prince Břetislav I of Bohemia, who attacked Poland, laid waste to Gniezno and took the relics of St Adalbert back with him to Prague. At that point the Polish Bolesław's plan might, therefore, have been realized from the Bohemian side. But once again King

←

Only remains of later alterations of the archbishop's cathedral at Gniezno, founded by Bolesław Chrobry (the Brave) around 1000, have survived together with a precious bronze door with relief scenes of the life of St Adalbert from the twelfth century.

On a peninsula in Lake Gopło in the Kujawy region stood Kruszwica in the tenth and eleventh centuries, one of the centres that upheld the might of the Polish Piast dynasty.

Henry III of Germany blocked the plan as he was afraid of a mighty Slav state as his neighbour and therefore rallied to the support of the exiled Piast Kazimierz (Casimir) I. The two nations — the Bohemian and the Polish — were very close to one another, but thus remained separated, each within its own state.

In the tenth century Gniezno became the first capital of the Polish state, but all we know of its beginnings come from legends. The medieval chronicler Gallus Anonymus relates that originally a Prince Popiel lived

here, who was, however, exiled and his place was taken by a poor ploughman named Piast. This story is highly reminiscent of that of Přemysl of Bohemia, who was likewise a ploughman. Piast became the founder of the Piast dynasty. The legend probably reflects developments on the territory of Poland some time in the second half of the ninth century. This period has been partly brought to light in the course of excavations. On a low hill called Lech Hill surrounded by marshy land between two lakes there stood a castle at the end of the eighth century. It had a fortified outer bailey and in front of this an open village spread along the lake shores. In the middle of the ninth century a change occurred which might possibly be associated with the arrival of the Piast dynasty. Part of the open village was changed into a second outer bailey, and the rest of the settlement was surrounded with a palisade. A whole group of settlements grew up in the vicinity, which

served as the economic hinterland of the centre. The part that underwent the most dramatic redevelopment lay to the east of the castle, where several routes crossed. First there would have been a market centre here, and later a medieval town grew up on this site. The entry of Poland into history, in the second half of the tenth century, is also revealed in finds resulting from excavations. The old fortifications were renovated and the palisade of the settlement below the castle was replaced by regular fortifications so that a whole complex of four parts came into being. Its core was the residence of the prince with the first Christian church of St George. In the first ward Bolesław the Brave built a cathedral to commemorate the establishment of the Gniezno archbishopric in 1000. Craftsmen inhabited the remaining outer wards. The high level of their work is proved by numerous finds, among them articles of wood, leather and bark, which have survived thanks to

←

The collegiate Church of SS. Peter and Paul has survived of the original architecture of Kruszwica. It has the shape of a Romanesque basilica with nave and aisles and a transept, and a semicircular apse in the presbytery (twelfth century).

A magnificent reliquiary in the form of a flat cabinet comes from Kruszwica. Decorated with scenes on the top and along the sides, it is made in enamel on a copper base (twelfth century).

Poznań on Dome Island in the river Warta held an outstanding position in political and cultural life in
early Polish history. It became the seat of a missionary bishopric in 968 with a St Peter's Church,
remains of which survive beneath the present cathedral.

the favourable soil conditions. There exists a report by the Prague chronicler Cosmas on the rich loot that the Bohemian Prince Břetislav found at Gniezno during his invasion of Poland in 1039.

Not all contacts with Bohemia took the form of conflicts. Christianity spread to Poland through the mediation of Bohemia, chiefly thanks to Dobrava (Doubravka), the sister of Boleslav II and wife of Mieszko I, and St Adalbert, the Bishop of Prague. He was originally buried in Gniezno after suffering a martyr's death in Prussia. His step-brother Radim (Gaudentius) became the first archbishop of the town. It is, therefore, not surprising that the first churches in that Polish centre were consecrated in the same manner as the oldest churches at Prague Castle, St George's and the Church of Our Lady. But nothing has so far been found of the original foundations of these buildings nor of the archbishop's cathedral. Only remains of later reconstruction were uncovered, including a coloured mosaic floor from the eleventh century and valuable twelfth-century bronze doors with relief scenes depicting the life of St Adalbert. Gniezno retained its important status into the thirteenth century when it became a typical medieval town.

Another pillar of Piast power in the early Middle Ages was Kruszwica, the centre of the Kujawy region. It stood on a narrow peninsula in Lake Gopło. In medieval legends it is linked with Popiel, who after being exiled from Gniezno died a miserable death here. Excavations begun in 1948 provide an idea of the development stretching back to the time before the Polish state came into being. Traces of life on the peninsula date back to the ninth century and the picture becomes clearer in the second half of the tenth century, when a castle with a fortified outer ward stood here and metalwork flourished. The wards were enlarged in the early eleventh century: a smaller outer ward by the castle with a church and a larger outer bailey with wooden dwellings of craftsmen. At the same time a group of settlements grew up on both shores of the lake. This underlines the growing importance of Kruszwica, which became the residence of a prince and under Mieszko II the seat of a bishop. The struggle between Władysław I Herman and his son Zbygniew in 1096 caused Kruszwica to lose its political significance. It retained only its economic importance, producing glass and clay articles with coloured glazes.

The third most important town in early Polish history was Poznań on Dome Island in the river Warta. In the north-western parts of the island a small castle already existed in the ninth century, and an open settlement is recorded at the end of that century. But Poznań did not become a mighty fortified centre until the time of the Piast dynasty. Soon after the adoption of Christianity in 968, it became the seat of a missionary bishop and, for a certain time, it probably served as the residence of Mieszko. Tradition has it that Mieszko's Czech wife Dobrava had the Church of Our Lady built there. In view of the densely built-up areas of the modern town it has not been possible to carry out full excavations in order to explain the topography in greater detail. But it is certain that a fortified outer bailey lay close to the castle on its eastern side. During the second half of the tenth century a bishop's Church of St Peter was erected here, of which the remains have survived below the present cathedral. Around it, as in the surrounding villages, stood the wooden houses of the craftsmen. The capital city of the Polish state was Gniezno, but Poznań held a leading political and cultural position far into the Middle Ages.

Apart from these main centres the power of the Piasts was based on a network of castles, whose significance was revealed only by excavations. Remains of stone architecture, both palaces and churches, survive in many of them. One example is at Płock in Mazovia where in the eleventh century the prince owned a palace built of stone. There were two rotundas there, to which a bishop's basilica with nave and aisle was added in the twelfth century.

In the very centre of Piast Poland there was another important locality — Łęczyca. It grew up on the site of an old palisaded and fortified settlement in the eighth century. Investigations point to an ancient tribal centre which was strongly fortified in the early twelfth century under Bolesław III Krzywousty (Wry-Mouth). The foundations of an eleventh-century monastery have been found close to the castle, on the right bank of the river Bzura.

Some Polish castles can pride themselves even on bridge constructions, as German archeologists discovered in the Slav castle of Mecklenburg. The castle

The intricate construction of the tenth-century fortifications at Poznań comprised a timber framework with chambers filled with stones. The framework was secured at this base by posts made from inverted sections of the trunks with the stumps of branches acting as hooks.

was built in the early tenth century on an island in Lednica Lake (Ostrów Lednicki) near Gniezno and was linked with the fortifications by a 600 metre (656 yard) long bridge. Apart from semi-subterranean dwellings excavations have brought to light the foundations of two interesting stone buildings: a church with a square nave, rectangular apse and attached dwelling places and a palace with a chapel with a central, cross-shaped ground plan and a cupola supported by four pillars.

This pairing palace and rotunda appeared on several other sites in Poland. One was discovered at Giecz, a hill-fort on the left bank of the river Moskawa, which protected the southern approaches to Gniezno. Excavations have shown that the buildings remained unfinished, probably as a result of the invasion by Břetislav I in 1039, during which part of the population was forced to move to Bohemia, where they founded the village of Hedčany. Another palace with a rotunda, also from the eleventh century, stood in the hill-fort of Przemyśl in south-eastern Poland. Here a building of an entirely different type was found, a church with a cupola on the Russian-Byzantine ground plan of a cross inscribed in a square. Remains survive below the castle. The hill-fort protected an important route to Kiev on the Russian-Polish border and therefore often changed hands.

Along the same route from Prague to Cracow and Russia lay the important crafts and trade centre of south-west Poland, Opole. The little fortified town on an island in the river Oder may originally have been the centre of the Opolanie tribe. In the tenth century a settlement with timber-reinforced earthworks arose here. It had three gates and wooden houses laid out along regular timber-paved streets. The trade contacts of this settlement are shown in finds of Byzantine silk, pearls from the Persian Gulf, fragments of broken Arabian dishes, Scandinavian fibulae, Russian Easter eggs, whorls and little bells, Rhineland bronze dishes and Moravian graphite vessels.

The ports on the coast of the Baltic Sea lived a busy life. The Slav tribes which settled the south coast of the Baltic established a number of ports: Starigrad (later Oldenburg) and Lübeck in the west to Gdańsk in the east, but none outdid the fame of Wolin, the famous Vineta or Jómsburg of the Western chroniclers and Northern sagas. Chronicler Adam of Bremen wrote that this harbour town, which flourished in the ninth to eleventh centuries, was the greatest European town inhabited by Slavs. It stood on an island of the same name at the mouth of the river Oder. Long years of excavations by German and, after the Second World War, Polish archeologists have filled in considerable detail to support Adam's enthusiastic description. It was shown that the town once had mighty fortifications.

Remains of its harbour were found by underwater archeologists. According to written reports there was

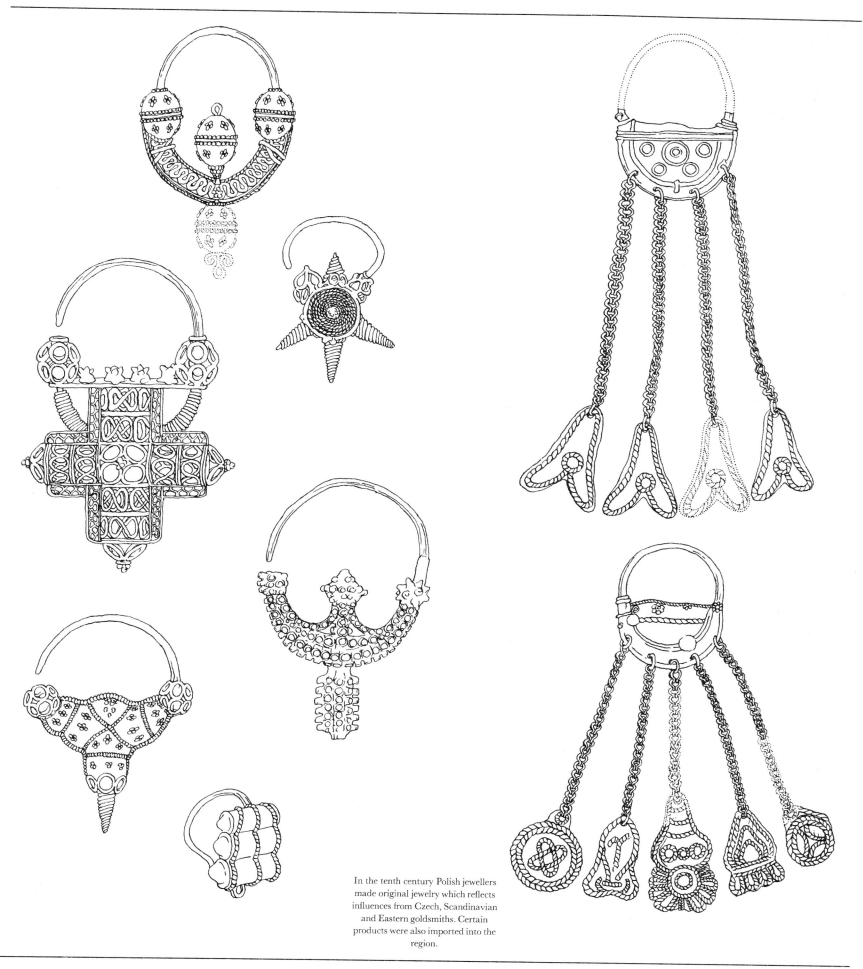

In the tenth century Polish jewellers made original jewelry which reflects influences from Czech, Scandinavian and Eastern goldsmiths. Certain products were also imported into the region.

even a lighthouse. How intensive the settlement was becomes clear from the fifteen strata of ruins of houses that were rebuilt over and over again. The wooden houses were set along narrow streets with timber paving. By the side of the merchants lived a great variety of different craftsmen: potters, smiths, goldsmiths, carpenters, glassmakers, carvers in bone and amber, and many others. Finds revealed trade contacts with the East as far as Novgorod, West to the Rhineland, and North to the towns of Scandinavia, especially Swedish Birka on Lake Mälaren. Wolin served as a major transhipment centre for all these regions, and it is not surprising that settlement stretched along the coast to a distance of four kilometres (two and-a-half miles) along both sides of the town.

Originally Wolin was a free town, but in the eleventh century it had to fight for its independance against the Polish state, to which in the end it succumbed. The final blow was struck by a Danish invasion in the twelfth century. Its role was then taken over by the economically and strategically more suitably located Stettin (or Szczecin). This town dates back to the ninth century and its history is a record of its changing roles. Stettin was at times independent, at others dependent on the Polish or the Pomeranian state. Later it became one of the most important harbours in Poland. The fortified town spread over three hills; the highest, where later a medieval castle was built, had once been a shrine to Triglav, and subsequently a prince's residence stood upon it. Stettin flourished in the twelfth century and, to judge by the built-up area, it must have had a population of roughly 5,000, which was large for that time.

←

Płock was the centre of Mazovia. It lay on a steep spur above the Vistula and was one of the many castles upon which the might of the Piast dynasty was based.

Remains of early medieval architecture have survived at Płock. Among them is an early Romanesque palace from the second half of the eleventh century.

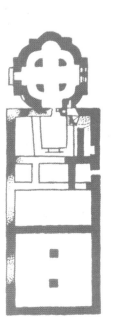

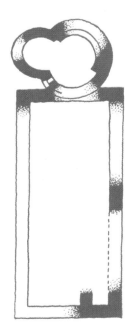

The harbours along the coast of eastern Pomerania include Kamień, Kołobrzeg and Gdańsk. The oldest written mention of Gdańsk is to be found in the *Life of St Adalbert* of the year 997. The Bishop of Prague set off on his mission to the pagan Prussians from this town, only to meet his death as a martyr there. As long years of excavations have shown, the fortified town with

Typical of the residences of the Polish princes was the pairing of palace and rotunda (Ostrów Lednicki, Giecz, Przemyśl).

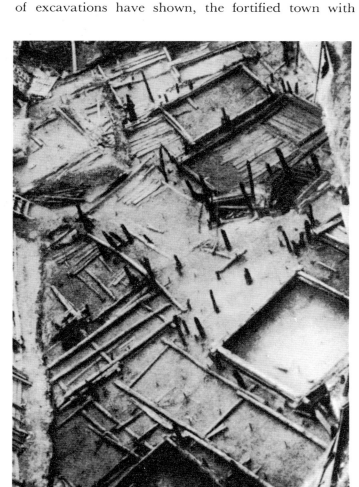

The log cabins in the little trading centre of Opole in Silesia were set out along streets with wooden pavements in the tenth to eleventh century.

a feudal residence lay originally on an island at the confluence of the Motława and the Vistula. The harbour was situated on the inner, western shore of the island facing the mainland, to which it was linked by a bridge. In the twelfth century a settlement grew up below the castle on the mainland shore, where the inhabitants built a harbour for trade and fishing. Excavations have revealed remains of its wooden piers. In the tenth and eleventh centuries Gdańsk with its timbered earthworks had about one thousand inhabitants living in wooden houses set along narrow streets. After a fire at the end of the eleventh century the whole town was rebuilt. In the twelfth century, when it was part of

the independent Pomeranian princedom, it grew considerably and became an important centre of craft production and international trade. Gdańsk is one of the few ancient ports on the Baltic Sea that have retained their importance to the present day.

The most recent Polish excavations have provided an idea of what the ships of the early medieval Slav seafarers on the Baltic looked like. They resembled Viking ships and even matched them in technical achievement. They were not as quick to manoeuvre as the Viking ships, from which their construction differed by having a flatter bottom. In this they resembled Friesian ships. The Slav ships had a smaller draught

A well fortified centre of craftsmen and traders, Opole, arose on an island in the river Oder in the tenth century. Excavations brought to light proof of the distant trade contacts of this little town, which lay on the important route from Prague to Cracow.

and the weight of the sails was shifted forward, which made them more stable so that they could stand up even to heavy seas. This picture was gained from wrecked ships, parts of ships and various tools that have been recovered, as well as by finds of models and even toy ships.

Seafaring, shipbuilding and the construction of harbours occupied all the Slav inhabitants of the southern coast of the Baltic Sea. This applies to the Polish and Pomeranian areas, which are nowadays on Polish territory, and the western, now German parts, which were once inhabited by Slav tribes that have long since vanished.

THE TRAGEDY
OF THE NORTH-WESTERN
SLAVS

A considerable part of what is today German territory (basically the whole of the German Democratic Republic and a large part of the German Federal Republic as far as Holstein, Hamburg, Hanover, Thuringia and north-eastern Bavaria) was once settled by Slavs. Their tribes flooded this land after the Germanic tribes had moved on at the time of the migration of nations. The Slavs then led a century-long struggle for their independence against the renewed Germanic penetration to the East. This ended with the Slavs being subjugated, exterminated or Germanized. Today all that remains are very small numbers of surviving Lusatian Sorbs, but there are no traces of the Polabian or Baltic Slavs other than numerous place-names and sites investigated by the archeologists.

The main cause of this tragic fate of the lost Slav tribes was their lack of political unity and consequent dispersion and ramification into a large number of separate units. They never became organized into a strong state that would have been able to withstand German pressure, as was the case of the Poles and the Czechs. Only two of their groups formed minor unions of tribes: the Veletians (or Liutizi) in Brandenburg and on the coast between the mouth of the Warnow and the Oder, in the tenth and the first half of the eleventh century, and the Obodrites (east Holstein and Mecklenburg [or Mikelenburg]) in the eleventh and the first half of the twelfth century. The Lusatian Sorbs remained permanently divided into individual tribes until they succumbed to the Germans in the tenth century. The Pomeranians (between the Oder and the Vistula) found themselves in the sphere of interest of the growing Polish state from the second half of the tenth century on. For a short period they existed as an independent princedom until, in the end, they found themselves subjugated by the Germans. It proved fatal to all these tribes that neither the Poles nor the Czechs managed to establish a strong state in Central Europe that would have unified all Western Slavs. This had been the dream of Bolesław Chrobry (the Brave) and Břetislav I of Bohemia, for that alone could have put up a barrier to the constant German expansion to the east. The Slavs' obstinate resistance to Christianity also played its part. Their dogged determination to worship nothing but their own gods laid these tribes open to the Christianizing efforts on the part of the Franks and Saxons, involving economic and political subjugation. All this finally led to the loss of nationhood.

The one-time home of the vanished Baltic Slavs was the melancholic landscape of Mecklenburg interwoven with numerous silver lakes and ponds shaded by pine or deciduous forests. All that remain of the Slavs' legacy are a large number of local names and ruins of castles, hidden in the marshland, on hillocks, peninsulas and on islands in the lakes.

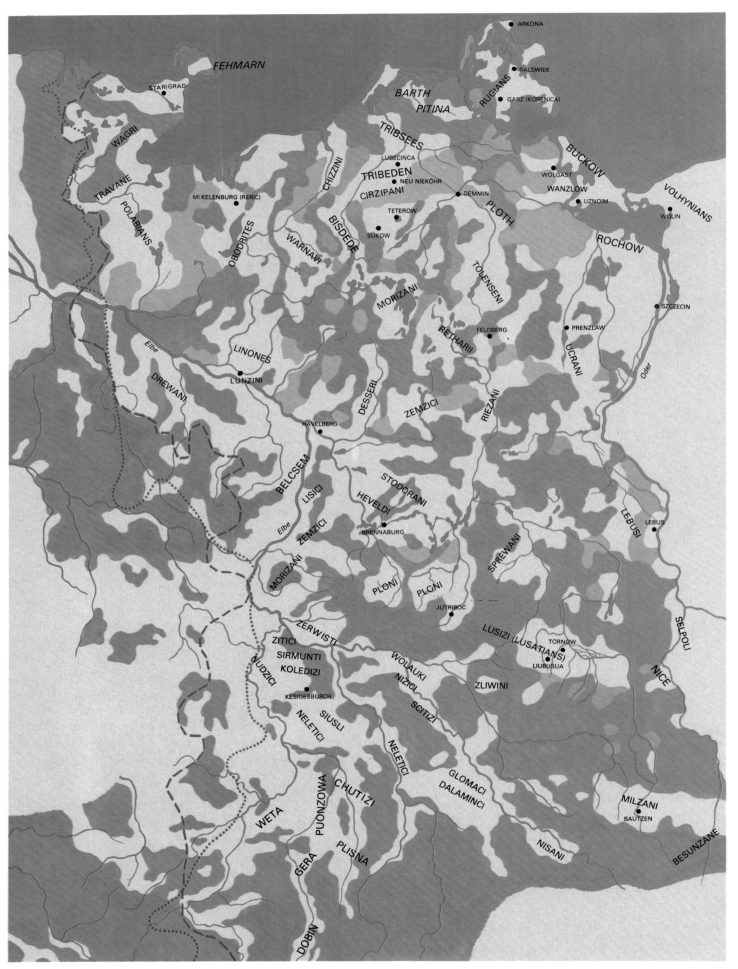

The Baltic and Polabian Slavs were split up into numerous tribes which formed only temporary tribal unions and never managed to set up a more permanent state as in the case of the Czechs and the Poles. This was one of the reasons why they vanished.

FEHMARN

STARIGRAD

ARKONA

RALSWIEK

BARTH
PITINA

RUGIANS

GARZ (KORENICA)

WAGRI

TRAVANE

TRIBSEES

POLABIANS

OBODRITES

CHIZZINI

LUBECINCA

TRIBEDEN

NEU NIEKÖHR

CIRZIPANI

BUCKOW

WOLGAST

WANZLOW

MIKELENBURG (RERIC)

BISDEDE

DEMMIN

PLOTH

UZNOIM

VOLHYNIANS

WOLIN

WARNAVI

TETEROW

SUKOW

ROCHOW

MORIZANI

TOLENSENI

LINONES

RETHARII

FELDBERG

SZCZECIN

PRENZLAW

LUNZINI

UCRANI

DREWANI

Elbe

DESSERL

ZEMZICI

RIEZANI

Oder

HAVELBERG

BELCSEM

STODORANI

LISICI

HEVELDI

LEBUSI

LEBUS

Elbe

ZEMZICI

BRENNABURG

SPREWANI

MORIZANI

PLONI

PLONI

JUTRIBOC

SELPOLI

ZERWISTI

LUSIZI (LUSATIANS)

TORNOW

NICE

ZITICI

SIRMUNTI

WOLAUKI

LIUBUSUA

KOLEDIZI

NIZICI

ZLIWINI

NUDZICI

KESIGESBURCH

SIUSLI

SCITIZI

NELETICI

NELETICI

GERA

PUONZOWA

CHUTIZI

GLOMACI
DALAMINCI

MILZANI

BAUTZEN

WETA

PLISNA

NISANI

BESUNZANE

DOBIN

The beauty of the jewelry from the region of the Baltic and Polabian Slavs in no way lags behind goldsmiths' work in the neighbouring Slav countries. This is proved by silver filigree ear-rings in the form of a cross and by a plaited necklace from Niederlandin near Angermünde (eleventh century).

Charlemagne already led a struggle with his eastern Slav neighbours, but he also managed to win them over as allies. He needed the Obodrites, for instance, in his effort to dominate the Saxons. These very Saxons, the immediate neighbours of the North-Western Slavs, involved them in many battles. Developments took a turn when the Duke of Saxony, Henry the Fowler, became King of Germany in 919. His name is linked with the beginning of the *Drang nach Osten* (desire for eastward expansion) which started nine years later. In his rapid advance Henry managed to conquer Brandenburg, the centre of the Heveldi or Stodorani, subdue the Veletians and the Obodrites and subjugate all the Sorbian tribes between the Elbe and the Saale.

His successor Otto I (936—973) was equally successful. He set up a network of castles and strengthened the German position between the Elbe and the Saale. Making use of the notorious Count Gero, whom he entrusted with the rule over this territory, he enlarged his domain as far as the rivers Neisse and Bober. The Christianization of the Slav tribes was supported by missionary bishoprics established along the borders with the Slavs, from Oldenburg as far as Meissen. The main centre was Magdeburg, to which all the Slavs between the Elbe and the Saale were to be ecclesiastically and politically subordinated.

Otto's plans came to nothing under his successor Otto II (973—983), whose defeat in the struggle against the Arabs in Calabria and death in 983 became a signal for a major Slav uprising. This swept away the German rulers between the Elbe and the Oder and put an end to all efforts for the conversion to Christianity of the local tribes. Only Holstein and the Sorbian territory remained under Germany. According to Helmold's *Chronica Slavorum* of the twelfth century the leader of the uprising was one Mstivoj, whose grandson Gottschalk organized the Obodrites into a state. Gottschalk was a Christian and co-operated with Archbishop Adalbert of Bremen to convert his country to Christianity in a peaceful manner — a form of missionary work begun by Otto III (983—1002) on the advice of his friend Adalbert, the Bishop of Prague, after the bitter experiences at the end of the tenth century. Gottschalk's aim was to form an independent Christian state on the Baltic coast in a feudal union with the German Empire.

On the initiative of the Veletians there was a new pagan regression in 1066 during which Gottschalk was assassinated and the Obodrites reverted to paganism. It was not until around 1093 that Gottschalk's son Henry defeated the pagans and became ruler of the Obodrites. After his death and a short period of Danish domination the Obodrite principality was divided between Pribislav and Niklot. Pribislav settled at Lubek (the Slavic predecessor of the present harbour town of Lübeck) and became renowned for his pirate expeditions along the Danish coast. Niklot became the founder of the princely dynasty of Mecklenburg, which in the course of time became German and remained in power until 1918.

Pribislav's and Niklot's territory was the main goal of a crusade against the pagan Slavs proclaimed by the well-known Abbot Bernard of Clairvaux in 1147. The Saxon nobility enthusiastically participated as they were interested in gaining new estates. The crusade was none too successful from a military point of view, but it broke the strength of the Slav tribes when large stretches of their country were laid waste. It ended with Pribislav and Niklot accepting Christianity and acknowledging the sovereignty of Henry the Lion, Duke of Saxony. For a time after the death of the Brandenburg Prince Pribislav in 1150, the Veletian territory came under the rule of Albert the Bear.

The last bastion of Slavonic paganism and independence — the island of Rügen — fell in 1168 to the Danish King Waldemar when he conquered Arkona. The entire region of the North-Western Slavs was then open to extensive colonization from the West, and thus it became Germanized.

This magnificent example of an iron stirrup decorated with silver inlay and gold comes from Baltic workshops east of the Vistula. It was lost by a Slav horseman on the river Havel near Pritzerbe not far from Brandenburg (first half of the eleventh century).

THE LUSATIAN CENTRE AT TORNOW

The few Lusatian Sorbs remaining today live in Upper Lusatia in the vicinity of the town of Bautzen and in Lower Lusatia in and about Cottbus. Once the Lusatian Sorbs were to be found in the whole southern area of the German Democratic Republic between the Oder, the Elbe and the Saale. Their villages even lay to the west of the Saale in north-eastern Bavaria and in northern Bohemia. They left behind a large number of settlements, cemeteries and fortified centres, where excavations have been carried out. One of the most important and most thoroughly excavated sites is the hill-fort of

The Lusatian tribe settled in the flat landscape with lakes and broad strips of forests which divided them from the territory of other related tribes. In the seventh to tenth century their land (today's Lower Lusatia) was densely scattered with hill-forts of a circular ground plan, evidence of an independent life which did not last long.

Tornow in Lower Lusatia. It best documents the culture of the Lusatian Sorbs in the period before they lost their independence.

Tornow lies on the territory of the Lusatian tribe south of the Spreewald. The southern tribal border ran along the Lusatian Hills, which divide Upper and Lower Lusatia. To the west their territory ended at the river Dahme and in the east along a bend in the middle course of the Spree near Cottbus. The landscape was flat with numerous watercourses and wide strips of forest that marked out other tribal areas. The Milzani lived to the south, the Sprewani to the north, in the east were the Selpuli and westwards lay the region of the Nisani.

Small hill-forts lie scattered all over this region. They have a circular ground plan no more than 30 to 40 metres (35 to 45 yards) in diameter and are located some 3—4 kilometres (about 2—2½ miles) apart. Most of them date from the time when these tribes lived an independent life, but from the tenth century on the whole region frequently changed hands and belonged in turn to the German or the Polish feudal state. The Lusatian tribe was first mentioned by name in the middle of the ninth century by the Bavarian Geographer, who cites twenty castles and their domains on this territory. Strangely enough, in contrast to other facts he gives, this tallies basically with what the archeologists found. Chronicler Thietmar of Merseburg mentioned a castle by the name of Liubusua conquered by Henry the Fowler in 932. The other names are not known to us, though one of them must, however, have been Tornow in the Calau district.

In the years 1961 to 1962 and in 1965 to 1967 excavations were carried out not only of the hill-fort itself but of the settlements in its surroundings so that a picture was built up of the development of the whole settled area. From this it became possible to draw important economic and social conclusions.

The hill-fort was constructed in two phases, which could be distinguished in the structure of the fortifications and the buildings inside the fort. In the earlier phase a construction of stakes stood behind the wooden frontal wall and there were casemates in the inner ward, where there stood dwelling houses, a mill and a well. It seems that the only permanent inhabitants were the family of the governor or warden of the castle, while the people in the surrounding villages used the castle casemates only in times of emergency.

This earlier hill-fort was destroyed by a fire, which must have broken out very suddenly as the inhabitants did not have time to remove supplies, which were burnt. A new castle was built relatively quickly on the ruins of the one that had burnt down. The new one followed the general layout of the older castle, but its fortifications were stronger while the inhabited interior area grew smaller. A large part of this inner area of the hill-fort was taken up by granaries. They replaced the casemates along the edge of the fortifications and contained large quantities of grain. In the centre of the hill-fort stood one large building, a wooden house with two storeys and a cellar, a small outbuilding and close by was a well. Three other dwelling houses were set into the fortifications alongside the granaries.

The difference between the earlier and later phase of Tornow can be explained by changes in social conditions. The larger inner area of the older fort, guarded simply by the family of the warden, provided the possibility of temporary abode for a larger number of people and their property. This points to its function of refuge for the peasant population in the surroundings where social differentiation was only just beginning. In the second phase the castle grounds were built up in

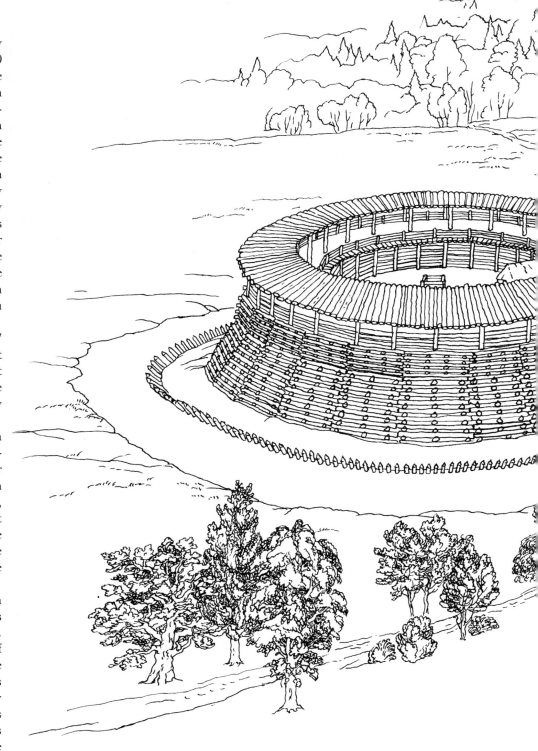

Excavations at Tornow in Lower Lusatia have made possible the reconstruction of the hill-fort and adjacent settlement. This documents the economic and social conditions of the Lusatians in the seventh to ninth century.

such a manner that there was no longer room for many other people. The entire central area was taken up by the residence of the lord of the castle who had a small retinue of about twenty men, who occupied the dwellings set into the fortifications. The rest of the area was taken up by storage facilities for food, mainly grain, levied from the population around the castle. In the same manner they acquired cattle (for bones form a large part of the refuse), honey, linen, furs, textiles, and other products made by village craftsmen, such as pottery, iron tools

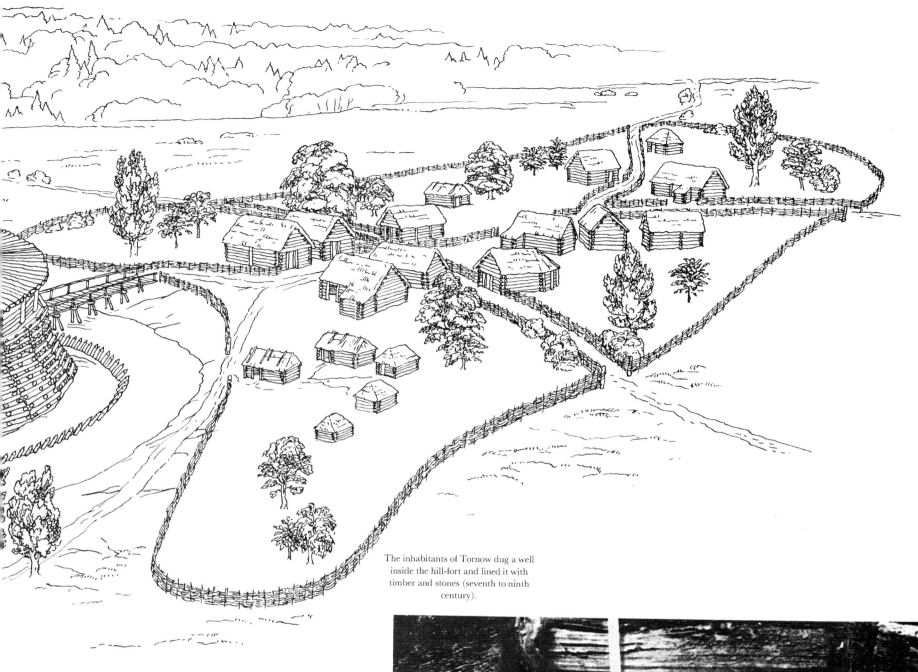

The inhabitants of Tornow dug a well inside the hill-fort and lined it with timber and stones (seventh to ninth century).

and weapons, wickerwork, as well as articles made by coopers and carpenters. They traded for millstones, made of porphyry, which is to be found in western Saxony, the region of the Chutizi. An analysis of finds using the radio-active C 14 carbon method dates the older castle at Tornow to the seventh and eighth centuries. The later one was built at the end of the eighth century but did not last longer than the first half of the ninth century when it, too, was laid to ashes by a fire.

Three villages, which shared its fate, were linked to

the hill-fort. Typical of the earlier phase are large farmsteads which probably belonged to single great families. On the other hand, in the later phase the large houses were replaced by a number of smaller dwellings. These were used by a lower stratum of the population dependent on the ruler of the castle. The fate of this region thus reflects on a small scale the social development of the entire Lusatian Sorbian region in the early Middle Ages.

←

The Teterow hill-fort of the Cirzipani tribe is a typical example of Slav fortification built on islands in the middle of the Mecklenburg lakes. It was linked to the mainland by a 750-metre (820-yard) long bridge.

Thanks to the properties of the soil the bridge at Teterow hill-fort is in excellent condition so that it is still possible to walk over it today, 1000 years later. All that is missing is the balustrade.

The reconstruction of Teterow, made possible by the excavations, is an attempt to evoke the way of life in the hill-fort, which was built in the ninth century and disappeared in the eleventh century.

TIMBER FORTRESSES IN MECKLENBURG

There is no other place where such numbers of early medieval castles have survived than the north, the region once inhabited by the Obodrites and Veletians (Liutizi) who have completely died out. One hundred and ninety-four such castles have been counted in the relatively small region of Mecklenburg. These monuments to the dramatic struggles of the Baltic and Polabian tribes against the overwhelming power of the Franks, Saxons, Danes and Poles form a characteristic feature of the beautiful Mecklenburg landscape where the rivers, lakes, villages and towns bear Slavonic names to this day. The castles were built soon after the arrival of the Slav tribes, i.e. in the seventh to eighth century, first as a place of refuge in restless times of inter-tribal conflict, and later as support for the power of local rulers, who organized resistance to external threats and competed against one another for domination over the subjected tribes. Life in the castles came to an end when their inhabitants lost their freedom in the twelfth century. The ruins of looted and burnt down castles now lie hidden among forest-clad hills, in the midst of inaccessible bogs, on peninsulas and islands in the numerous lakes, hidden in pine and damp deciduous woods.

The Slav castles in Mecklenburg underwent a certain development in the course of centuries. The oldest lie in the eastern parts of the region. They stand on high points and have extensive fortifications. None of these castles is mentioned in written records. They date from the eighth to the ninth century if not from an earlier period. The second, slightly later group comprises circular castles and citadels (known as *Ringwall*). They are sometimes surprisingly small, 30 to 50 metres (about 35 to 55 yards) in diameter. Most of them were built in the lowlands, on the banks of rivers and lake shores. Since they served as family seats of the rising tribal

Another important hill-fort of the Cirzipani, at Behren-Lübchin, might rightly be called the Mecklenburg Pompeii. The timber fortifications and buildings from the eleventh to twelfth centuries sank into the bog, which has preserved them up to the present day.

220

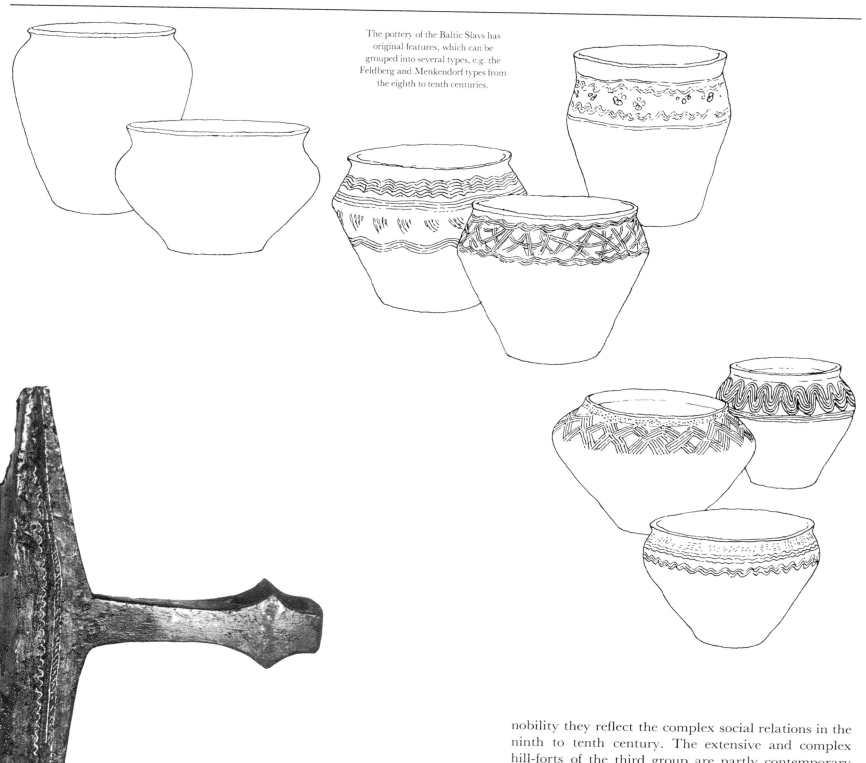

The pottery of the Baltic Slavs has original features, which can be grouped into several types, e.g. the Feldberg and Menkendorf types from the eighth to tenth centuries.

The axes of the Baltic Slavs not only served as working tools but were favourite weapons. Their blades were very broad and they were inlaid with silver, as this magnificent example from Behren-Lübchin shows.

nobility they reflect the complex social relations in the ninth to tenth century. The extensive and complex hill-forts of the third group are partly contemporary with the former, but lasted into the eleventh and even the twelfth century. Finally, the last type are castles established in barely accessible places, especially on islands in lakes as silent witnesses to the last desperate struggle of the Slav tribes in the eleventh and twelfth centuries.

Intensive investigations have been carried out on the territory of one of the main tribes of the Liutizi union, the Cirzipani. They lived in a marshy region between the rivers Reknitz, Trebel and Peene. The most important excavations were undertaken on hill-forts at Teterow, Behren—Lübchin, Sukow and Neu-Nieköhr.

221

marshy mainland opposite. The exceptionally favourable soil conditions have preserved its construction almost intact, so that it could still be used today. Only the supporting posts have remained on the bottom of the lake where they rise above the surface at a low water level. On the mainland only the balustrades are missing as a result of having been covered over by a causeway at some later stage. We can thus reliably reconstruct its appearance. The discovery of this bridge and the appearance of the entire hill-fort serve as an eloquent illustration to a report by Ibrāhīm ibn Yaʿqūb in which he described Slav castles in these regions. It may even be that one of the castles that he visited during his travels in the tenth century was, in fact, Teterow.

An even more comprehensive picture of the vanished life of the Cirzipani was given by excavations of the hill-fort at Behren-Lübchin. This can probably be identified with the *urbs Lubekinca* mentioned by the Danish chronicler Saxo Grammaticus in connection with an expedition under the Danish King Cnut VI and Archbishop Absalon of Lund to the Slav regions on the Baltic in 1184. The Rani tribe from the island of Rügen joined this expedition, and they reached this town in the Cirzipani bogs where the army began looting. The hill-fort, built on the shore of the now dry lake, was composed of two separate parts linked by a wooden bridge: a smaller castle on the narrow peninsula and a larger outer ward on the mainland. Since there were frequent floods on the peninsula its ground level was raised with the aid of a thick layer of tree trunks on which peat and soil had been piled to act as foundation for the houses. This timbered layer in time sank into the soft substrata so that in places it has survived almost in its entirety. All that was needed for reconstruction was to erect the fallen parts.

Teterow hill-fort was constructed on a picturesque site on an elongated island in the centre of a lake bearing the same name. The castle proper stood at the northern end of the island. It was not very large and was surrounded on all sides by a mighty wall, which is still 8 metres (over 26 feet) high today. The larger outer ward, surrounded by a similar wall, was inhabited primarily alongside the fortifications while the inner hill-fort was densely built-up. The remaining parts of the island revealed traces of an open village, from which a raised timbered road led to the marshy shores.

A great surprise for the archeologists was the discovery that this road was, in fact, the end of a bridge, which crossed the water of the lake to a total length of 750 metres (820 yards) and continued over a stretch of

In one of the oldest hill-forts in Mecklenburg, Alte Burg near Sukow, excavations exposed a well paved way which linked the hill-fort with the settlement close by as early as in the eighth century.

→
An insight into the manner of constructing roads was gained from the remains of the paved way at Sukow, which survives in good condition. It led across the local boggy lands for a distance of 1,200 metres (1,300 yards).

The large number of objects found here include valuable wooden articles which do not usually survive in other soil conditions: shovels, cudgels, even axes with handles, wooden dishes, buckets, wagon wheels, sticks with decorative handles, little carved figures (e.g. a dragon's head which was probably an ornament on a wagon or sledge) and other objects that provide an indication of the level of local craftsmanship in the eleventh and twelfth centuries.

223

Hill-fort Alte Burg near Sukow is one of the most ancient in Mecklenburg. Here was a chance to gain an insight into the manner of road building. There was a timbered road, 1,200 metres (over 1,300 yards) long, that linked the castle hidden on a hillock in the bog with the unfortified settlement. The timbered way has survived in excellent condition in the wet soil. It was rebuilt on several occasions. The most interesting alterations date from the period when the castle was the centre of an estate with a whole group of settlements. There was a substratum of tree trunks laid crosswise on top of one another. On this lay thick, broad, painstakingly cut planks, which were attached with oak posts to the surrounding terrain along the edge. The result was a road of double width strewn with fine sand which rose half a metre (nearly two feet) above the boggy land as a causeway. It was possible for two wagons to use it to go simultaneously in and out of the castle. In this more recent form the road served until the castle was abandoned, when it became overgrown and has thus survived in almost its original form. All this must have taken place in the eighth to ninth century. To judge by finds of undecorated pottery typical of the older hill-forts and their settlements in Mecklenburg, Sukow fortress might even date back to the seventh century.

→
Until the Danish invasion in 808 Reric, probably to be identified with hill-fort Mecklenburg, was the destination of Frankish trade caravans. Later it became the centre of the Obodrite princes.

Iron shackles with a lock, found at Neu-Nieköhr hill-fort, were used to bind prisoners or slaves (eleventh to twelfth century).

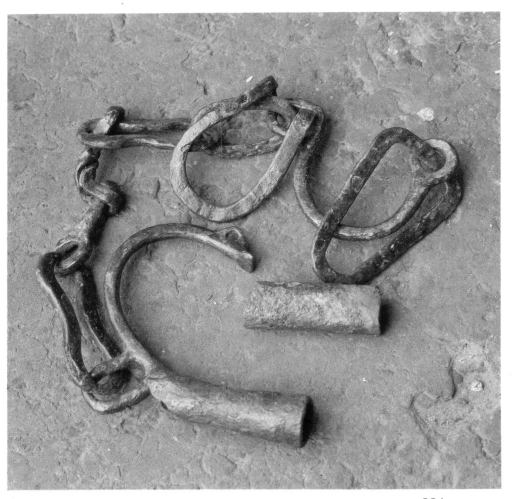

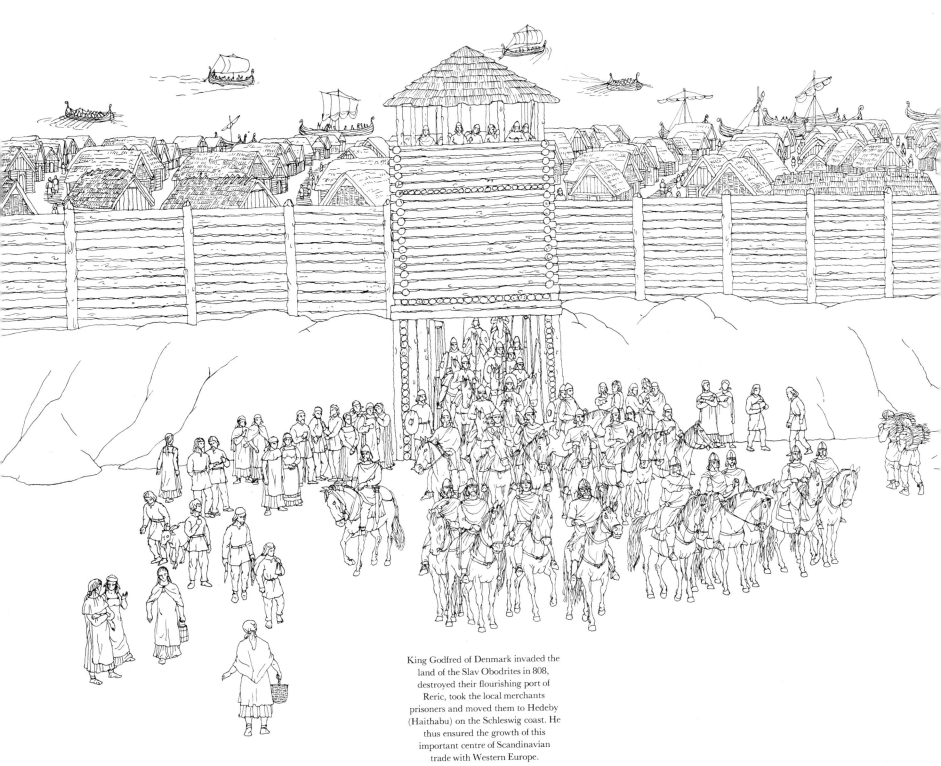

King Godfred of Denmark invaded the land of the Slav Obodrites in 808, destroyed their flourishing port of Reric, took the local merchants prisoners and moved them to Hedeby (Haithabu) on the Schleswig coast. He thus ensured the growth of this important centre of Scandinavian trade with Western Europe.

It has already been said that there existed a Liutizi union. After the victorious uprising of the Slav tribes of the Polabian and Baltic regions in 983 it was joined by the Cirzipani and also the Chizzini, Tolenseni and Retharii, and played an important political and military role until the middle of the eleventh century. Then civil war broke out between the Chizzini and the Cirzipani on the one side and the Tolenseni and the Retharii on the other, which ended with the first two being drawn into the realm of the Obodrites. As late as in 1151 we still hear of an unsuccessful struggle on the part of these two tribes against the Obodrite Prince Niklot. Soon after, they shared the fate of all the Slavs between the Elbe and the Oder, who finally lost their independence and in the course of the next two or three centuries even their nationhood. All that remains are the ruins of timber castles, unearthed by the shovels of the archeologists, which provide evidence of their former glory.

The Slav princes in the Polabian and Baltic regions began to mint their own coins in the twelfth century. One of the first to do so was Pribislaw-Heinrich of Brandenburg who reigned in the years 1127—1150. Later coins bore the portrait of the princes: Jazca of Köpenick (1153—57) and Jaromar I of Rügen (1170—1217).

→
The Slav tribes had a good deal of contact with the Scandinavian region, both in the form of trade and in warfare. This is proved by a bronze disc with a bas-relief of a mythical beast, done in the Jelling style (Carwitz, eleventh century).

SEAFARERS AND PIRATES IN THE BALTIC SEA

Ships and harbours of the types we found in the eastern parts of the Slavo-Baltic coast were also built in the western regions, in Mecklenburg and Holstein. Records speak of the existence of the oldest known Slav harbour, Reric, on the territory of the Obodrites. Its name is Danish and means "reed-bed", but it was an Obodrite centre which the Saxons called Mikelenburg, from which the present-day Mecklenburg is derived. The original Slavonic name was Veligrad. The power of the Obodrites grew after they fought against the Saxons as allies of Charlemagne. They were given land as far as the mouth of the Elbe, where Hamburg now stands. The Frankish merchant caravans which crossed the region from the Elbe to the Baltic Sea made this Reric-Mecklenburg their destination. Such rivalry in trade was regarded with dislike by the Danish King Godfred. In 808 he invaded the territory of the Obodrites, destroyed Reric, whose wealth had been a thorn in his side, and moved the local merchants to Hedeby (Haithabu), a harbour town that he had founded on the Schleswig coast. From that time on Hedeby, which has been the centre of interest of German archeologists for several decades now, became a centre of Viking trade with Western Europe. But Reric did not vanish. It became the seat of the Obodrite princes and is still mentioned in the twelfth century, even though its importance had receded into the background by that time.

The most exposed westerly tribe of the Baltic Slavs were the Wagri. Their main centre was Starigrad, called Oldenburg by their western neighbours. It grew up in the seventh or eighth century and developed into

a harbour town that carried on a brisk trade with Scandinavia. This fact is proved, among others, by a number of treasures found in its surroundings. Like Mecklenburg and other harbour towns Oldenburg did not lie right on the coast but at a distance of about five kilometres (about three miles) from Kiel Bay and roughly fifteen kilometres (about nine miles) from Lübeck Bay, which could be reached by ship along the Oldenburg canal. In 968 a bishopric was founded here as the centre of the mission to the local Slav tribes. In the eleventh to twelfth century Starigrad and the whole of Wagria became part of the Obodrite state and was then gradually overshadowed by growing Lübeck, which took over the role played by Starigrad-Oldenburg and Reric-Mecklenburg in the twelfth century.

Old Lübeck lay four kilometres (about two and a half miles) to the north of the later medieval town. It became prosperous under the Obodrite Prince Henry (1093—1127), who chose it for his residence. The town has frequently attracted archeologists, who clarified its situation during major excavations in the years 1947 to 1959. Inside the castle walls they unearthed the foundations of a church with an elongated ground plan and in it eight tombs of princes. They contained eleven gold discs and gold hairpins. Next to the church stood the princes' palace and close by were the living quarters of the garrison, a mint, goldsmiths' workshops, storerooms, granaries and a well. Outside the walls lay three settlements, in which the craftsmen, servants and merchants dwelt. They were mainly of Danish and German nationality and, according to the *Chronicle* of Helmold, they even built their own church. Old Lübeck did not flourish for long. The settlement vanished before the middle of the twelfth century together with the

Obodrite state, and in 1158 Henry the Lion founded the present town of Lübeck close by.

The spiritual centre of the Baltic Slavs was the island of Rügen with the Svantovit temple at Arkona. The location and shape of the island with its numerous bays where ships could run ashore made Rügen ideal for seafaring. One of the harbours was discovered at Ralswiek in Jasmund Bay. The settlement was protected by marshland and extended over more than half a kilometre (about 550 yards). It was inhabited by both the local population and foreign merchants who brought, among other imports, Scandinavian fibulae and Norwegian talc. Silversmiths were active here and finds of writing tools suggest that people knew how to write. Seafaring was confirmed when three ships from the ninth or tenth century were discovered. The largest was 13 to 14 metres (nearly 15 yards) long, 3.4 metres (3.7 yards) wide and was constructed of oak battens joined with iron rivets and attached to the frame of the ship with wooden pegs. The holes were caulked with hemp fibre and resin. This ship was of a type used to carry cargo.

The Slavs on the Baltic Sea were good seafarers and managed to establish a whole network of fortified, economically prosperous harbours. For that reason the Vikings did not manage to gain control over the southern coast of the Baltic even at the time of their greatest expansion nor did they settle permanently here as they did in the British Isles, Iceland, Normandy, Sicily and in Eastern Europe. By contrast to the Vikings the Slavs at the onset were not interested in piracy. They had no reason to be as their land was far more fertile than Scandinavia. Chronicles relate that even vines grew in Pomerania. Agricultural produce transported

In the early twelfth century Old Lübeck became an important port of the Obodrite tribe. Excavations brought to light a prince's residence with a church, a mint, and three settlements of craftsmen and traders.

on Slav ships was a major commodity in their trade with Scandinavia where they exchanged it for weapons, jewelry, coins and the like. In this way the Slavs even acquired Arabian silver. In the tenth century the Jewish-Arab merchant Ibrāhīm ibn Ya'qūb, who visited the Obodrites, did not know anything about the existence of Slav pirates. But he speaks of their long voyages across the seas to the Russians, as far as Constantinople, even perhaps on the Atlantic Ocean, for he mentions icebergs, on which some Slav seafarers were wrecked. In the early period the Slavs were allies of the

Vikings in their struggles against the Saxons and the Angles. A radical change occurred in the second half of the eleventh and in the course of the twelfth century. After exhausting battles against the Germans, Danes and Poles, and hemmed in on all sides on the mainland, the Slavs were forced to abandon their ravaged homes, seek refuge on the sea and live by piracy. Some harbours, especially those on the islands of Fehmarn and Rügen, turned into feared pirates' nests and became the departure points for devastating raids to the vulnerable Danish islands, the Swedish and Norwegian coast, the island of Gotland and on Lübeck, colonized by the Germans. A change of fortune took place in the year 1157 when a large Slav fleet of 1,500 ships was wrecked in a storm off the Norwegian coast. Since this weakened the power of the Slavs at sea, King Valdemar of Denmark was able to begin a ten-year offensive against the main base of the sea pirates on the island of Rügen. After the fall of Arkona in 1168 the Pomeranian fleet under Bohuslav suffered a heavy defeat by the Danes off the island of Koos in 1184. This disaster put a definite end to the activities of the Baltic Slavs at sea.

The ships of the Baltic Slavs resembled those of the Vikings, but they had a flat bottom, a shallower draught, and the mast with the sails was moved further forward. A wreck found at Ralswiek on Rügen was 13—14 metres (nearly 45 feet) long and 3.4 metres (about 11 feet) wide (ninth to tenth century).

Towards the end of their independent life
the Baltic Slavs were forced to abandon
their homes, devastated by never-ending
wars, and to take to the sea, where they
lived by piracy. They mainly raided the
islands of Denmark and the coast of
Scandinavia until they were defeated near
the island of Koos in 1184.

The coast of the Baltic Sea is attractive for its dream-like and
melancholic beauty which seems to evoke the dramatic
struggle and tragic events that took place here in the early Middle
Ages.

In the dramatic struggles where gains alternated with losses, the Slavs held a strong place in European history during the early Middle Ages. They emerged in the sixth century as an unknown third wave of colonists after the Celts and the Germans and spread across almost half of the continent in the course of a few generations. Their immense pressure shook the walls of ancient cities, broke down the frontiers of Roman provinces and scattered the original population. The Slavs arrived on the scene with a unified but not very striking culture of simple peasants, of cattle breeders seeking new pastures. To begin with, all the strength of the Slavs was exhausted by these endeavours, so that they did not form any powerful political organization nor important cultural centres. They remained split up into a number of groups for a long time and only temporarily formed tribal unions. Like other barbarian tribes in Europe they first assumed the role of pupils who on settling in new places eagerly adopted the ways of their new environment, particularly where they came into contact with the ancient seats of culture — the Black Sea, the Mediterranean region, the Danube valley and the Rhineland.

It did not take long before a change occurred. The pupils matured into independent masters, who actively re-created the influences they had adopted. A decisive turning point took place in the ninth and tenth centuries when the first Slav states arose in Central, South-Eastern and Eastern Europe. All of them had ambitions to compete with the great powers of the time. New cultural centres grew up where Slavonic literature was written, an original form of architecture was adopted, craftsmen created a style of their own and other forms of culture developed. Certain common features can be traced all over the Slav world deriving from a roughly equivalent social and economic level and linguistic and cultural relations. At the same time, certain signs of differentiation appeared which led to the emergence of individual Slav nations. These differences came to the fore roughly in the twelfth and thirteenth centuries. It might be said that since that time the Slav nations have gone their own way and made their own specific contribution to European history.

The preconditions for this later development were established in the early Middle Ages as we have tried to show in giving a picture of this process.

BIBLIOGRAPHY

D. ANGELOV, Die Entstehung des bulgarischen Volkes, Berlin 1980

Arkheologicheskoye izucheniye Novgoroda (ed. B. A. Kolchin, V. L. Yanin), Moscow 1978

M. BERANOVÁ, Zemědělství starých Slovanů (The Agriculture of the Ancient Slavs), Prague 1980

I. BORKOVSKÝ, Die Prager Burg zur Zeit des Přemyslidenfürsten, Prague 1969

H. J. BRACHMANN, Slawische Stämme an Elbe und Saale, Berlin 1978

V. A. BULKIN — I. V. DUBOV — G. S. LEBEDEV, Arkheologicheskiye pamyatniki Drevney Rusi IX—XI vekov, Leningrad 1978

B. CHROPOVSKÝ, Slovensko na úsvite dejín (Slovakia at the Dawn of History), Bratislava 1970

D. CSALLÁNY, Archäologische Denkmäler der Awarenzeit in Mitteleuropa, Budapest 1956

J. DEKAN, Veľká Morava. Doba a umenie (Great Moravia. Its Time and Art), Bratislava 1976

H. D. DÖPMANN, Das alte Bulgarien, Leipzig 1973

F. DVORNIK, The Slavs, Boston 1956

J. EISNER, Rukověť slovanské archeologie (Manual of Slavonic Archeology), Prague 1966

J. GĄSSOWSKI, Dzieje i kultura dawnych Słowian (The History and Culture of the Ancient Slavs), Warsaw 1964

M. GIMBUTAS, The Slavs, London 1971

B. D. GREKOV, Kiyevskaya Rus', Moscow 1949

W. HENSEL, Die Slawen im frühen Mittelalter, Berlin 1965

W. HENSEL, Ur- und Frühgeschichte Polens, Berlin 1974

J. HERRMANN, Zwischen Hradschin und Vineta, Leipzig-Jena-Berlin 1971

V. HRUBÝ, Staré Město, velkomoravský Velehrad (Staré Město, Great Moravian Velehrad), Prague 1965

M. K. KARGER, Drevniy Kiyev, vols. 1, 2, Moscow-Leningrad 1958, 1961

J. KUDRNÁČ, Klučov, staroslovanské hradiště ve středních Čechách (Klučov, an Old Slav Hill-Fort in Central Bohemia), Prague 1970

G. LÁSZLÓ, Steppenvölker und Germanen, Berlin 1971

L. LECIEJEWICZ, Słowiańszczyzna Zachodnia (Western Slavdom), Wrocław—Warsaw—Cracow—Gdańsk 1976

T. LEHR—SPŁAWIŃSKI, O pochodzeniu i praojczyźnie Słowian (The Origin and Homeland of the Slavs), Poznań 1946

I. I. LYAPUSHKIN, Slavyane Vostochnoy Yevropy nakanune obrazovaniya Drevnerusskogo gosudarstva, Leningrad 1968

H. ŁOWMIAŃSKI, Podstawy gospodarcze formowania się państw słowiańskich (The Economic Basis of the Development of the Slav States), Warsaw 1953

J. NALEPA, Słowiańszczyzna północno-zachodnia (North-Western Slavdom), Poznań 1968

L. NIEDERLE, Manuel de l'antiquité slave, vols. 1, 2, Paris 1923, 1926

K. ONASCH, Gross-Novgorod und das Reich der heiligen Sophia, Leipzig 1969

I. PLEINEROVÁ, Březno, vesnice prvních Slovanů v severozápadních Čechách (Březno, a Village of the First Slavs in North-Western Bohemia), Prague 1975

J. POULÍK, Mikulčice, sídlo a pevnost knížat velkomoravských (Mikulčice, Seat and Fortress of the Great Moravian Princes), Prague 1975

I. P. RUSANOVA, Slavyanskiye drevnosti, Moscow 1976

B. A. RYBAKOV, Remeslo drevney Rusi, Moscow 1948

B. A. RYBAKOV, Early Centuries of Russian History, Moscow 1965

E. SCHULDT, Behren-Lübchin, eine spätslawische Burganlage in Mecklenburg, Berlin 1965

V. V. SEDOV, Proiskhozhdeniye i rannaya istoriya slavyan, Moscow 1979

Die Slawen in Deutschland (ed. J. Herrmann), Berlin 1972

Słownik Starożytności Słowiańskich (Dictionary of Slavonic Antiquities), vols. 1—5, Wrocław—Warsaw—Cracow 1961—75

Á. SÓS, Die slawische Bevölkerung Westungarns im 9. Jahrhundert, Munich 1973

M. ŠOLLE, Stará Kouřim a projevy velkomoravské hmotné kultury v Čechách (Old Kouřim and the Great Moravian Culture in Bohemia), Prague 1966

P. N. TRET'YAKOV, Finno-ugry, balty i slavyane na Dnepre i Volge, Moscow—Leningrad 1966

R. TUREK, Böhmen in Morgengrauen der Geschichte, Wiesbaden 1974

Z. VÁŇA, Einführung in die Frühgeschichte der Slawen, Neumünster 1970

Z. VÁŇA, Objevy ve světě dávných Slovanů (Discoveries from the World of the Ancient Slavs), Prague 1977

Zh. VŬZHAROVA, Slavyanski i slavyanobŭlgarski selishta v bŭlgarskite zemi VI—XI vek (Slav and Slavo-Bulgarian Settlements on the Territory of Bulgaria in the 6th—11th Centuries), Sofia 1965

Zh. VŬZHAROVA, Slavyani i prabŭlgari po danni na nekropolite ot VI—XI v. na teritoriyata na Bŭlgariya (Slavs and Proto-Bulgars on the Basis of Finds in Graveyards from the 6th to the 11th Century on the Territory of Bulgaria), Sofia 1976

J. WERNER, Slawische Bronzefiguren aus Nordgriechenland, Berlin 1953

J. WERNER, Slawische Bügelfibeln des 7. Jahrhunderts, Reinecke-Festschrift, 1950, pp. 150—172

E. WIENECKE, Untersuchungen zur Religion der Westslawen, Leipzig 1940

J. ZEMAN, Nejstarší slovanské osídlení Čech (The Oldest Slav Settlement in Bohemia), Památky archeologické LXVII, 1976, pp. 115—235

237